RURAL CRIMINAL JUSTICE

Conditions, Constraints and Challenges

Thomas D. McDonald
North Dakota State University

Robert A. Wood
North Dakota State University

Melissa A. Pflüg
University of Wisconsin-Eau Claire

Sheffield Publishing Company

Salem, Wisconsin

For information about this book, write or call:
Sheffield Publishing Company
P.O. Box 359
Salem, Wisconsin 53168
(414) 843-2281

ISBN 1-879215-29-2

Printed in the United States of America

7 6 5 4 3 2 1

TABLE OF CONTENTS

ABOUT THE EDITORS

THOMAS D. MCDONALD (B.A. Suffolk University, M.A. University of Maine, Ph.D. Southern Illinois University) is a professor of sociology and director of the criminal justice program at North Dakota State University. His research includes analysis of criminal justice policy impacts (e.g., DUI legislative changes) and the emergence of intensive supervision programs. His publications have appeared in numerous journals, such as *Western Sociological Review, Journal of Gambling Behavior, Sociological Practice Review, Adolescence, The Great Plains Sociologist,* and *Sociology and Social Research.* He has been employed as an instructor in the Illinois State Penitentiary, Chester, Illinois and presently serves as a member of the North Dakota Parole Board.

ROBERT A. WOOD (B.S. and M.S. Pittsburg State University, Kansas, Ph.D. University of Missouri-Columbia) is an associate professor of political science at North Dakota State University, chair of the department and acquisitions editor for the North Dakota Institute for Regional Studies. As an instructor at Lincoln University, he taught at the Missouri State Penitentiary. His research focuses on right-wing extremist groups and terrorism in the United States, the impact of DUI laws on the judicial process, and constitutional issues as they apply to university students. He has published articles in *Terrorism, Violence, and Insurgency; Adolescence; Sociology and Social Research; Sociological Practice Review;* and *The Great Plains Sociologist.*

MELISSA A. PFLÜG (B.A. University of California at Santa Barbara, M.A. University of California at Los Angeles, Ph.D. Wayne State University) is an assistant professor of anthropology and American Indian studies at the University of Wisconsin-Eau Claire. Her research has involved extensive fieldwork among the contemporary Algonkian-speaking Indians of the rural Great Lakes region, particularly the Odawa (Ottawa). She has published articles in *Religion, Michigan Historical Review,* a chapter in *Questioning the Secular State* (edited by David Westerlund, Hurst Publishing, London and St. Martin's Press, New York), has a book in progress, an article forthcoming in *American Indian Quarterly,* as well as having written several book reviews dealing with various issues related to American Indians.

ABOUT THE CONTRIBUTORS

Curt R. Bartol (Ph.D. Northern Illinois University) is professor of psychology at Castleton State College, Castleton, Vermont. He is a licensed police psychologist, providing psychological and research services to numerous rural and small-town law enforcement agencies for over 20 years. He has co-authored with Anne M. Bartol *Juvenile Delinquency: A Systems Approach* (1989, Prentice-Hall), *Psychology and Law* (1994, 2nd edition, Brooks/Cole) and authored *Criminal Behavior: A Psychological Approach* (1995, 4th edition, Prentice-Hall). His current research and publishing interests focus on psychological issues involved in small-town and rural law enforcement.

Anne M. Bartol (Ph.D. State University of New York-Albany) is a professor of criminal justice and coordinator of the criminal justice program at Castleton State College, Castleton, Vermont. In addition to research and teaching interests in the judicial process, she studies juvenile justice issues, gender issues in criminal justice and mental health systems. She is co-author of two textbooks (with Curt R. Bartol, see above), *Juvenile Delinquency* (1989) and *Psychology and Law* (1994).

Randall R. Beger (Ph.D. Southern Illinois University-Carbondale) is an associate professor of sociology, specializing in criminology and juvenile delinquency, at the University of Wisconsin-Eau Claire. He has had extensive field experience working in the juvenile justice system. His research interests include gender disparities in juvenile court referral and punishment, southeast Asian gangs in the midwest, and the job satisfaction of police officers. He has published articles in *Crime and Delinquency; Juvenile and Family Court Journal;* and *Journal of Crime and Justice* on the application of contempt power in juvenile courts and community service programs for juvenile offenders.

Carroll Edmondson (M.A. University of Wisconsin) has been a fellow of the Institute for Court Management since 1986. He has served as a statistical clerk for the Wisconsin Supreme Court; an assistant professor of political science at North Dakota State University; an assistant court planner and then director of personnel and training for the North Dakota State Administrator's Office; and a trial court administrator for a four-county rural district in eastern North Carolina. Currently, he is the district court administrator for a six-county judicial district in Iowa.

Lois A. Guyon (Ph.D. Illinois State University) is an assistant professor of criminal justice sciences at Illinois State University and director of the LaSalle County, Illinois Mental Health Board 708. Previously, she was employed as a correctional sociologist for the Illinois Department of Corrections, as a rehabilitation counselor for the Illinois Department of Rehabilitation Services, and as the executive director of the Drug Education and Information Resource Center in Milwaukee, Wisconsin. Her research focuses on drug abuse, the corrections system, history of corrections, and teaching materials for criminal justice students. She has authored numerous journal articles, research reports and books, and has presented her findings at several professional conferences.

Victor H. Sims (Ph.D. University of Southern Mississippi) is an associate professor in the department of criminology at Southern Oregon State College. Author of *Small-Town and Rural Police* (1988, Charles C. Thomas), he has been a member of police departments in Berkeley, California; Anchorage, Alaska; Nome, Alaska where he was chief of police; and Phoenix, Arizona. His research interests include small-town police departments, the interrelationships between police officers and others (e.g., victims), and rural policing.

Sanford Schwartz (Ph.D. Washington University in St. Louis, Missouri) is an associate professor in the school of social work at Virginia Commonwealth University. A former probation officer, he also has been the project director of a school-based juvenile delinquency program. Currently conducting research in the areas of chemical dependency and AIDS, his work has appeared in *Social Work, Journal of Drug Issues, Administration in Social Work,* and *Administration Policy in Mental Health*.

Kevin M. Thompson (Ph.D. University of Arizona) is an associate professor in the department of sociology/anthropology at North Dakota State University. He has worked in juvenile probation, and has served on several juvenile and criminal justice task forces. His research interests include empirical testing of causes of crime and delinquency, assessing causes of adolescent substance abuse, and evaluating criminal and juvenile justice policies. He has published articles related to crime and criminal justice in the *American Journal of Sociology, Social Problems, Criminal Justice and Behavior,* and the *Journal of Canadian Criminology*.

Nanci Koser Wilson (Ph.D. University of Tennessee), currently at Indiana State University of Pennsylvania, is a member of the department of criminology, and is on the women studies faculty. Co-founder of the American Society of Criminology's Division on Women and Crime, she has done research in the field for several years. Other interests include environmental ethics and law, ecological crime and ecofeminism.

Herman Wood (M.S.W. Washington University, St. Louis) is an adjunct professor at the department of criminology and criminal justice, University of Missouri-St. Louis and is the director of the Midwest Counseling Service. He previously served as a St. Louis County probation officer and jail superintendent. A past president of the Missouri Corrections Association and a former board member of the American Corrections Association, he has conducted research on the processing of the mentally retarded offender and on the counseling of shoplifters. His work has been published in the Conference Proceedings of the American Corrections Association and *Social Work*. Currently, he is conducting research in chemical dependency.

ACKNOWLEDGMENTS

We wish to express our appreciation to the managing editor at Sheffield Publishing Company, Stephen R. Nelson. It is largely due to his patience and encouragement that we were able to see this project to its successful completion. Additionally, we also wish to especially thank Cindy Mudrak at the University of Wisconsin-Eau Claire, Jill Blazek and Kate Ulmer at North Dakota State University for their valuable assistance in helping prepare the manuscript.

INTRODUCTION

Today, a number of supplemental texts are readily obtainable to augment the core choices of instructors in both criminal justice and judicial politics courses. In teaching our own classes, we have received many requests for information on rural criminal justice issues. Our colleagues at other institutions have informed us of similar student interest, and of their difficulty in providing adequate coverage in the field. Thus, the interest and need for rural criminal justice materials seems widespread. We believe that *Rural Criminal Justice: Conditions, Constraints and Challenges* is appropriate for these courses because it helps fill a void in the present inventory of available resources.

In 1982, Carter et al. edited a volume titled *Rural Crime: Integrating Research and Prevention* that systematically detailed the scope of rural crime and its prevention. Additionally, as Weisheit and his colleagues recently note, other works of the decade and before have focused on comparisons of rural versus urban data or even rural crime alone (1994). Despite these efforts, many Americans tend to view illegal activities in general (Watson 1985), and violent crime in particular (Committee on the Judiciary 1991), as primarily urban phenomena.

These public perceptions are substantiated by most data. For example, the 1990 Uniform Crime Reports (UCR) demonstrate that crime is less pervasive in rural locales. Additionally, the 1990 National Crime Survey (NCS) found the percentages of households victimized by crime were 30%, 23% and 17% respectively for urban, suburban and rural areas (Weisheit et al. 1994).

Recently, there has been considerable debate over whether or not the gap between urban and rural crime rates is decreasing. Again, Weisheit and his co-authors compare UCR data from 1980 through 1990 and conclude that the distance between the two rates has varied little during the decade of the 1980s (1994). Likewise, they report that longitudinal data from the NCS do not support the thesis that rural-urban differences are narrowing.

Some evidence to the contrary is provided by the results of a study by the Judiciary Committee of the United States Senate, which concluded that violent crime is growing at a greater rate in rural America than in the large urban states (1991). A major deficiency in the report is,

xiii

however, that data and concomitant increases only were compared between 1989 and 1990.

In addition to a relative analysis of rates of crime, it is important to note that a comparision of the contextual setting of urban and rural locales yields interesting similarities as well as differences. Major cities exhibit a great deal of variation in terms of culture, occupational status, wealth, physical geography and day-to-day living. The same categories or variations have been noted by Murray and Keller in terms of rural America (1991). For instance, they detail how distinctions exist between the sparsely settled areas of the southwest and rural New England. They also explain that some rural communities contain large numbers of minorities, while yet others are characterized by extreme poverty, both of which are phenomena that we most commonly associate with metropolitan areas.

Major rural-urban distinctions also are found when one considers the physical setting within which crimes occur. Relevant environmental factors that have been cited for rural locales include geographic isolation, the greater availability and likelihood of owning guns, disproportionate socio-economic problems, and the social climate or culture (Murray and Keller 1991; Weisheit et al. 1994).

The articles that follow seek to introduce undergraduate students to these and other complexities concerning rural criminal justice. It is our goal to further student understanding of both the criminal justice agencies and related issues within the rural environment, and to enhance an appreciation for rural communities themselves (Bishop and Harvie 1982).

In helping to make a contribution in this area, we bring together a number of differing viewpoints in a compilation of original pieces of scholarship. The approach that we employ is decidedly eclectic. Thirteen individuals have contributed manuscripts representing a number of states in diverse regions of the nation. The work as a whole has a multi-disciplinary orientation with contributors from anthropology, criminal justice, political science, psychology, social work and sociology. Several authors have specialized areas of research and many have had extensive experience working with criminal justice agencies. As a result, a combination of academic and applied scholarship is present.

The six sections of this book focus on a number of major areas of concern in understanding rural criminal justice and are organized along the lines of many introductory texts in the field. The reader will find that each of the selections is organized around the themes of "Conditions,

Constraints and Challenges." We begin with general observations on the nature and extent of crime in rural America, and the economic constraints associated with agencies in rural communities. The next three sections examine the institutional context, with six chapters discussing issues related to rural law enforcement, courts and corrections. The fifth section examines four "Special Issues" as they relate to rural criminal justice: women, juvenile courts, American Indians, and right-wing extremist groups. Last, we discuss the implications of the articles for the future of rural America and criminal justice. Each major portion of the book is preceded by a brief overview of the readings found in that section.

THOMAS D. MCDONALD
ROBERT A. WOOD
MELISSA A. PFLÜG

REFERENCES

Bishop, L., and R. Harvie. "Major Crime in Three Rural Counties of Montana, 1895-1915," *Journal of Police Science and Administration*, 10, No. 1, 1982: 83-91.

Carter, T., G. Phillips, J. Donnermeyer, and T. Wurschmidt, eds. *Rural Crime: Integrating Research and Prevention*. Totowa, NJ: Allanheld, Osmun, 1982.

Majority Staff Report. *Rising Casualties: Violent Crime and Drugs in Rural America*. Monograph prepared for the Committee on the Judiciary, United States Senate. Washington, DC: 1991.

Murray, J., and P. Keller. "Psychology and Rural America: Current Status and Future Directions," *Psychology in the Public Forum*, 46, No. 3, 1991: 220-231.

Watson, G. "Rural and Urban Crime Patterns—A Twelve-Year Study." Unpublished manuscript, 1985.

Weisheit, R. A, D. N. Falcone, and L. E. Wells. "Rural Crime and Rural Policing," in *National Institute of Justice: Research in Action*. Washington, DC: United States Government Printing Office, 1994.

PART I

TRENDS AND FOUNDATIONS OF RURAL CRIMINAL JUSTICE

The two chapters in this section are intended to serve as a foundation for the readings that follow. We begin with Kevin M. Thompson's piece on "The Nature and Scope of Rural Crime." By examining data from the Federal Bureau of Investigation's Uniform Crime Reports (UCR) and the United States Department of Justice's National Crime Victimization Survey (NCVS), Thompson compares patterns that emerge in rural areas with those of urban centers along several dimensions. These include the scope and nature of crime; how arrest patterns are impacted by such variables as gender and age; and victimization rates. One major theme that emerges from his work is that individuals in rural America may be more vulnerable to certain forms of crime, such as those against property, than are their urban counterparts.

The second chapter, titled "Some Economic Realities of Rural Criminal Justice," is authored by Thomas D. McDonald. He begins by reviewing the general similarities and differences between rural and urban criminal justice agencies. Next, law enforcement, courts and juvenile justice are discussed in the rural context. McDonald contends that the general conditions of the economic and political environment exert considerable influence on the structure and procedures in all three of the above areas, producing important challenges and constraints. For example, as a result of these forces, the county sheriff is expected to fulfill a greater variety of functions when compared with police officers in urban law enforcement. Further, judges and prosecutors may be part-time and view their activities in the criminal justice system as being secondary to other careers. Finally, the adult and juvenile systems are often merged, with professionals performing multiple roles. Overall, practitioners operate as generalists in a relatively non-bureaucratic environment.

CHAPTER 1

The Nature and Scope of Rural Crime

by *Kevin M. Thompson*

INTRODUCTION

Almost universally, crime is visualized as an urban problem. When citizens read or hear reports about gangs, drive-by shootings, the drug trade, defaced public buildings and burglaries, frequently they visualize the dilapidated inner city. When news of a double homicide or a drug ring surfaces in rural areas, citizens express astonishment since heinous crime and drug trafficking usually are not associated with the rural environment.

Because of the more pacific image of rural areas, people who study the distribution and causes of crime often have neglected the rural setting. This chapter presents trends in rural crime, and then compares these trends with the nature and extent of crime in urban areas. One thesis of this chapter is that the nature of some forms of crime may make rural residents more vulnerable to victimization than urban residents. For example, Wilkinson concluded that the average murder rate in rural areas exceeds the rate in most small cities (1984). This pattern may be due to the more frequent and intense familial interaction patterns experienced by people who reside in more remote settings. Rural residents also may be somewhat vulnerable to property crimes. Because rural residents are required to traverse greater distances to purchase goods and services than urban residents, their households are more susceptible to theft and burglary. Smith (1980) found that 25% of victimizations of rural residents took place while they were away from their dwellings compared to 10% for urban residents. Rural households also tend to be more isolated, which lessens the ability of neighbors to monitor homes and impedes the mobilization of law enforcement officials.

Law enforcement officials also recognize that rural areas may be crime attractive because these settings are fairly insulated from government and citizen monitoring. For example, rural settings frequently harbor groups that propagandize against the government. Such

3

hate or bias groups establish footholds in rural areas where they can more safely direct attacks against persons or groups based on the victim's race, religion, ethnicity, gender or sexual orientation. Marijuana cultivation also tends to be a largely rural practice (Weingarten and Coates 1989; Weisheit 1993), as are crimes such as agricultural theft and poaching (Swanson and Territo 1980; Weisheit, Falcone and Wells 1993).

Some of the difficulties experienced by rural citizens and law enforcement personnel in monitoring criminal activity also make estimates of the nature and extent of rural crime somewhat problematic. One source of crime is the Uniform Crime Report (UCR). This is the annual report that chronicles the nation's crime and arrest incidents. Since we can never know the true rate of crime, we derive estimates of this figure from law enforcement officials, who in turn receive much of their crime information from citizens. Weisheit, Falcone and Wells suggest that this process of estimating crime might be impeded in rural areas by a culture that is distrustful of government and oriented toward solving problems informally instead of officially (1993). This rural emphasis on informal control suggests that crime might be more underestimated in rural areas than in urban areas. Since the inception of the UCR, rural law enforcement officials reputedly are less cooperative in reporting crime to the FBI than city or suburban officials (Federal Bureau of Investigation 1993). Cooperation rates vary from a high of 98% in urban areas to 89% in rural areas (Federal Bureau of Investigation 1993). Moreover, the greater distrust of outsiders makes it difficult for survey researchers to collect information on self-reported crime and victimization rates in rural areas.

Nevertheless, it is possible to assemble characteristics about rural offenders and rural crime with some degree of confidence. This chapter presents national data on the nature and extent of rural crime. The presentation of national data facilitates statistical comparisons with urban areas, but in the process obscures crime differences across rural counties. Thus, readers who wish to assess how much crime exists in a rural county of their interest should be encouraged to consult the library's copy of the Uniform Crime Report.

THE NATURE AND SCOPE OF RURAL CRIME
The Uniform Crime Report is a nationwide program that combines the efforts of over 16,000 city, county and state law enforcement agencies

reporting data on crimes brought to their attention. The FBI has administered this program since 1930 and, while there have been some changes in the program through the years, the seven offenses originally chosen to serve as Part I crimes have remained unchanged. These offenses include the violent crimes of murder, robbery, rape, aggravated assault, and the property crimes of burglary, larceny-theft and motor vehicle theft.

The FBI defines a rural area as "that portion of a county outside the Standard Metropolitan Statistical Area excluding areas covered by city police agencies" (Federal Bureau of Investigation 1993). This definition excludes suburbs. Figure 1 presents trends in the Part I crime rate from 1974 through 1993 for our nation's rural areas, expressed as a rate per 100,000 inhabitants. A straightforward interpretation of a rate is that in 1993 for every 100,000 inhabitants residing in rural areas, there were 1,971 crimes reported to the police. Overall, the graph indicates that rural crime rose 13% during the 20 year period. This growth in crime is much slower than the rural crime rate growth during the 20 year period from 1960 through 1979, in which rural crime increased nearly 450% (Carter 1982). The graph shows that rural crime reached its zenith in 1980. In 1984, the rural crime rate was 22% lower than in 1980. Crime then began a steady rise from 1984 to 1991, followed in the next two years by another decline.

How do these trends compare with trends in urban crime? Figure 2 contrasts the ratio of urban to rural crime for the Part I offenses and for the four crimes of violence. The overall urban-rural crime ratios appear to be remarkably stable over the 20 year period, suggesting that rural crime has kept pace with urban crime. We can say definitively that in any given year, urban crime is about three times more common than rural crime. The ratios for violent crime, however, show larger urban-rural differences, ranging from a low of 3.2 to 1 in the mid 1970s to a high of 4.2 to 1 in the mid 1980s. The ratios also show that urban violence began to increase faster than rural violence beginning around 1986. In part, this pattern is a function of the problems that large, metropolitan areas began to experience with large shipments of crack-cocaine entering the United States around late 1984. This surge in urban violence could also be attributable to the increase in the urban gang menace around the mid 1980s.

FIGURE 1

Trends in Rural Crime (1974-1993)

Crimes Known to the Police (per 100,000 inhabitants)

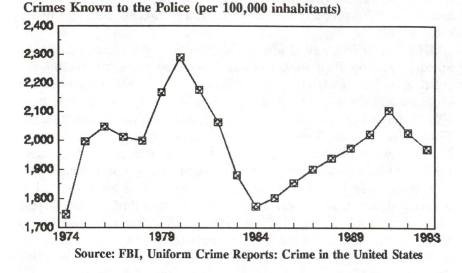

Source: FBI, Uniform Crime Reports: Crime in the United States

There is a disturbing trend that is not entirely evident in these data: that while the rate of violence has declined in urban areas in the last two years, it has continued to climb in rural areas. Since 1986, the urban rate of violence increased 16%, while violence in rural areas increased 27%. Why violence has continued to escalate in rural and not urban areas is not readily apparent. One hypothesis is that the urban causes of violence are beginning to "spill over" into rural areas. For instance, a number of rural sheriffs are beginning to express concern about gang activity in the popular media (Coates and Blau 1989; Mount 1992). Some sheriffs speculate that rural youths are being targeted by urban and suburban gangs as an untapped source of drug distributors and users. Fischer maintains that rural areas experience cultural trends much later than urban and suburban areas. If this pattern holds true, then rural violence, hopefully, will dissipate in the coming years (1980).

Table 1 presents urban-rural crime rates and expresses differences in rates as a ratio of urban to rural crime. Among violent crimes, the

FIGURE 2

Ratio of Urban to Rural Crime (1974-1993)

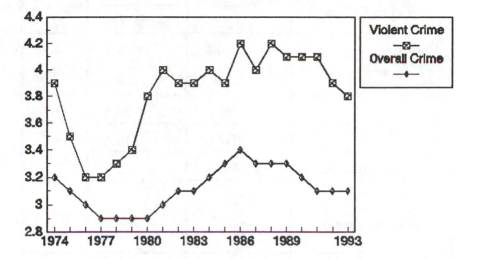

Source: FBI, Uniform Crime Reports: Crime in the United States

largest urban-rural difference appears for robbery. In 1993, robbery was 19 times more common in urban areas than in rural areas. Overall, violent crimes accounted for a larger proportion of Part I crimes in urban areas than in rural areas (14.1% versus 11.3%). It also should be pointed out that while the rate of overall violence was generally four times higher in urban areas (see Figure 2), the homicide and rape rates in rural areas were less than 50% of the rates in urban areas.

The largest property crime differences in Table 1 appear for motor vehicle theft. Motor vehicle theft is six times higher in urban areas than in rural areas. Both robbery and motor vehicle theft tend to increase with a rise in population density. Increasing opportunities for people to cross paths with other people or come in contact with automobiles increases the odds of taking possessions by force or taking automobiles unlawfully.

Table 2 expresses crime rates as a proportion of all Part I crime. Overall, property offenses account for 85% of crime in urban areas and 89% of offenses in rural areas. One pattern that is noteworthy in this

Table 1: Crime Rates in Urban and Rural Areas, 1993

Violent Crimes	Urban Areas	Rural Areas	Ratio
	Crime Rate	Crime Rate	
Murder & Nonnegligent Manslaughter	10.6	5.4	1.9
Rape	43.2	24.9	1.7
Robbery	312.0	16.4	19.0
Aggravated Assault	486.4	175.7	2.8
Property Crimes			
Burglary	1,182.3	633.4	1.9
Larceny-Theft	3,289.3	1,005.7	3.3
Motor Vehicle Theft	721.4	109.9	6.6

Source: FBI, Uniform Crime Reports: Crime in the United States, 1994.

table is the urban-rural proportion of burglary. While rural residents have lower odds than urban residents of being burgled, burglary accounts for a much larger proportion of Part I crimes in rural areas than in urban areas. Almost one-third of all Part I crimes reported to the police are burglaries, compared to roughly 20% in urban areas. Other patterns evident from this table show that murder and rape account for a slightly larger share of Part I crimes in rural areas than in urban areas.

**Table 2: Crime Rate Proportions in Urban and
Rural Areas, 1993**

	Urban	Rural
Murder	0.17	0.27
Aggravated Assault	8.0	8.9
Rape	0.71	1.3
Burglary	19.5	32.1
Robbery	5.2	0.83
Motor Vehicle Theft	11.9	5.6
Larceny-Theft	54.4	51.0

Source: FBI, Uniform Crime Reports: Crime in the United States, 1993.

RURAL ARREST PATTERNS

Whether a person gets arrested for the commission of a crime depends on a number of factors. Most criminal events come to the attention of the police via citizen reports. Research shows that the reporting patterns of citizens increases with the seriousness of the event, whether citizens are acting as witnesses, victims or both (Black and Reiss 1970). However, serious crimes tend to be exceptional. Homicide, robbery and rape, for instance, constitute less than 1% of *all* arrests in rural counties in a given year (this includes Part II crimes). Most criminal events in rural areas are quite ordinary and, therefore, result in more reporting discretion by citizens and law enforcement officials. Crimes such as theft, simple assault, fraud, drug abuse violations and driving under the influence (DUI) comprised almost 50% of all arrests in rural counties in 1993. Thus, any characteristics of the rural environment that might influence the probability of these crimes being reported and cleared will shape what we can say with respect to arrest patterns.

One question that interests criminologists is how arrests in different locations might vary by gender and age. Since its inception, the UCR has revealed that males are disproportionately represented in arrest statistics. This is true as well in rural areas. In 1993, males accounted for 82.5% of all rural arrests. Since males account for roughly 50% of the rural population, they are overrepresented in rural arrest statistics by about 33% (Bureau of the Census 1990). In urban areas, males accounted for 80.2% of all arrests in 1993. Since males account for roughly 48% of the urban population, they are overrepresented in urban arrest statistics by 32%. Thus, gender is implicated in arrest figures somewhat similarly for rural and urban areas.

Arrests by age tell a somewhat different story. Generally, juveniles (10-17 year olds) tend to be overrepresented in arrest statistics (Federal Bureau of Investigation 1993). This tends to be less true in rural arrest patterns. Juveniles accounted for about 10% of arrests in rural areas in 1993 and compose roughly 13% of the population (Bureau of the Census 1990). Nineteen percent of all arrests in urban areas, however, involve juveniles, whereas juveniles comprise roughly 11% of the urban population (Bureau of the Census 1990). Hence, juveniles are actually underrepresented in rural arrest figures by 3% and are overrepresented in urban arrest figures by 8%. This difference may be due to the more law abiding nature of rural youths or it may be that the types of crimes rural youths commit do not as frequently come to the attention of law enforcement officials as the types of crimes committed by urban youths.

Similar comparisons are offered for various types of crime in Table 3. This table depicts the arrest rate for the crimes that produced the largest and smallest urban-rural differences, expressed as a ratio of urban to rural arrests.[1] Thus, the offense in 1993 for which the urban-rural arrest difference was largest was prostitution. Arrests for prostitution were over 80 times more frequent in urban areas than in rural areas. Of the five crimes exhibiting the largest urban-rural ratios, only robbery could be considered a serious crime. For crimes such as rape and burglary, urban-rural arrest ratios are smaller, with most ratios approaching one.

There are also several offenses in the Uniform Crime Report for which the urban-rural arrest ratios are reversed. These offenses include driving under the influence (DUI) and fraud. The higher rural DUI

---

[1] Excludes arrests for vagrancy, arson, and unclassified offenses.

Table 3: Urban-Rural Arrest Patterns, 1993[2]

Largest Ratios	Arrest Rate (per 100,000 inhabitants)		
	Urban	Rural	Ratio
Prostitution	57.7	.7	82.4
Robbery	93.6	11.3	8.2
Curfew/Loitering	55.7	7.6	7.3
Larceny-Theft	723.6	207.3	3.5
Disorderly Conduct	364.6	136.2	2.7
Smallest Ratios			
Rape	16.6	13.7	1.2
Burglary	171.4	135.9	1.3
Liquor Law Violations	229.2	176.5	1.3
Forgery/Counterfeiting	46.1	32.6	1.4
Murder/Nonnegligent Manslaughter	10.8	6.5	1.7
Reversed Ratios			
Driving Under the Influence	517.7	886.3	1.7
Fraud	141.4	204.2	1.4

Source: FBI, Uniform Crime Reports: Crime in the United States, 1994.

---

[2] Excludes vagrancy, arson and unclassified offenses.

arrest rate is in part a function of the greater distances that rural drinkers are required to travel from drinking establishments to home. This increases the odds that rural drinking drivers will be pulled over and arrested by law enforcement officials. Rural drinking drivers also must traverse roads that often are in poor condition and provide fewer on and off road safety features for drivers (e.g., signs, guardrails). These conditions also increase the odds of a DUI arrest but more regrettably increase automobile fatalities among rural drinking drivers. Among the nation's alcohol related automobile fatalities in 1992, 57% occurred in rural areas (National Highway Traffic Safety Administration 1992). If we eliminate the number of pedestrians killed by drunk drivers in 1992, the proportion of alcohol related fatalities in rural areas rises to 63% (National Highway Traffic Safety Administration 1992). This figure is even more remarkable when one considers that urban areas house many more residents and handle much more traffic than rural areas. Taking into consideration these population differences, a rural driver's chances of experiencing an alcohol related driving fatality are roughly 4.5 times greater than that of an urban driver.

The higher rural fraud rate could be due to a number of factors. Greater distrust of government could lead to higher rates of tax fraud, for instance, among rural citizens. Rural areas also tend to suffer from greater levels of poverty than urban areas (Garkovich 1991), which might contribute to alternative, albeit illegitimate, sources of wage earning (e.g., postal fraud, credit fraud). Finally, rural residents may be more trusting of fellow residents and may be more vulnerable to some of these deceptions.

RURAL CRIME VICTIMS

Amidst criticism in the early 1970s that the Uniform Crime Report (UCR) was missing a significant volume of crime, the Department of Justice initiated the National Crime Victimization Survey (NCVS). The NCVS inquires about the criminal victimization experiences of over 100,000 individuals. As well as providing details about the extent and nature of victimization, the NCVS also provides details on victim variation by location of residence (United States Department of Justice 1994).

Table 4 depicts the urban-rural victimization rates in 1992. For any crime, urban residents were almost twice as likely as rural residents to

Table 4: Urban-Rural Victimization Rates, 1992
(per 1,000)

	Urban	Rural	Ratio
Robbery	10.9	2.7	4.0
Assault	31.5	22.1	1.4
Aggravated	12.1	7.8	1.5
Simple	19.4	14.3	1.3
Rape[1]	.8	.6	1.3
Larceny			
Personal	73.3	47.2	1.5
W/Contact	4.4	.6	7.3
W/O Contact	68.9	46.6	1.5
Household[2]	114.5	61.6	1.8
Burglary	60.1	41.7	1.4
Motor Vehicle Theft	35.3	6.2	5.7

[1] Incidents per 1,000 females.
[2] Incidents per 1,000 households.

Source: U.S. Department of Justice, Bureau of Justice Statistics, Crime and the Nation's Households, 1992.

be a crime victim in the preceding 12 months. For crimes which offer straightforward comparisons with the Uniform Crime Report (e.g., robbery, burglary, larceny, assault, rape, motor vehicle theft), the NCVS tends to minimize urban-rural crime differences. On average, the urban-rural ratio in the UCR is about 5.8 to 1 while the NCVS places this ratio at about 2.1 to 1. Partly this difference is a function of the larger urban-rural ratios in the UCR for robbery. Recall that robbery is 19 times more common in urban areas than in rural areas in the UCR but is only four times more common in urban areas in the NCVS. If we remove robbery from the calculations, we still see that the urban-rural differences in crime are almost twice as large in the UCR than in the NCVS.

What accounts for the differences in these urban-rural ratios from one crime reporting method to another? One possibility is that rural residents simply are less likely than urban residents to alert law enforcement officials to criminal incidents. This underreporting pattern might be part of a tendency of rural residents to resolve problems informally, instead of trust their fate to government officials. For instance, urban-rural burglary ratios are much smaller in the NCVS than in the Uniform Crime Report. Rural residents may be underreporting burglary because they may carry a false confidence about their chances of being burgled and, so fail to carry insurance. Moreover, rural dwellers do not have the urban advantages of having neighbors, and hence witnesses in close proximity to observe their property while they are away. For crimes such as rape, rural women often are not provided the support network to diminish the stigma attached to rape reporting. For domestic assault, women in the countryside likely expect little official intervention in an environment that tends to be more traditional. For assaulted males, there may be more of a rural tradition to resolve the dispute informally. All of this adds up to possibly more underreporting in rural areas, which further shields offenders and denies rural victims the protection they deserve.

SUMMARY

Data from several sources allow us to draw several conclusions about the extent and nature of rural crime.

1) Rural crime tends to resemble trends in urban crime over time. From year to year, urban crime roughly is three times greater than rural crime. This ratio tends to be slightly higher when the comparison involves crimes of violence.

2) Burglary tends to account for a larger proportion of Part I crimes in rural areas than in urban areas. Robbery and motor vehicle theft tend to account for a much larger proportion of Part I crimes in urban areas than in rural areas.

3) Juveniles are less likely to be represented in arrest statistics in rural areas than in urban areas.

4) There are fairly large urban-rural arrest ratios for public order offenses (e.g., prostitution, curfew, disorderly conduct). Smaller urban-rural ratios are observed for more serious crimes (e.g., homicide, rape, forgery).

5) Rural residents are more likely than urban residents to be arrested while they are under the influence of alcohol. Moreover, rural drinking drivers have greater odds of perishing in a crash than urban drinking drivers.

6) Urban-rural crime differences are smaller in victimization surveys than in the Uniform Crime Report (UCR). This could be due to the underreporting of criminal events to law enforcement officials that stems from rural residents' greater distrust of government officials.

These data suggest that while rural areas remain safer environments than urban areas, it is not clear if rural areas will provide their residents with as safe a haven in the near future.

A number of sheriffs have expressed concern in recent years regarding the spread of urban gangs and drugs to the hinterlands. Because of their more remote nature, rural areas may be fertile territory for the growth of a variety of criminal activities, including: 1) drug growing and peddling; 2) chop shops; 3) burglary and fencing rings; 4) confidence games.

It also is foreseeable that urban areas could be negatively impacted by activities in rural areas as urban and suburban populations begin to creep closer to the countryside. These "collar counties" might facilitate markets for drugs from illegal crop growing, racial and ethnic intolerance from hate groups, and markets for fur bearing animals from poachers. Thus, it will be important in future years to monitor how the nature and extent of rural crime affects, and is affected by, urban sprawl.

REFERENCES

Black, D., and A. Reiss. "Police Control of Juveniles," *American Sociological Review*, 35, 1970: 63-77.

Bureau of the Census. *General Population Characteristics, United States: Census of the Population*. United States Department of Commerce. Washington, DC: United States Government Printing Office, 1990.

Carter, T. "The Extent and Nature of Rural Crime in America," in T. J. Carter, G. H. Phillips, J. F. Donnermeyer, and T. N. Wurschmidt, eds., *Rural Crime: Integrating Research and Prevention*. Totowa, NJ: Allanheld, Osmun, 1982.

Coates, J., and R. Blau. "Big-City Gangs Fuel Growing Crack Crisis," *The Chicago Tribune*, September 13, 1989: 1, 8.

Federal Bureau of Investigation. *Uniform Crime Reports: Crime in the United States, 1993*. Washington, DC: United States Government Printing Office, 1993.

Fischer, C. "The Spread of Violent Crime from City to Countryside, 1955 to 1975," *Rural Sociology*, 45, 1980: 416-434.

Garkovich, L. "Governing the Countryside: Linking Politics and Administrative Resources," in K. E. Pigg, ed., *The Future of Rural America: Anticipating Policies for Constructive Change*. Boulder, CO: Westview Press, 1991.

Mount, C. "Counties Planning a United Effort to Combat Gang Problems," *The Chicago Tribune*, February 23, 1992: 23.

National Highway Traffic Safety Administration. *Alcohol Involvement in Fatal Traffic Crashes, 1992*. National Center for Statistics and Analysis, United States Department of Transportation, Washington, DC: United States Government Printing Office, 1994.

Smith, B. "Criminal Victimization in Rural Areas," in B. R. Price and P. J. Baunach, eds., *Criminal Justice Research: New Models and Findings*. Beverly Hills, CA: Sage, 1980.

Swanson, C., and L. Territo. "Agricultural Crime: Its Extent, Prevention and Control," *FBI Law Enforcement Bulletin*, 49, 1980: 8-12.

United States Department of Justice. *Sourcebook of Criminal Justice Statistics, 1993*. Bureau of Justice Statistics. Washington, DC: United States Government Printing Office, 1994.

Weingarten, P., and J. Coates. "Drugs Find Home in Heartland: Crime, Addictions Destroying Small-Town Way of Life," *The Chicago Tribune*, September 10, 1989: 1, 8.

Weisheit, R. "Studying Drugs in Rural Areas: Notes from the Field," *Journal of Research in Crime and Delinquency*, 30, 1993: 213-232.

Weisheit, R., D. Falcone, and L. E. Wells. "Rural Crime and Rural Policing: An Overview of Selected Issues," *Roll Call: Newsletter of the National Sheriff's Association*, November, 1993: 1-16.

Wilkinson, K. "A Research Note on Homicide and Rurality," *Social Forces*, 63, 1984: 445-452.

CHAPTER 2

Some Economic Realities of
Rural Criminal Justice

by *Thomas D. McDonald*

INTRODUCTION

Rural America has changed significantly during the 20th century. At the onset of this century, rural America was the nucleus of American life and home to most of its citizens. While rural America remains a vital segment of our country, it is instructive to realize that it comprises "...83 percent of the nation's land and is home to 21 percent (51 million) of its people" (United States Department of Agriculture 1995: 2). With this snapshot in mind, the purpose of this chapter is to review some economic conditions, constraints and challenges of the rural criminal justice system that is charged with the responsibility of serving and protecting the residents of rural America and watching over this vast landscape.

In reviewing economic aspects of rural criminal justice in the United States, it is wise to refrain from two assumptions. First, while it may be conceptually tempting to assume that the rural context is extremely homogeneous, many jurisdictions contain substantive heterogeneity in their economic base and demographic profile. As Eisenstein recognizes, this sets the stage for important considerations about the infrastructure of rural criminal justice (1982). Second, it is wise to avoid assuming that the agencies in non-urban regions are totally distinct from their urban counterparts. Such an assumption is incorrect. In order to guard against this over-generalized dichotomy, it is important to review some similarities and dissimilarities between the rural and urban criminal justice agencies.

Similarities in Rural and Urban Criminal Justice

Political authorization for the criminal justice system to control crime and punish criminals is found in legislative statutory codes. The authorized administrative control of this system frequently is found at the local level, and by the ideological design of the colonialists, is subject to local political and economic constraints. For example, both rural and urban law enforcement are controlled where the command of this power is exercised, "...which means primarily locally, and most often by elected persons" (Kaplan and Skolnick 1991: 171). Local political influence also can be found in prosecutorial and adjudicatory units (Eisenstein 1982). The overall goal of the rural and urban criminal justice systems is the same, namely, order maintenance. Differentiating among agencies is the business of identifying their respective objectives: that is, law enforcement, prosecution, adjudication, sentencing, and custody/corrections. Variance in assigned objectives among agencies also reveals different bases of jurisdictional authority, which means that the various agencies must utilize different economic bases. Each agency is subject to budgetary pressures and pulls that reflect a social and political-economic context. Authorizing the political priorities of public services that include, but are not limited to, criminal justice services "...is what practical politics is all about" (Christenson and Taylor 1982: 160). Within these budgets, criminal justice personnel in both rural and urban America have been subject to productivity pressures.

Finally, since the late 1960s, there has been a "rediscovery" of criminal justice in the United States. Originally, through the Safe Streets and Crime Control Act, this "rediscovery" has tried to improve the effectiveness of the criminal justice system. While the lion's share of this interest remains with the urban criminal justice system, some attention is being directed to rural contexts (see, for example, Sigler and Singleton 1984).

Dissimilarities in Rural and Urban Criminal Justice
Social control in the rural setting is more reliant on informal means instead of on the official, bureaucratic machinery of the urban criminal justice system. Informal constraints seem to work with more cost-effectiveness in small social settings where people know one another well and interact with each other continually (Clinard and Meier 1989: 22).

Constant (24 hours per day, seven days a week) and costly reliance on law enforcement, for example, is seldom prioritized. Thus, Wilson's "legalistic" police style is not a hallmark of rural areas (1968). This allows enforcement agencies to provide other types of service foci. To quote Wilson:

> The localistic police forces of small towns...work satisfactorily largely because they need not handle profound social conflicts; little is expected of them except to perform in middle-class areas a service function or in working-class areas a watchman function.
>
> —1968: 290

As a result of this service expectation "...rural police may face even greater citizen expectations for a variety of services not connected with law enforcement" (Reid 1993: 173).

With low demand for constant and costly criminal justice protection, many vital positions in rural criminal justice are staffed by part-time personnel. For example, in the North Dakota system, all municipal judges and most county/district prosecutors work part-time. One important economic impact of this trend is that numerous rural criminal justice agencies are vulnerable to major socio-economic development. Part of the difficulty exists in coping with a rapid influx of laborers and resulting rise in crime, especially by outsiders. Personnel and physical plant resources can be intensely strained during periods of economic boom, such as the energy development that occurred in many rural areas during the 1970s. Salary levels for laborers in the energy industry have been known to easily recruit many deputy sheriffs. Part-time prosecutors, facing an upsurge in their case load, are unwilling (understandably so) to continue in public service and sacrifice the more lucrative rewards of private practice (Schriner et al. 1976).

Finally, the ability to recruit and retain well-educated and trained personnel (especially in law enforcement) is more challenging in rural than urban jurisdictions. For example, while urban police departments are demonstrating a continuing trend to hire college graduates, rural communities face a dilemma in establishing such educational standards. Qualified people may be difficult to locate in a small labor pool; or, because of educational background, the young qualified person may be mobile with an accompanying preference to live and work in a metropolitan area (Carter et al. 1989: 20).

LAW ENFORCEMENT IN THE RURAL ARENA

News and entertainment media, along with many research publications, create an image of law enforcement as large organizations employing highly specialized, task-specific personnel who number in the hundreds, if not thousands, per department. While such circumstances exist in *some* jurisdictions, it is a misleading statistical and functional profile. In reviewing data from the Bureau of Justice Statistics, Weisheit et al. (1994a: 57) point out that of the 15,383 police departments surveyed, 89.1% reported having less than 50 officers on their staff. Table 1 presents the distribution.

TABLE 1: Number of Police Officers in all Local Police Departments
in the United States for 1990

Number of Police Officers	Number of Police Departments	Percent of Police Departments
1-9	7,461	48.5%
10-49	6,245	40.6%
50-99	877	5.7%
100-249	554	3.6%
250 and More	246	1.6%
TOTAL:	15,383	100.0%

While the majority of law enforcement departments are small-town agencies, in rural areas the county sheriff has been, and remains, the primary means of law enforcement and also is a central political figure (Esselstyn 1953; Eisenstein 1982; Reid 1993). In the approximate 3,000 counties in the United States, then, most law enforcement units are independent agencies and the senior administrator is the elected sheriff whose authority is, in the main, provided by the state's constitution. For a few rural locales, law enforcement is rendered by the county police. Chartered by the county commission, it is administered by a county-commission-appointed chief of police. This appears to be particularly the condition in southern and western regions (Reid 1993).

Modern sheriff's departments have evolved since the time of Alfred the Great and the "posse comitatus" ("power of the county"). No longer does the sheriff rely on the surety for custody of the accused and the salary structure is not based on the collection of service fees. Today, and still working within the peace-keeping function, a sheriff's department provides three important objectives. First is the responsibility of enforcing the law, and in many rural areas this means "...rural police must be summoned because they do not patrol" (Eisenstein 1982; Reid

1993). "Typically, a sheriff's department's law enforcement functions today are restricted to unincorporated areas within a county, unless a city or town police department requests its help" (Senna and Siegel 1993: 222).

The second responsibility involves providing personnel who function as officers of the court: for example, bailiffs and executors of criminal and civil papers. Finally, the sheriff's department is responsible for the administration of the county jail.

Bearing in mind that the sheriff's department tends to be small, and that it has a breadth of responsibilities, the personnel are expected to perform a more generalized set of duties with a greater range of tasks than the specialized law enforcement officer in a large, bureaucratically specialized urban police department. As Eisenstein describes:

> With only a handful of officers, many working only part-time, none specialize and expertise in any aspect of police work is rare. Significant obstacles exist even to participating in training programs. Internally, these departments have a less elaborate hierarchial structure, fewer official rules, a shorter chain of command and greater informality in inter-personal interaction.
>
> —1982: 116

More recently, Sims (1988) along with Weisheit and his colleagues (1994b) have pointed out that the concept of community policing, which is becoming increasingly prevalent in urban areas, has a long standing acceptance in many rural communities and police departments. Perhaps some ideas about effective policing can be provided by rural police to their urban associates.

As a result, the personnel of rural law enforcement have a greater set of expectations regarding their functional competence than is the case with their urban colleagues who are more highly educated, trained, specialized and salaried. Perhaps these differences partly explain why "per capita costs for police protection are higher for large than for smaller cities" (Bureau of Justice Statistics 1988: 116).

Some Budgetary Conditions and Constraints

Funding for law enforcement primarily is the burden of state and local governments that supply approximately 90% of the costs for criminal justice. Within this, the dominance of municipal spending is declining. From the 1970s through 1993, the state share of criminal justice costs has increased from the mid-20 percentile range to slightly better than one-third, and the county budgets have grown from about 20% to approximately 25%. During this same period, the municipal contribution to the cost of criminal justice has declined from the 40 percentile range to less than 33%. In 1993, the 3,000 counties of the United States dedicated about 35% of their budget for law enforcement protection services, which usually means the sheriff's department; and about an additional one-third for "correctional services" that primarily means for the operational costs of the county jail (Bureau of Justice Statistics 1994). Available evidence indicates that while our urban jails are likely to be overcrowded, the rural jails are likely to house fewer inmates than their functionally authorized capacity (Klofas 1990). As close to one-third of a county's justice budget is used for "correctional services" (primarily jail operations), it is important to briefly review some related economic matters.

*Approximately 50% of the 3,300 jails in the country are more than 35 years old.

*As the courts find an increasing number of jails to be in violation of constitutionally acceptable standards, more and more county commissions are faced with the question of costly jail renovation or costly jail construction.

*Construction costs for a new jail average $8.1 million, and every construction cost dollar requires $10 million in operating costs for the next 30 years. The efficiency of this issue is much more of an economic strain in rural areas than urban centers.

*Unfortunately, some counties have pursued new jail construction without adequate planning and alertness to court decreed constitutional matters. The ability of rural counties to withstand the cost of litigation and/or renovation of newly constructed jails is a questionable matter (National Institute of Corrections 1988: 1-3).

Finally, it is important to realize that rural law enforcement personnel easily can become immersed in the heated political-economic battles of budget priorities. Their urban colleagues are, for numerous reasons (e.g., personal residence and political culture), more likely to be shielded, if not isolated, from such tensions by the cultural and organizational structures of large cities.

COURTS IN THE RURAL ARENA

Much of the structural and procedural attributes of our rural courts are determined by statutory codes, prior court decisions and state or federal court administrators. Within these externally decreed boundaries, the rural courts and their personnel operate with a keen alertness to the internally determined conditions and priorities.

Criminal justice annals continually chronicle that both the volume and nature of crime and delinquency in rural regions are significantly different from the urban scene. Research specific to the rural jurisdictions suggests a prevalence of "minor crimes" (misdemeanors and lower level felonies). Much attention appears to be involved with traffic offenses, disorderly conduct, crimes of youthful error and livestock theft. The socio-cultural system of rural areas prefers to handle these matters with as much informal response as possible and hold down the use and concomitant costs of the official apparatus (see, for example, Warner 1982; Reid 1993; Weisheit et al. 1994c). While differences in the extent and nature of crime between rural and urban regions exist, processing pressures seem to operate in both court systems. One investigator suggests that:

> Case pressure results from the interaction of the cases brought and the resources (especially time and personnel) available to handle them. The scarcity of resources and the shortage of personnel in small jurisdictions may produce as much or more pressure to dispose of these cases expeditiously.
> —Eisenstein 1982: 119

In short, the economy of scale yields similar organizational inducements for efficient handling of the case load.

When the official machinery of the rural criminal justice system is invoked, the sheriff's department commonly is involved in the early stages. The question of whether to set bail, and if so how much, can be importantly influenced by the sheriff. Ginsberg suggests that pre-trial matters such as bail are, to some degree, impacted by the sheriff's knowledge and assessment of the defendant's background (1974).

Regarding the role of prosecutors, it is important to realize that they significantly influence the total criminal justice system; that is, before the commencement of case processing. To begin with, they are among the most formally educated people in rural jurisdictions. As attorneys, they perform "...an important social role as allocators of authority and definers of legitimate political argument..." (Melone and McDonald 1978: 21). In many rural areas, it is common to find people who attend law school in-state and "...return home upon graduation and practice among old friends and neighbors" (Melone and McDonald 1978: 32). Thus, rural attorneys are members of, and subscribers to, the "...values, traditions, and community life of established institutions and interests" (Eisenstein 1982: 113). As members of the criminal justice system, and holding central management positions in this system, they are heavily relied on by members of the town council, county commissioners, municipal judges, (who in many rural areas are not law school graduates), and others for legal education and advice.

Judges also are part of the upper-level community political infrastructure. Many judges, as is the case with prosecutors, are part-time public servants whose career priority may exist elsewhere. They too sense pressure to maintain harmonious working relationships (Eisenstein 1982; Fahnestock and Geiger 1993). Municipal judges may be attorneys or some other type of business person, e.g., banker, pharmacist, grocery store or service station owner. County judges are likewise linked to the community power structure and possibly more so as the county court is of principal importance in our rural jurisdictions (Reid 1993).

These socio-economic and political-economic circumstances (for example, the practical politics of budgetary allocations) contribute to the high degree of inextricably interwoven relationships of familiarity which, in turn, produce reciprocal pressures to handle issues and cases informally or with as little official ado as possible. As Eisenstein discerns:

> Familiarity or lack of impersonality or anonymity, combined with economic dependence, facilitates informal coercion and intimidation.... Thus, both self-induced and external social pressures add their weight to tacit (and sometimes explicit) economic intimidation.
>
> —1982: 109

This economic pressure also is present in the assignment of defense counsel for indigent defendants. Remuneration for contracted services is of such a financially depressed level that it provides pressure to dispose of cases with effortless efficiency. This contract situation involves a flat fee for services. Some observers suggest that the fee is so meager that in many jurisdictions attorneys may be expected to view their legal responsibilities as an unwanted burden, with little inclination to serve the defendant and no incentive to develop court room skills via such cases (Smolowe 1994). How different this is from the urban setting of court-appointed attorneys is in need of research, however.

The context of personal and political closeness influences the rural court room proceedings (Reid 1993). Several observers have suggested that one symptom of this familiarity and related informality is that of "individualized" attention. Ginsberg, for example, relates that insofar as judges know the accused, and at least something about the crime incident, they may be expected to provide a substantive inquiry at the arraignment proceedings (Ginsberg 1974: 39). Whether this signals alertness to matters of procedural criminal law and enhances the principle of fairness is, however, unclear (Eisenstein 1982: 125).

Recruitment of the two principal functionaries (prosecutors and judges) in the rural court system is a challenge. To begin with, attorneys in the rural setting have "...less need for specialization given the relative sparsity of social conflict" (Melone and McDonald 1978: 26). Scant but available evidence suggests that recruiting these key personnel involves working with a limited pool of potential candidates who, particularly for prosecutors, are likely to be inexperienced in matters of criminal law. Most attorneys may be expected to have more experience in issues of probate, taxation and estate planning than criminal law (Melone and McDonald 1978: 25-26). For the prosecutor's office, this means a likely predominance of young attorneys who are, in addition to being inexperienced, more interested in building a successful career which, if it is to develop, is unlikely to evolve via the narrow boundaries of criminal law experience. As suggested earlier, the pool of municipal judges may mean reliance on the local business people; that is, state law permitting. Recruiting judges for county court also can prove to be difficult, as this line of public service may involve considerable personal sacrifice.

It is interesting to note that the above difficulty does not appear to be the case with recruiting of probation officers to rural areas. In an Illinois study, Colley and her colleagues found that compared to urban agents, probation officers in rural areas are more generalists in their task performances (thus similar to earlier points made about law enforcement and court personnel) (1986). However, they also report that: "Rural departments are as capable as urban departments at attracting and retaining well-educated individuals to probation work" (Colley et al. 1986: 69). Part of this may be due to state funding instead of local budgeting.

Whether such is generalizable from Illinois to states that have a different cultural standard for the funding of services and salaries is unknown. Furthermore, it is important to realize that in some states (e.g., Minnesota), probation officers in the more rural districts are assigned both adult and juvenile offenders.

Some Budgetary Conditions and Constraints

Across the country the funding of court services primarily is through the county level of government; that is, 33%-35%. An additional 12% of these court costs are provided by municipal governments. Thus, close to one-half (45%-47%) of the nation's costs for court services are very much under the influence of local socio-economic and political-economic pressures. State governments contribute about 33% and the federal government supplies the final 20% of court costs (Bureau of Justice Statistics 1994). Within the county budget for all criminal justice expenditures, the national profile indicates that approximately one-third of this is designated for court services, about 10% for prosecutorial related costs, and slightly over 3% for public defense.

Rural socio-economic and political-economic conditions exert noticeable influence on the court structure and procedures that are externally mandated. Responding to these external challenges tends to occur more slowly and unevenly than the announced time-tables of state and national leaders.

RURAL JUVENILE JUSTICE

The juvenile justice system that emerged in the urban sector about 100 years ago is a sub-system of the larger criminal justice organization. Its main structural, policy and procedural trappings originate from laws and regulations that rise primarily from the state and national levels. Very much akin to the conditions of rural law enforcement and rural court matters, the rural juvenile justice system mirrors the perceived needs and priorities of the local social and political-economic contexts, and it adapts accordingly.

The profile of rural delinquency suggests that its volume and nature differ markedly from the urban context; for example, there is less per capita violence. Because of this and the generic conditions of the larger rural criminal justice system, there is little organizational and personnel specialization in handling rural delinquents. As we saw previously, law enforcement and court personnel do not engage in the task specific expertise of their urban brethren. Law enforcement agencies seldom budget for a "juvenile bureau." Juvenile court personnel will not engage in a specialized division of labor; for example, intake, hearing and probation.

In a longitudinal study of delinquent processing in North Dakota, the juvenile court was staffed by one person who performed multiple roles; that is, he was "...the juvenile commissioner, the supervisor, the referee and the probation officer for an eight county region of jurisdiction" (McDonald et al. 1977: 46). Clerical matters were handled by several of the county or district court personnel as need dictated or convenience permitted. The challenge of serving an eight county region prohibits, obviously, frequent visits between the probation officer and the juvenile. This was handled by the reliable use of unofficial but functionally equivalent "probation officers." Depending, then, on a juvenile's needs and community contacts, this person heavily relied on municipal police, the county sheriff, the clergy and others to perform much of the work of a probation officer and supply periodic feedback. In the rural setting, such cost effective cooperation is, generally speaking, "surely" available. Specialized, expensive law enforcement, court operations and correctional services are not perceived to be necessary budgetary items. These conditions, constraints and challenges of providing adequate monitoring and correctional services also are characteristic of working with adult offenders on probation or parole in the rural regions (see, for example, the work of Ralph and her associates, 1994).

For rural juvenile justice, adaptation to, and full compliance with, the legislative and constitutional mandates of the past 25 years has been slow and uneven. Insufficient research on this system, its evolution, and quality of services exists (a substantive contribution being Jankovic et al. 1980).

Of particular concern is the incarceration of juveniles in municipal lockups and adult jails, which is a national crisis. "This is particularly the case in rural counties" (Soler 1986/1987: 14). Federal regulations (the Juvenile Justice and Delinquency Prevention Act of 1974 and its 1980 Amendment), along with several state laws, have attempted to eliminate this problem. However, these efforts have proven "...to be a far more difficult task to accomplish than anyone envisioned" (Schwartz 1988: 131). This difficulty is frustrating in Minnesota, which "...is nationally recognized for its enlightened criminal justice policies" (Schwartz et al. 1988: 133). While Minnesota law seriously restricts incarcerating juveniles and forbids the "...incarceration of status offenders in adult jails and lockups..." this has not eliminated the problem because "...there are insufficient alternative programs to serve them (e.g., shelter care, crisis intervention services), particularly in rural areas" (Schwartz et al. 1988: 136). This difficulty generates even more concern when considering the multiple dangers encountered by the incarceration of females (Chesney-Lind 1988).

Recruiting personnel for juvenile justice in rural regions does not appear to be a problem. Specialists in juvenile justice are not perceived as a necessity. Probation officers for juvenile court systems are, in many areas, budgeted by the states and, based on the findings by Colley and her colleagues, should not be a recruiting challenge. Juvenile commissioners and supervisors, however, may not be law school graduates in the rural area, and, as we discussed earlier, they will be expected to rely on prosecutors (and perhaps judges) for legal advice.

Some "Cost" Considerations

Budgeting for the juvenile justice system mainly is contained within the larger criminal justice system. Rural budgets mask this due to their use of non-specialized personnel and facilities. For some observers it is important to realize that the economic cost of housing juveniles in adult jails or lockups is "...more expensive than placing them in community based alternatives.... Some communities spend over three times as much to incarcerate children in jails as they do to place children in supervised programs in the community" (Soler 1986/1987: 14). Litigation costs resulting from cases involving assaults and suicides have increased significantly (Soler 1988).

Part of the slowness in adapting to statutory mandates perhaps can be at least partly understood if we view "cost" as a multidimensional concept. Constructing and using special juvenile facilities (detention centers) can be viewed as not cost-effective. Periodically sheriffs have to choose between the responsibilities of law enforcement and jail administration.

While Minnesota has had a measure of success with the use of multi-county regional detention centers, these have not totally eliminated incarcerating juveniles in adult jails. Other types of cost operate and do so with pressure. Thus, the "cost" of releasing a staff member to take a juvenile to a detention center hours away is unappealing. Schwartz and his colleagues summarize the problem:

> Minnesota is a large state, most of which is rural.... This means that law enforcement officials in many jurisdictions have to transport juveniles long distances in order to access appropriate services and facilities. This is a task they are often unable or unwilling to do.
>
> —Schwartz et al. 1988: 145

The composite result of these multidimensional costs functions as a powerful disincentive to comply with federal and state statutes. When juvenile detention centers are constructed on a multi-county model with expectations about referrals and associated billings, and the rural county agencies do not follow through, then in addition to the primary problem of juvenile safety, the economic feasibility of the facility becomes jeopardized. Inter-agency relations will be uneven, professional practitioners will become frustrated, and the quality of juvenile services will limp along while the conditions, constraints and challenges of rural juvenile justice remain and in some regions appear to be intensifying.

SUMMARY

Although research on rural criminal justice is much less than the inventory on the urban sector, some important similarities and differences between these two exist. While the profile of crime differs between the extremes of rural and urban America, local perceptions of needed priorities and actual budgetary constraints influence the practical politics of budgetary decisions. Relative conditions yield economies of scale which contribute to serious respective pressures for cost effectiveness.

Practitioners in the rural system do not function within a heavy, bureaucratic, task specific environment. Generalists, instead of specialists, predominate the rural work force. To modify and extend Radelet's (1995) proposition on some urban police, rural criminal justice generalists seem to be much more *a part of their communities* than their urban brethren who appear to be more *apart from their communities.* Perhaps the rural professional practitioner can provide some valuable insights to the urban administrators and functionaries who are seriously challenged by the public's alienation from metropolitan, sophisticated criminal justice services. In many instances, recruitment and retention of capable functionaries are more challenging for rural agencies. Evidence seems to suggest that the rural criminal justice system seriously is constrained in its ability to fully comply with federal and state provisions. Adequate allowance for indigent defense and the safe incarceration of juveniles are two illustrations. This evidence seems to indicate that externally decreed legislative and administrative policy mandates have a perceived asymmetrical relationship with locally and internally controlled political-economic realities. When this occurs, the latter may be expected to resist and do so effectively—at least in the short term. Understanding this can be partially accomplished by consideration of all the dimensions which create costs for the thinly budgeted and staffed rural system.

Changing socio-economic conditions contribute to the need for reassessing the operations and budgetary needs of rural criminal justice. As shifts in population along with changes in the economic strengths of rural jurisdictions occur, the opportunity exists for reassessing basic assumptions about political-jurisdiction lines determining the operational scope of organizational-jurisdiction lines. Multi-jurisdictional operations such as regional jails and detention centers need increasing consideration by cooperative political leaders.

Economic constraints should not serve as excuses for inadequate facilities. Marengo County, Alabama, is testimonial evidence as to what can be achieved via dedicated, imaginative leadership (Haley and Smith 1982). Administrators of rural criminal justice agencies can more effectively and efficiently serve the public through greater attention to the principles of "management by objectives." This necessitates more focused analyses in clearly identifying an agency's conceptual mission, obtaining the necessary political and economic resources, managing the agency's operations and measuring the results. Policymakers, business leaders, agency administrators and interested citizens will need to anticipate and respond to challenging questions about rural criminal justice, and other rural services, as we move into the 21st century (Murdock 1995). This challenge, it seems, will remain both more pressing and more complex in those rural counties characterized by persistent poverty levels; that is, rates of 20% or higher. This profile is found most disproportionately in the south and to some degree in scattered areas of the southwest and northern plains (Cook and Mizer 1994: 24). Chronic poverty in these counties is accompanied by numerous other interwoven human and social problems which, in part, constrain the scope and depth of tax resources while increasing the need for publicly funded services.

Researchers in criminal justice have advanced numerous descriptive and analytical models which include the rural system. While such analyses have been somewhat valuable, greater progress can be made via a more holistic framework. Research on the perceptions about the total public service sector and how criminal justice ranks within these considerations is needed. As research on rural criminal justice proceeds, perhaps it will be wise to determine if we can agree on the conceptual and operational definitions of "rural." The literature is characterized by different operational boundaries ranging from 2,500 to 100,000 people. Lack of precision in the research community is of limited value to political leaders, agency administrators and the field staff of our rural criminal justice agencies.

Rural criminal justice practitioners face serious economic challenges. Opportunity exists for confronting delicate questions with responsible political leadership and imaginative organizational management. Should these opportunities be addressed, valuable lessons may, then, become available to the urban professional practitioners.

REFERENCES

Bureau of Justice Statistics. United States Department of Justice. *Report to the Nation on Crime and Justice, 1988.* Washington, DC: United States Government Printing Office, 1988.

_____. *Sourcebook of Criminal Justice Statistics, 1993.* Washington, DC: United States Government Printing Office, 1994.

Carter, D. L., A. D. Sapp, and D. W. Stephens. "Higher Education as a Bona Fide Occupational Qualification (BFOQ) for Police: A Blueprint," *American Journal of Police,* 4, 1989: 1-27.

Chesney-Lind, M. "Girls in Jail," *Crime and Delinquency,* 34, 1988: 150-168.

Christensen, J. A., and G. S. Taylor. "Determinants, Expenditures, and Performance of Common Public Services," *Rural Sociology,* 47, 1982: 147-163.

Clinard, M. B., and R. F. Meier. *Sociology of Deviant Behavior.* Chicago: Holt, Rinehart and Winston, 1989.

Colley, L. L., R. G. Culbertson, and E. Latessa. "Probation Officer Job Analysis: Rural-Urban Differences," *Federal Probation,* 50, 1986: 67-71.

Cook, P. J., and K. L. Mizer. *The Revised ERS County Typology.* Washington, DC: United States Department of Agriculture, 1994.

Eisenstein, J. "Research on Rural Criminal Justice: A Summary," in S. D. Cronk, J. Jankovic, and R. K. Green, eds., *Criminal Justice in Rural America.* Washington, DC: United States Department of Justice, 1982.

Esseltyn, T. C. "The Social Role of the County Sheriff," *The Journal of Criminal Law, Criminology and Police Science,* 44, 1953: 177-184.

Fahnestock, K., and M. D. Geiger. "We All Get Along Here: Case Flow in Rural Courts," *Judicature* 76, 1993: 258-263.

Ginsberg, M. "Rural Criminal Justice: An Overview," *American Journal of Criminal Law,* 3, 1974: 48-49.

Haley, M., and W. H. Smith. "Marengo County Jail Inmate Services Program," in S. D. Cronk, J. Jankovic, and R. K. Green, eds., *Criminal Justice in Rural America.* Washington, DC: United States Department of Justice, 1982.

Jankovic, J., ed. *Juvenile Justice in Rural America.* Knoxville, TN: University of Tennessee, 1980.

Kaplan, J., and J. H. Skolnick. *Criminal Justice.* Mineola, NY: Foundation Press, 1991.

Klofas, J. M. "The Jail and the Community," *Justice Quarterly,* 7, 1990: 69-102.

McDonald, T. D., J. J. Thilmony, and E. C. Schriner. "Rural Delinquents: A Ten Year Assessment of Their Disposition Patterns," in T. N. Ferdinand, ed., *Juvenile Delinquency: Little Brother Grows Up.* Beverly Hills, CA: Sage Publications, 1977.

Melone, A. P., and T. D. McDonald. "Lawyers in a Rural Setting: Community Size and the Sociology of the Bar," *North Dakota Quarterly,* 46, 1978: 21-39.

Murdock, S. H. *An America Challenged.* Boulder, CO: Westview Press, 1995.

National Institute of Corrections. *Planning of New Institutions.* Washington, DC: United States Department of Justice, 1988.

Radelet, L. A. *The Police and the Community.* New York: Macmillan, 1995.

Ralph, P. H., R. M. Hoekstra, and T. R. Brehm. "Community Corrections in Rural States: Reinvolving the Community," in J. Smykla and W. S. Selke, eds., *Intermediate Sanctions: Sentencing in the 1990s.* Cincinnati, OH: Anderson Publishing Company, 1994.

Reid, S. T. *Criminal Justice.* New York: Macmillan, 1993.

Schriner, E. C., J. N. Query, T. D. McDonald, F. Keogh, and T. Gallagher. "An Assessment of the Social Impacts Associated with a Coal Gasification Complex Proposed for Dunn County, ND," *Report to the National Gas Pipeline Company of America.* Chicago: 1976.

Schwartz, I. M. "Introduction," *Crime and Delinquency,* 34, 1988: 131-132.

Schwartz, I. M., L. Harris, and L. Levi. "The Jailing of Juveniles in Minnesota: A Case Study," *Crime and Delinquency,* 34, 1988: 133-149.

Senna, J. J., and L. J. Siegel. *Introduction to Criminal Justice.* Minneapolis/St. Paul: West Publishing Company, 1993.

Sigler, R., and R. Singleton. "LEAA's Impact on a Nonurban County," *Federal Probation,* 48, 1984: 16-21.

Sims, V. H. *Small Town and Rural Police.* Springfield, IL: C. C. Thomas, 1988.

Smolowe, J. "The Trials of the Public Defender," in J. J. Sullivan and J. L. Victor, eds., *Criminal Justice: 94/95.* Guilford, CT: Dushkin Publishing Company, 1994.

Soler, M. "The Hard Facts About Children in Jails," *Perspectives,* 11, 1986/1987: 14-15.

_____. "Litigation on Behalf of Children in Adult Jails," *Crime and Delinquency,* 34, 1988: 190-208.

United States Department of Agriculture. *Understanding Rural America.* Washington, DC: United States Department of Agriculture, 1995.

Warner, J. R., Jr. "Rural Crime, Rural Criminals, Rural Delinquents: Past Research and Future Directions," in S. D. Cronk, J. Jankovic, and R. K. Green, eds., *Criminal Justice in Rural America.* Washington, DC: United States Department of Justice, 1982.

Weisheit, R. A., L. E. Wells, and D. N. Falcone. "Crime and Policing in Rural and Small-Town America: An Overview of the Issues," Washington, DC: National Institute of Justice, 1994a, Draft.

Weisheit, R. A., L. E. Wells, and D. N. Falcone. "Community Policing in Small-Town and Rural America," *Crime and Delinquency,* 40, 1994b: 549-567.

Weisheit, R. A., D. N. Falcone, and L. E. Wells. "Rural Crime and Rural Policing," Washington, DC: National Institute of Justice, 1994c.

Wilson, J. Q. *Varieties of Police Behavior.* Cambridge, MA: Harvard University Press, 1968.

PART II

LAW ENFORCEMENT

The next three major sections of the text focus on agencies that help shape the character of the rural criminal justice system: Law Enforcement (Part II); Rural Courts (Part III); and Corrections (Part IV). The current law enforcement section presents two selections.

Victor H. Sims presents an overview of small town and rural policing in Chapter 3, which is titled "The Structural Components of Rural Law Enforcement: Roles and Organizations." He begins his presentation by briefly describing the distinguishing characteristics of rural life and discussing several aspects of rural law enforcement. One of his major arguments is that law enforcement in such settings contains many of the same qualities as rural society in general. In addition to describing these conditions, the author views the major challenge to law enforcement agencies as being able to provide quality policing within the constraints of limited resources and a lack of skilled leadership.

In the second piece, Curt R. Bartol examines the origins and character of "Stress in Small Town and Rural Law Enforcement." He briefly defines the concept of "stress," describes how it is measured and presents an overview of what the research in the field has concluded. The causes of stress, differences in the types and quantity of stressors, and gender differences are cited as a set of important conditions for those in rural law enforcement. Four major factors are identified as constraints that inhibit coping with stress effectively: 1) a lack of knowledge; 2) insufficient resources; 3) politics; and 4) the general character of small communities themselves. Last, Bartol cites the need for further research into the topic of stress in law enforcement agencies, attracting the interest of more researchers, and interesting students in rural police and small town psychology as major challenges.

CHAPTER 3

The Structural Components of Rural Law Enforcement: Roles and Organizations

by *Victor H. Sims*

INTRODUCTION

The police reflect their parent community, and the limited available evidence suggests that rural law enforcement is no exception. The rural regions of the United States constitute an important, and absolutely essential, segment of our society and culture. Consequently, rural law enforcement, although frequently neglected and ignored by scholars and criminal justice experts, is a crucial and indispensable member of the whole police family. Just as certain characteristics of cities vary with their size and population density, so do law enforcement agencies differ. Policing does not appear to be the same from one city to the next, or from one region of the country to another. This variability echoes the sociological diversity and change that have been hallmarks of history and culture in the United States. To better understand the unique features and milieu of rural law enforcement, this chapter: 1) examines the world of rural people; 2) synthesizes that with what is known about the police in rural communities and small towns.

First, the chapter briefly reviews the major characteristics that distinguish rural life in the United States, and then it explores the many dimensions of rural law enforcement. Despite the popular perception that rural law enforcement exists far from mainstream policing, rural police are closely integrated with their respective communities. This interaction and interdependence is discussed and analyzed. Finally, to help us better understand rural law enforcement, the chapter synthesizes our knowledge of rural living with information concerning the dynamics of rural policing.

Armed with increased knowledge of rural law enforcement, the reader will possess a greater understanding of rural criminal justice. A greater awareness of the workings of the rural criminal justice system means a broader appreciation of criminal justice, generally. Increased knowledge of rural law enforcement also will give the student of policing some penetrating insights into the moment-of-truth that occurs: when any individual police officer helps another person; when he or she influences another in an approved fashion; plus, how in some way, no matter how slight, he or she improves the community and serves justice.

After more than half a century, the Rural Sociological Society still struggles with attempts to develop a precise universal definition of "rurality." As in other areas of the social sciences, great effort is expended collecting subjective data and converting those to objective data for analysis, only to later strain over and speculate about the implications of the findings for the subjective aspects of the study's focus. Nonetheless, such efforts are not wasted. Working to assess that which cannot easily be measured helps to grasp unique features of the rural setting that have not been previously understood.

The United States Bureau of the Census classifies areas and, therefore, individuals living in those areas, as "metropolitan" and "nonmetropolitan." The term "rural" is not interchangeable with "nonmetropolitan," and "metropolitan" does not always translate to "urban." Considerable overlap exists. Rural pockets might be found within urbanized areas, extended cities or even in metropolitan statistical areas (MSA). Urban cities also sometimes prosper in nonmetropolitan counties. The classifications of "nonmetropolitan" and "metropolitan" each may have a rural and urban component.

"Rural," initially, is defined by the Census Bureau as any population outside of unincorporated or incorporated places of more than 2,500 people and/or outside urbanized areas. Those pockets of rural territory inside metropolitan areas usually receive law enforcement service from a relatively large police bureaucracy and, therefore, they will not be included in this chapter. Some of the small towns in nonmetropolitan areas, even though classified as urban, depend on nonbureaucratic or rural law enforcement to provide them with services. These small towns, therefore, must be considered in a study of rural criminal justice. This chapter concentrates on what the Census Bureau labels as either rural or urban, in nonmetropolitan areas.

THE RURAL-URBAN CONTINUUM:
CHARACTERISTICS AND CONDITIONS

The Bureau of the Census must have numbers and precise definitions but there are other approaches to the study of rural sociology. Allowing census figures to constrain the definition of rural law enforcement restricts its study and ignores many important theoretical issues. For example, rurality goes beyond low density living. Many scholars suggest that rurality is a matter of degree. Rural characteristics vary from one extreme that everyone seems to agree is rural, to the opposite extreme where few find anything that appears to be rural. The rural-urban distinction is more of a continuum than a concrete datum point. Rural and urban are not discrete variables. If the rural-urban measure were a yardstick, for example, rural would extend from the 1" end of the measuring instrument to some indiscernible point located at about 23", 24", or 25"; while urban would begin at another invisible point somewhere around 11", 12", or 13" and extend to the 36" end of the yardstick. As the rural-urban distinction becomes increasingly blurred, this convergence results in greater rural and urban interdependence and interpenetration, but not necessarily greater similarity. Stereotypes and common images of rural people and rural law enforcement can prevent an appreciation of the enormous variation displayed in the total rural world.

The differences found between rural areas frequently are significantly greater than the differences between nonmetropolitan and metropolitan places (Brown 1978). Change and diversity always have characterized rural communities and small towns but in recent years these factors have accelerated. Economic vitality, preference for low-density living and modernization are three reasons why approximately one of every five residents in the United States today lives in a rural or small town community (Brown 1978; Bureau of the Census 1994). Retirement, recreation, decentralization of employment, improved communications, transportation and public services also attract new residents to some rural settings.

The changing conditions of the rural population alter people's needs and introduce fresh challenges for each community. No single master plan will work for every rural community. No one policy is guaranteed for each rural law enforcement agency: each program must be tailored to fit specific conditions and needs. The characteristics and limitations of each rural community must be addressed.

Rural counties and communities of the United States have experienced gains in areas other than population and employment, but still they lag behind nonrural settings in some measures. Median family income of nonmetropolitan families is only about 75% that of metropolitan families (Leistritz and Hamm 1994). Poverty in some rural counties soars to 3.5 times the average in metropolitan locations (USDA 1995). A disproportionate share of the nation's poor live in rural sections of the country (Horton et al. 1994). Many of these are the working poor who do not qualify for financial assistance. Nonmetropolitan populations have a higher percentage of younger and older age brackets compared to the working age range. Rural residents also average less formal education than the metropolitan population.

Rural housing frequently is deficient in commonly accepted modern conveniences. A greater percentage of rural homes lack some plumbing. About 200,000 rural homes in the United States were beyond the reach of telephone services less than a decade before the beginning of the twenty-first century (Johnson September 8, 1991).

In contrast to such economic gloom, rural life offers much. Rural families follow more traditional roles and patterns of relationships (Brown 1978; Fuguitt et al. 1989). A traditional nuclear family or extended family household structure characterizes rural areas. Compared to urban areas, a greater proportion of rural households contain a married couple and a lesser percentage includes a single parent. A smaller percentage of rural residents live alone, and of those who do, a greater proportion are elderly (Fuguitt et al. 1989).

Impersonality and bureaucracy frequently are less pronounced in rural communities. When bureaucracies are found in rural parts of the country, they tend to treat individuals more personally and less formally as compared to metropolitan bureaucracies. Self-reliance remains high in nonmetropolitan communities, and traditional American values such as good neighborliness, involvement in community endeavors, sobriety, clean living, hard work and a sense of fair play all appear stronger in rural sections of our nation (Carlson et al. 1981).

Despite the many ways in which rural areas lag behind nonrural settings, studies have shown repeatedly that the majority of United States citizens, if given a choice, would prefer to live in areas of low population density (Brown 1978). Some of the attractions of rural life do not lend themselves to easy empirical assessment. Some of the many expected benefits of low-density living include: 1) a strong sense of community; 2) values of self-reliance and independence; 3) less crime; 4) a cleaner and healthier environment; 5) schools with more personal attention; 6) better surroundings in which to raise children; 7) traditional values; 8) something called "quality of life."

THE RURAL-URBAN POLICE DISTINCTION: CHARACTERISTICS AND CONDITIONS

Rural police, like all other law enforcement officers, mirror the policed population. Urban police tend not to live where they work, while rural officers do. Rural police are more personalistic and less bureaucratic. Rural law enforcement involves less formality and more face-to-face interaction and communication. Additionally, it includes a greater relative percentage of police-acquaintance contacts and a lesser relative fraction of police-stranger contacts. These and other conditions bring unique challenges and constraints to rural law enforcement.

Rural law enforcement officers are many things but commuting police they are not. Most officers in the United States work in a larger city but live in the suburbs or lower density areas. Therefore, most police officers are commuter police. They do not live in the same areas as the people with whom they work. Commuter police monitor strangers and they do not necessarily share a vested interest in the affairs of that community. Rural law enforcement is different. Rural police identify with individual community members. As nonmetropolitan, noncommuting peace officers, they share a genuine interest in the welfare of the community because it is their home.

As stated, rural law enforcement is personalistic and nonbureaucratic, in contrast to the formality, impersonality and bureaucratization of urban police. The structural components of rural law enforcement seem as diverse and varied as the rural people they serve but always within certain parameters. The structural components of rural law enforcement are constrained and controlled by the principles of small group dynamics and interpersonal relationships, just as the principles and properties of bureaucracy dictate the structural components of urban policing (Hummel 1977; Ridgeway 1983; Sims 1988; Weisheit et al. 1994a).

Rural policing differs from urban policing in the same way that small groups differ from bureaucracies. Small group dynamics empower and explain rural law enforcement, just as bureaucratization defines much of urban policing. The organizational components of rural police reflect the great diversity of rural society. For example, Texas has 254 counties and it has been said the Texas sheriffs' offices display 254 kinds of organization.

Rural police agencies are not bureaucracies but they are small groups. Generally, rural officers are closer to each other, and to individuals in the community, than are their counterparts in urban areas. This recurring face-to-face interaction within the law enforcement agency sometimes leads to a semi-democratic organization. Many rural law enforcement agencies are top heavy in their ranks because a quasi-military tradition and expectations of the occupation create an artificial rank-consciousness.

Urban police bureaucracies encourage specialization, while rural law enforcement cultivates and encourages officers to become generalists. As a result, the rank-heavy nature of some rural police agencies seems to have little or no detrimental effect, since virtually all rural police officers are generalists. In a rural setting, it is not unusual to see the police chief taking a vehicle accident report, investigating a felony, talking with children, working routine patrol on the street or giving directions on the interstate to a lost motorist. Similarly, the rural patrol officer, with no rank, would not feel out of place having lunch in the only cafe in town with the banker, mayor or greasy-shirted auto mechanic. Like the chief, the rural patrol officer is a generalist, and he/she is quite confident performing the very same roles reserved for the detective-specialist or Special Weapons Assault Team member in urban departments. These differences prompt some observers to conclude that "... urban police tend to be efficient; rural police tend to be effective" (IACP 1990: 8).

Roles in a bureaucracy are specific and clearly defined. In rural law enforcement, roles are broad, general, ill-defined and interchangeable. Urban police departments, like all bureaucracies, have written policy. It details the rules of the organization and what is expected of each person. Rural law enforcement agencies frequently appear to perform adequately in the absence of any written policy.

RURAL LAW ENFORCEMENT:
CONSTRAINTS AND CHALLENGES

Clearly, the two greatest constraints on rural law enforcement are insufficient fiscal resources and a lack of talented leadership (Carlson et al. 1981; Organization for Economic Co-operation and Development 1986). Metropolitan areas continue to receive a disproportionately large share of national tax-generated resources (Carlson et al. 1981), while local tax bases leave only a small share for many rural governments. Per capita dollars spent for rural police services are 40% of that spent for urban police services (Carlson et al. 1981). It has been estimated that a population of 10,000 is the minimum required for a rural community to comfortably finance a 24 hour, around-the-clock, police operation (Brown 1978). When this author was the police chief of Nome, Alaska, the town—with a population of about 2,500—maintained a full-time police service, which raises two considerations: 1) the tremendous variation in rural law enforcement; 2) the practical issue that governments in rural regions can and do survive with less.

A survey by this author of the police agencies in Mississippi—a rural state—found that police department size was the strongest predictor of police officer salaries. The fewer officers employed by a municipal police department or sheriff's office, the lower the average salary for members of that agency. In contrast, for example, today some of the larger police agencies in Southern California begin their officers with a first year salary that is three times the amount paid to four or five year veteran law enforcement officers who serve rural communities in the Old South.

Such a seemingly unfair imbalance in salaries is explained neither by the occupation nor the size of the police department but instead by the rural setting. Dentists, doctors, public school teachers, judges, truck drivers, small-retail-store owners and carpenters who work in rural communities or small towns also are underpaid in comparison to their counterparts in higher density metropolitan towns. Perhaps lower salaries are a part of the opportunity cost for the improved quality of life in rural society.

The constraints caused by limited revenues are exacerbated and perpetuated by a lack of talented leadership in rural public management. Frequently, rural management systems lack the personnel with the skills necessary to effectively lead and organize. Often, rural public management neither understands the need for planning nor the complex relationship between proper planning and solving interrelated problems.

Developing an atmosphere that encourages the refinement of leadership skills remains one of the challenges for rural administrations. A challenge for rural law enforcement is obtaining advanced and current training for its administrators. Rural communities will realize a handsome return on their investment when they support a police administrator's attendance at any type of school or workshop designed to teach or hone management skills. Administrators of rural departments sometimes tend to handle problems as they occur with little thought given to planning, long range solutions and how rural problems are interrelated (IACP 1990; Marenin and Copus 1991).

Other times, rural administrators try to apply urban solutions to rural problems with absolutely disastrous results. During the nineteenth century, small town and rural police practices were forced on newly formed metropolitan police departments and the problems were exacerbated. During the twentieth century, big city police procedures too frequently were hammered onto rural law enforcement. Today, without their own data bases, rural governments often try to utilize urban solutions (Cronk 1977).

Inadequate initial training of rural law enforcement officers, however, is not the problem it was only a few years ago. The establishment of offices or commissions to oversee police training, and the regulated minimum police standards by individual states contributed to somewhat uniform training for all new police officers. A study of all the police departments in one rural state revealed no correlation between department size and average training for officers. This is remarkable in light of the fact that at the time of the survey, 1982, the state had no minimum requirements, training or otherwise, for its police officers.

In an ironic twist of rural versus urban police training, the Chief of Police of Dallas, Texas, was found unqualified to wear a police uniform and legally carry a pistol (*The Houston Chronicle* September 2, 1991). This occurred in 1991 in a state with strict extensive minimum standards for police training.

One of the challenges confronting the rural police administrator today is producing acceptable results within budgetary constraints—doing more with less. Avoiding cynicism, and the inactivity resulting from it, perhaps is the greatest negative challenge confronting rural police today. Continuing to strengthen relationships with individual community members, and increasing the number of such bonds, possibly are the most important positive challenges facing the individual rural officer.

Rural law enforcement officers fill many roles and wear many hats. One recurring role of the rural peace officer is that of social worker. The rural officer often matches needs with resources (Weisheit et al. 1994b). Rural police officers recognize faces more frequently than do their urban peers and are, therefore, probably more likely to attempt to help others.

Human nature makes it difficult to ignore a need or a call for help when that person wears a familiar face.

As a generalist police officer and as a social worker, the rural peace officer has more occasions than does a metropolitan officer to interact face-to-face with citizens that the officer will see again. This interpersonal relationship forms the basis of all law enforcement. Policing is interpersonal communication or it is nothing. This interpersonal strong suit of rural policing is the core of all effective policing. The conditions of rural society that foster relationships between individual officers and citizens also suggest possible ways to improve policing nationwide.

Community-based policing is a concept of a co-active arrangement between the police and the community—individuals and groups working together to improve the overall well-being and environment of a community or city. Community-based policing is many things and has many definitions but they all pivot on the idea of the individual officer in the field interacting in a personal fashion with people. Rural law enforcement never strayed far from community-based policing and in those few exceptional cases when it did, the offending officer or agency found itself ostracized and rendered ineffective, a victim of its own undoing (Weisheit et al. 1994a).

This relationship between the individual officer and citizen is what makes for effective policing. Strong interpersonal relationships between individual officers and persons in the community certainly are not an exclusive domain of rural police departments. However, all the evidence suggests that this meaningful police interaction does occur with a greater relative frequency in rural communities and small towns.

Many writers and scholars define the concepts of police and policing but only a few tackle the challenge of defining effective policing and what makes a good police officer. In *Police: Streetcorner Politicians*, William Muir, Jr. constructs a widely cited and discussed definition of a good police officer. A good police officer is one who does two things: 1) grasps and understands the nature of human suffering; 2) resolves to one's own satisfaction the paradox every police officer must face of using coercive means to achieve just ends (1977). Additionally, Muir wrote that becoming a good police officer depends to a great degree on the officer's love of talking. Muir's book makes a strong argument that the effective officer is one who cares about people, their lives and their problems both small and large.

Although Muir studied the police of a bureaucratic police department in a metropolitan location, the ideas seem universal. The conditions and constraints, principles and practices, of good policing that Muir addresses appear to be the same as those so frequently found in the delivery of rural police services. Rural law enforcement officers tend to be less bureaucratic and more personalistic. The fact that they are generalists literally forces them to interact on a face-to-face basis with people, and the fact that they are rural inhabitants causes them to repeat these face-to-face encounters with the same people. As mentioned earlier, it is difficult not to care or feel sympathy when suffering wears a familiar face. Rural law enforcement officers possibly accept the tragic nature of the human drama with a greater frequency than do their urban counterparts simply because rural law officers are closer to human suffering and they have fewer protective devices.

Bureaucracy builds distance between the street officer and the needs and suffering of those the police are supposed to serve (Hummel 1977; Lipsky 1980). The bureaucracy attempts to insulate and protect the officer from feeling the human despair so unavoidable in police work.

In contrast, rural law enforcement officers care about people. Rural public servants know that they must live with the results of their work. When the police officer in a big city takes a juvenile into custody or has to make an unpleasant disposition with a case involving an adult, the officer is guided by the knowledge that probably s/he will never see this offender again. In the very same situation, the rural peace officer is guided by the understanding that s/he will likely see this person again and again under totally different circumstances. Such forces cause the officer to consider all possible consequences before taking action and, therefore, these forces influence the officer's decision.

Muir contends that a good police officer is one who loves to talk. Perhaps it is worthwhile to note that Muir does not use the words "enjoys," "likes" or "prefers" but "loves." His book makes a moving case that a good police officer is, indeed, the officer who genuinely loves interpersonal communication. More than a hint of passion emerges. The good police officer sincerely and totally immerses all concentration and focus in talking with people—talking, listening and hearing—engaging in a process of give and take. During the 1960s and 1970s, years before Muir's book, this author was a police officer with the Berkeley, California Police Department. There the necessity and importance of getting out of the patrol car and interacting and talking with citizens were constantly emphasized. The credo was "you can't be a police officer while sitting in a car."

Bureaucracy works in such a way as to limit, and even intentionally decrease, communication between the officer (functionary) and another human being: victim, offender, client, complainant, and the like (Hummel 1977; Lipsky 1980). Unfortunately, too often this occurs at the expense of effective policing in larger cities. Comparing and contrasting urban to rural policing provides insight and understanding of rural law enforcement.

Clear distinctions in attitudes and behaviors exist between rural and urban groups (Carlson et al. 1981). Rural people tend to depend on friends and acquaintances, and to be somewhat distrustful of impersonal bureaucracies. Factors of rural sociology suggest that rural law enforcement officers talk with and seem to care more about their fellow citizens (Carlson et al. 1981). Factors of interpersonal communication indicate that rural peace officers enjoy a relatively higher degree of success in talking with people—and hence in effective policing—because of the greater proportion of interpersonal relationships involved (Emmert and Emmert 1984).

Rural communities often enjoy the benefits of effective policing because so many rural peace officers are good police officers by a definition used and accepted in the occupation. Despite low salaries, derogatory stereotyping, occasional long hours of boredom, and absence of fiscal and tangible rewards, rural police officers experience the same personal gratification that comes to conscientious police officers the world over. In addition to this self-satisfaction, rural law enforcement officers know the contentment of living in low density areas with a spirit of community—where people still matter, and people still care. Rural law enforcement personnel reap all the benefits of a low density environment where the quality of life assumes a different value.

Rural law enforcement is significantly different from mainstream policing in the United States. Rural policing differs from metropolitan policing in much the same fashion as rural living differs from urban life. Rural policing is less bureaucratic and more personalistic. Police officers in rural areas remain closer to the people they serve, and this relationship provides the explanation for much of the effectiveness of rural policing. Law enforcement officers in low density areas feel a sense of common responsibilities and obligations because they work in their home community.

SUMMARY

Policing nationwide will not realize its full potential until each segment reaches perfection, which of course, in the real world is impossible. However, policing nationwide can be improved. Police agencies, urban and rural alike, must seize the initiative to meet the opportunities and face the challenges presented by the hard work and problems that lie ahead. A thousand mile hike begins with one step. One individual can make a difference. One police officer, rural or urban, one police administrator, metropolitan or nonmetropolitan, who cares can improve the delivery of police services. What one police officer says and does can, and will, effect what other people say and do.

This chapter first reviewed some of the attempts that have been made to define rurality. It quickly became clear that "rurality," or ruralness, is somewhat of an abstract, and certainly a subjective, construct. The blurring of the rural-urban convergence reflects the homogenization of the United States' population and society. However, diversity and change remain the normal condition in rural society. We would make a mistake if we were to try and predict the future of the rural parts of our country based on past decades or on this decade.

Next, this chapter discussed rural demographics. Education, income, government services, housing, management and revenues were some of the measures mentioned that differ from rural to urban.

Rural law enforcement was examined and found to contain many of the same properties of rural society. Interpersonal communication, caring, talking with people, being an integral part of the community and identifying with the community set rural law enforcement on the fringes of policing. These same characteristics explain the effectiveness of rural law enforcement. Limited revenues and a lack of skilled leadership are the toughest constraints of the many trying conditions in the world of rural law enforcement. Delivering quality police service with limited resources remains the supreme challenge for both the chief and patrol officer in rural areas.

Roles and organization also reflect their rural environment. Rural peace officers are generalists and social workers who fill many roles beyond the expected law enforcement and police stereotypes. They are truly public servants. Rural law enforcement organization is diverse, again reflecting the diversity of rural areas in the United States.

Finally, the essence of all policing—good policing—was outlined and defined. Rural law enforcement was put to the test and passed with a high score. Possibly urban police could improve by studying their rural counterparts.

REFERENCES

Brown, D. L., ed. *Rural Development Perspectives*. Washington, DC: United States Government Printing Office, 1978.

Carlson, J. E., M. L. Lassey, and W. R. Lassey. *Rural Society and Environment in America*. New York: McGraw-Hill, 1981.

Cronk, S. D., ed. *A Beginning Assessment of the Justice System in Rural Areas*. Washington, DC: National Rural Center, 1977.

"Dallas Chief Studying to Meet Police Standards," *The Houston Chronicle*, September 2, 1991: A25.

Emmert, P., and V. J. L. Emmert. *Interpersonal Communication*. Dubuque, IA: Wm. C. Brown, 1984.

Fuguitt, G. V., D. L. Brown, and C. L. Beale. *Rural and Small Town America*. New York: Russell Sage Foundation, 1989.

Horton, P. B., G. R. Leslie, R. F. Larson, and R. L. Horton. *The Sociology of Social Problems*. Englewood Cliffs, NJ: Prentice Hall, 1994.

Hummel, R. P. *The Bureaucratic Experience*. New York: St. Martin's Press, 1977.

International Association of Chiefs of Police (IACP). *Managing the Small Law Enforcement Agency*. Dubuque, IA: Kendall/Hunt, 1990.

Johnson, D. "Nebraska Village Symbolizes Death of America's Small Towns," *The Houston Chronicle*, August 25, 1991: 8A.

_____. "Telephone Service Unavailable to 200,000 Rural Households," *The Houston Chronicle*, September 8, 1991: 20B.

Leistritz, F. L., and R. Hamm. *Rural Economic Development 1975-1993*. Westport, CT: Greenwood Press, 1994.

Lipsky, M. *Street-Level Bureaucracy*. New York: Russell Sage Foundation, 1980.

Marenin, O., and G. Copus. "Policing Rural Alaska: The Village Public Safety Officer (VPSO) Program," *American Journal of Police*, 10, 1991: 1-26.

Muir, W. K. *Police: Streetcorner Politicians*. Chicago: University of Chicago Press, 1977.

Organization for Economic Cooperation and Development. *Rural Public Management*. Paris: Author, 1986.

Ridgeway, C. L. *The Dynamics of Small Groups*. New York: St. Martin's Press, 1983.

Sims, V. H. *Small Town and Rural Police*. Springfield, IL: Charles C. Thomas, 1988.

United States Bureau of the Census. *Statistical Abstract of the United States: 1994*. United States Department of Commerce, Washington, DC: United States Government Printing Office, 1994.

United States Department of Agriculture, Economic Research Service. *Understanding Rural America*. Agriculture Information Bulletin No. 710. Washington, DC: United States Department of Agriculture, 1995.

Weisheit, R. A., L. E. Wells, and D. N. Falcone. "Community Policing in Small Town and Rural America," *Crime and Delinquency*, 40, 1994a: 549-567.

Weisheit, R. A., D. N. Falcone, and L. E. Wells. *Rural Crime and Rural Policing*. National Institute of Justice, Washington, DC: United States Government Printing Office, 1994b.

CHAPTER 4

Stress in Small-Town and Rural Law Enforcement

by *Curt R. Bartol*

INTRODUCTION

For several decades law enforcement work was believed to rank among the top of all occupations in the amount and variety of stress it promotes. Spurred on by the underlying assumption that law enforcement work is the most stressful of all occupations, considerable research interest and federal funding have been directed at studying stress among males in metropolitan or urban law enforcement. This research has generated a substantial collection of papers, articles and books about stress. However, research focusing on stress experienced by rural or small-town law enforcement officers largely has been neglected. Considering that 85% of the 20,000 law enforcement agencies in the United States employ less than 25 full-time officers, the lack of research interest in stress among rural and small-town law enforcement officials is surprising (Bartol 1991). Perhaps the research neglect stems from the unwarranted assumption that the causes and nature of stress are the same for all law enforcement officers—large city or small city, metropolitan or rural, deputy sheriffs or municipal officers, men or women.

This chapter focuses on the causes and nature of stress encountered by individuals working in small-town and rural law enforcement. In this context, "small-town" refers to communities and municipalities with populations of less than 50,000 and located away from any urban sprawl. "Rural" law enforcement refers to the work performed primarily by county sheriff's departments. Although highway patrol and state police agencies also deal with rural areas, our focus is restricted to the more localized small-town and rural agencies. The chapter begins by briefly defining "stress" and how it is typically measured. Next, it summarizes what is known about stress in law enforcement generally. Then it focuses on what we know about stress in rural law enforcement, the constraints for dealing with the issue and the challenges.

Definition of Stress

"Stress" first was used as an engineering term that referred to any external force directed at a physical object (Lazarus 1966). It was introduced into the life sciences in 1936 by endocrinologist Hans Selye who became one of the world's leading researchers of biological stress (Appley and Trumbull 1967). Selye directed most of his attention to effects of biological stress on the physiological and biochemical functions of the living organism. He defined stress as "the nonspecific response of the body to any demand" (Selye 1976: 15). The bodily reaction to stress is presumed to be generalized, with the whole body system as a unit engaged in reducing or eliminating "agents" that cause stress. The agents, which Selye called "stressors," may be external to the organism (exogenous) or within the organism (endogenous), and they may develop from a virus, physical injury or disease-causing agent. The effects that these stressors create are called "stress."

Recently, the term "stress" has been extended to include "psychological stress." The term "stressor(s)" has come to mean any stimulus or stimuli that generates self-reported feelings of frustration, threat, conflict or pressures that threaten the individual's ability to cope. Psychological stress occurs when a stimulus initiates a response that does not lead to greater perceived or actual control over the stimulus. With the exception of extreme and sudden life-threatening situations, it is unlikely that any particular stimulus is a stressor to all individuals exposed to it. Whether stress develops greatly depends on how the person perceives and appraises the stimulus in combination with the person's coping strategies and life experiences. Typically, stress results in sympathetic activity of the autonomic nervous system that often produces a variety of physical ailments; from backaches and headaches to digestive problems and ulcers. Thus, among the standard equipment found in the glove compartment of many small-town police cruisers is an assortment of antacids.

In psychology the most common response to stressors is called "anxiety," a term often used interchangeably with stress reaction. Anxiety is an unpleasant emotional state marked by worry, fear, anger, apprehension and muscular tension. The anxious person may stammer or display other speech disturbances, may chainsmoke, display irritability, avoid a situation or assume any number of other behavioral patterns.

Measurement of Stress

To conduct effective research on stress and bring it out of the realm of speculation, it would be helpful if social and behavioral scientists were able to measure it. Ideally, this measurement calls for methods of discovering how much stress a person is going through at a particular time, and how much cumulative stress the person has faced. Stress seems to accumulate: a group of relatively minor stressors, called "micro-stressors," can build toward a serious stress reaction over time.

Psychological stress is a highly subjective experience and, consequently, there is no satisfactory objective way to measure it. We can measure it only indirectly, and the best measure currently available is to ask individuals to report their perceived stressors and their reactions to them. This method is called a "self-report survey" or questionnaire.

In the self-report survey, people tell researchers what feelings they are experiencing or have experienced, what they think precipitated these feelings, and in some instances, what they are doing to adjust. However, due to individual differences in how one appraises stress conditions, comparable, quantifiable data often are difficult to obtain unless the researcher sets up objective, standardized surveys that limit the variety of responses.

A number of standardized surveys have been developed to measure the subjective appraisal of psychological stress elicited by various stimuli and everyday events. James Sewell, for example, developed a stress scale specifically designed for law enforcement (1983). The scale, called the Law Enforcement Critical Life-Events Scale (LECLES), lists 144 events that may be stressors for officers; from the pursuit of a traffic violator, to the death of another officer in the line of duty. The officers are asked to indicate on a scale of 1 (no stress) to 100 (extremely high stress) the stress they experienced when confronted with a given event. Sewall found that the most stressful event for large-city or metropolitan officers was the violent death of a partner in the line of the duty (rated an average of 88), followed by dismissal (85) and taking a life in the line of duty (84) (More 1992). Many researchers, however, find the LECLES inadequate to address certain issues, and they have developed their own self-report surveys (Bartol and Bartol 1994).

THE CONDITIONS FOR STRESS IN LAW ENFORCEMENT
A common strategy employed in the police stress literature is to divide stressors into four major categories: 1) organizational; 2) external; 3) task-related; 4) personal (Kroes et al. 1974; Wexler and Logan 1983).

Types of Police Stress
Our category of police stress includes "organizational stressors" which generally refer to the policies and practices of the law enforcement agency itself. They include: poor pay, excessive paperwork, insufficient training, inadequate equipment, weekend duty, limited promotional opportunities, incompetent supervision and nonexistent administrative support, and strained relationships with supervisors or colleagues. Several surveys also have reported shift work as a major organizational stressor (Hilton 1973; Margolis 1973; Eisenberg 1975; Kroes 1976). Shift work interferes with sleep and eating habits, and with family life. Irregular hours often preclude social get-togethers and family activities, a job characteristic that socially isolates the law enforcement officer even more. The organizational structure of large police departments often promotes office politics, lack of effective consultation, non-participation in decision making and restrictions on behavior (Cooper and Marshall 1976).

"Task-related stressors" refer to the nature of police work, such as: inactivity and boredom; situations requiring the use of force; responsibility of protecting others; the use of discretion; the fear that accompanies danger to oneself and colleagues; dealing with violent or aggressive individuals; making critical decisions; frequent exposure to death; continual exposure to people in pain or distress; and constant need to keep one's emotions under close control. It is likely that task-related stressors found in large-metropolitan policing are significantly different from those found in small-town and rural law enforcement. For example, Stotland makes a connection between workload and stress (1991). He divides law enforcement careers into two categories, depending on the amount of fast-moving action they experience on a daily basis while on the job. Those officers who are exposed daily to shootings, crime, drugs and violent incidents are called "high-workload" officers. "Low-workload" officers are exposed to much less violent and high-paced incidents, so they experience a different kind of stress. Low-workload officers serve the community by engaging in more ordinary tasks, such as we would find in small, low-crime communities or rural areas. These ordinary tasks often result in sheer boredom, which produces its own stress. While it is different than the stressors found in fast-paced policing, boredom can carry many of the same discomforts and burnout rates as "high-workload" stressors.

"External stressors" include frustration with: the courts, the prosecutor's office, the criminal process, the correctional system, and the media and public attitudes. For example, for every 100 felony arrests, 43 typically are dismissed or not prosecuted, a situation that can result in considerable frustration for the arresting officers (Witkin 1990). Many law enforcement officers feel that court appearances are excessively time consuming, and often they are frustrated over judicial procedures and inefficiency. It has been suggested that one of the predominant stressors confronting law enforcement officers is alienation (Niederhoffer 1967). Jirak found that alienation due to perceived lack of support from political groups, the press, the courts and the public was a dominant stressor for New York City law enforcement officers (1975). He found that feelings of alienation usually increased throughout an officer's career, reaching a peak about the fifteenth year of service, at which point they decreased, apparently due to anticipated retirement. This trend also was reported by Lotz and Regoli (1977). Law enforcement-community relations are presumed to be important contributing factors to feelings of alienation (Skolnick 1973). In a survey study of United States police by Chappell and Meyer, only 2% of the officers polled believed the public held them in high esteem (1975). Related to this perceived alienation is the often-reported role conflict between what law enforcement officers think they *should* be doing (e.g., crime detection and arrest), and what the public *believes* they should be doing (e.g., protecting citizens, settling family disputes, chasing unleashed dogs) (Wilson 1968).

"Personal stressors" involve: marital relationships, health problems, addictions, peer group pressures, feelings of helplessness and depression, and lack of achievement. Research in this area has focused almost exclusively on male officers but the exceptions will be discussed later in the chapter. In a survey conducted by Kroes et al., 79 of the 81 married police officers interviewed felt that the nature of their work had an adverse effect on their home life (1974). More specifically, the officers thought that police work gave a negative public image to their family, that their spouses worried regularly about their safety, that they took the tremendous pressures of the job home, that it made them less able to plan social events, and that the job inhibited non-police friendships. A survey of 100 police spouses—all women—revealed that nearly one-fourth were dissatisfied with their husbands' careers and that particular aspects of the job resulted in frequent family arguments (Rafky 1974).

What Category of Stressors Is Most Stressful?

Kroes et al., using semi-structured interviews, found that perceived sources of stress for Cincinnati male police officers largely were organizational in nature (1974). Task-related stressors did not emerge as a major source of stress, contrary to what commonly is supposed (see, for example, Somodevilla 1978).

In one of the few studies examining stress in smaller departments, Crank and Caldero investigated self-reported stress in eight medium sized Illinois municipal police departments ranging from 40 to 100 full-time officers (1991). The researchers passed out a questionnaire to officers present at roll call for all shifts. Their study focused on one item in the questionnaire that requested officers to write a statement "about what you think is your greatest source of stress, and why" (Crank and Caldero 1991: 341). Only 6 of the 162 officers were identified as women, precluding a meaningful comparison by gender. More than two-thirds of the respondents (68.3%) perceived the organization as their principal source of stress, which was reflected particularly in problems with superior officers, usually their immediate supervisors. The second most frequent stress source identified was task-related (16.2%), followed by the court system, which is an external source (7.2%). Level of stress intensity was not measured.

Stressors of Small-Town and Rural Law Enforcement

The variety and amount of stressors faced by small-town police officers and rural-county sheriffs appear to be significantly different from those encountered by metropolitan or urban police officers. For example, informal discussions with rural officers in Maine by Sandy and Devine suggest that at least four stressors are unique to small-town or rural patrol (1978). Three of these stressors are task-related: 1) security; 2) working conditions; 3) inactivity. The fourth stressor, social, is external.

"Security stressors" center around the extreme sense of isolation experienced by officers confronting incidents in the field, especially domestic disturbances. Rural and small-town officers usually work alone, without readily available backup. They quickly must decide when encountering dangerous situations whether to deal with the situation themselves or to call and wait for backup, which may take 30 minutes or longer to arrive. Metropolitan or urban officers, on the other hand, if working alone are encouraged—as a matter of policy—to call for backup, which typically arrives within minutes. Moreover, contributing to perceived lack of security is the observation that a majority of homes in rural areas contain a collection of firearms purchased either for protection, hunting or both.

"Working conditions stressors" include low salary and marginal benefits, plus inadequate equipment and resources. Additionally, as mentioned earlier, inactivity and boredom can be significant stressors. Sitting alone in a cruiser night after night while a small, isolated, lonely town closes down can, indeed, be stressful.

"Social stressors" in the rural context involve the absence of anonymity that officers experience, both on and off patrol. Like those of other residents of a small community, the habits and behaviors of law enforcement officers are open to public scrutiny. Frequently, officers refer to this phenomenon as the "fishbowl factor." A majority of small-town and rural officers have been born and raised within the community in which they work and live. Residents have known them since kindergarten. Enforcing the law against people they have known all their lives often produces dilemmas that may be highly stressful.

For over 17 years, I have been conducting a longitudinal study on the careers of 869 small-town police officers and rural-county sheriffs (Bartol 1991). A recent study based on these data examined the stressors and problems faced by officers in small-town municipal law enforcement (Bartol et al. 1992). The study examined: the sources of stress for these officers; whether female and male officers in the same department experience the same stressors; how stressors affect performance; and whether there are identifiable predictors of susceptibility to police-related stress. Performance was measured by supervisory evaluations of 11 behaviors believed to be critical for adequate performance in small-town or rural law enforcement. The level of stress for each officer was measured by observations of supervisors (usually police chiefs) and the responses to a self-report questionnaire from the police officers themselves. Personality susceptibility to stress also was measured by scores on a standard personality inventory (Minnesota Multiphasic Personality Inventory) that were obtained prior to hire and, generally, before they received any law enforcement experience.

The results of the analysis revealed that external stressors emerged as the category that small-town police officers, both men and women, found the most stressful, followed closely by organizational stressors. Based on comments by the officers, the "liberal" attitude of the courts, dealing with prosecutors who are "always playing let's make a deal" and "constantly being in the public eye" (the "fishbowl factor") were among the leading specific external stressors. These small-town officers found that working and living in a small community where everyone knows your business—including what clothes you washed at the laundromat— can be surprisingly stressful. One officer remarked, "You are never off duty and when you tell someone—who wants something at that moment— that you are off duty, they remind me that they pay my salary."

Specific organizational stressors included: constant politics within the department; lack of recognition for good work; inadequate retirement plans and poor pay; insufficient personnel to do the job effectively; and colleagues not carrying their fair share of the load. A majority of the 46 departments that we surveyed were staffed by less than five full-time officers. It is imperative, therefore, that the officers get along reasonably well and do their fair share of the work load. If an officer did not feel that he or she fit in, the level of stress experienced usually resulted in their leaving the department, often for another in a nearby town. Generally, officers find their niche in large urban departments but in small departments they do not have that luxury because there is only one niche. Another stressor that continually cropped up was the poor pay and retirement benefits that small-town departments provided. In fact, this stressor was one that often contributed to constant moving by officers from one department to another, in a chronic but largely unsuccessful, search for a better pay package.

In this project, we found that the perceived stress caused by the job itself (task-related) was significantly less than external or organizational stress; a finding also reported by Crank and Caldero for medium-size police departments in Illinois (1991). So, it is not the job itself that causes most of the stress, it is the peripheral aspects of the job.

Gender Differences in Law Enforcement Stress

Policewomen and policemen reported the same magnitude of stress for the usual organizational, external and personal stressors reported in law enforcement. There were, however, significant gender differences in the task-related stressors as well as in the type of stressors within the other categories. With task-related stressors, policewomen experienced more stress than policemen in those areas requiring sensitivity and empathy. Specifically, the policewomen indicated that they strongly were affected by the tragedy, pain and death they encounter in police work. In fact, many of the female officers noted that frequently encountering abused and dead children was one of the most stressful aspects of the job and one to which they never adjusted. A similar finding was reported by Wexler and Logan in their study of large-city policewomen (1983). In contrast, policemen with experience seem to become more calloused and less affected by these personal tragedies. Female officers also reported more stress than their male counterparts as a result of the sense of responsibility they have for the lives and safety of the public, as well as for the safety of their police colleagues. Nevertheless, these higher levels of stress reported by female officers did not translate into poor or substandard performance. The chiefs and supervisors evaluated their performance to be as effective and competent as their male counterparts. More often than not, the policewomen in small departments performed better in all phases of policing than their male peers.

Although the small-town policewomen generally reported the same level of stress for the three other stress categories commonly reported in the police literature, they did identify different kinds of stressors. Women entering the male-dominated occupation of law enforcement are likely to face an array of stressors usually not experienced by men. This especially is the case in small-town or rural law enforcement where the "ol' boy" system and the town "fathers" continue to have a strong influence on—if not control over—the law enforcement agency's operations, which include: hiring practices, promotional opportunities, training, pay and retirement benefits, and assignments. These small-town and rural stressors include sexual harassment, discrimination, rumors, negative attitudes of male officers and supervisors, working as the sole female officer, and lack of role models. Little is known about how male police administrators, usually who have been hired through the ranks, view female officers (Weisheit and Mahan 1988). In small-town law enforcement, this is a critical variable because the chain of command is direct and uncomplicated. Additionally, we know very little about how small-town policewomen view their supervisors.

Much of the contemporary research, beginning in the 1970s, on women in law enforcement has concentrated on comparing the job performance of men and women to determine if women physically and psychologically can handle the rigors of law enforcement work, particularly patrol assignments. This research consistently has found that women can do law enforcement work at least as effectively as men in large metropolitan departments (Pendergrass and Ostrove 1984; Feinman 1986; Balkin 1988), and in small-town departments (Bartol et al. 1992). Despite the growing research that continually finds women capable of law enforcement work, women officers still face many obstacles and stressors. Interestingly, one of the greatest barriers to accepting women into law enforcement does not come from the public but from male officers, particularly male supervisors (Wexler and Logan 1983; Bartol et al. 1992).

In another project focusing on why women leave small-town law enforcement, we discovered that 43% of the women who left law enforcement said that the high amount of stress associated with sexual harassment from male officers, particularly male supervisors, was the primary reason for their leaving (Bartol and Urzillo 1993b). Another 33% said that they had been sexually harassed by male officers, mostly supervisors, but these women stated that harassment was not the primary reason for leaving the department. In our interviews with the policewomen who left the force specifically because of sexual harassment, they indicated that the constant onslaught of sexual harassment made job situations uncomfortable, stressful and not worth pursuing. The other policewomen who experienced sexual harassment but who did not leave because of it found harassment a very stressful and disrupting influence on relationships within the department.

Researchers have studied how women adapt and adjust to the barriers and gender discrimination found in male-dominated police culture. Some writers have asserted that female officers go through a period of stages, running from the "honeymoon" stage, to the "ambivalent" stage, to the "transition" stage (see, for example, Berg and Budnick 1986; More 1992). However, it is an oversimplification to assume that members of any group go through a series of stages and adapt to environments the same way. Another research approach is to identify the various strategies that women use to adapt to law enforcement work.

Judie Gaffin Wexler, in her study of a large metropolitan department in northern California, identified four role styles adopted by women in law enforcement: 1) neutral-impersonal; 2) feminine; 3) semi-masculine; 4) mixed (1985). The largest number of women officers in her sample adopted the "neutral-impersonal" style, where a businesslike attitude toward their male colleagues was apparent. Women who followed this style wanted to be treated with respect as full and equal members of the work group, and they shunned special treatment from colleagues or administrators. Wexler found, however, that the women in this group believed some aspects of law enforcement work had to be approached differently than the traditional approach used by their male counterparts. For example, they believed that force often was unnecessary in accomplishing certain goals, such as making arrests. Wexler discovered that women who adopted the neutral-impersonal style typically did not do much socializing with their male colleagues, and 50% of them described their relationships with the male officers as distant and tenuous.

Wexler defined the "semi-masculine style" as a tendency to be professional and do the job well, while believing that as policewomen they would not be totally accepted as equals in this male-dominated profession. The women who adopted this style did expect to be treated as individuals, however. In contrast to the neutral-impersonal officers, the semi-masculine officers believed that they could be accepted as individuals by socializing with the male officers, by joking with them, by going out after work for drinks, and by cheering for or participating in departmental sports teams.

Women who adopted what Wexler called the "feminine style" put more emphasis on the fact that they were women in the physical sense. "Being attractive at work was important to them" (Wexler 1985: 752). Interactions with male officers often carried sexual undertones, in which these women used their femininity to gain acceptance. Policewomen in this group accepted or desired special treatment from colleagues and supervisors, and they accepted male protectiveness on the job. Wexler observed that women who followed this style really were not accepted in the informal work group, and they were not taken seriously enough by the male officers for information to be shared with them.

The "mixed style" is characterized by women using all three styles, with no particular style dominating. These female officers wanted to gain respect by hard work and interpersonal distance, but they often resorted to a combination of conscientious hard work, flirting and teasing to reach their goals. They also wanted to be treated as equals and refused special treatment. Wexler found that very few of the policewomen used the mixed style.

We tested Wexler's classifications on small-town policewomen, examining style and strategies used in the field, as well as within the department (Bartol and Urzillo 1993a). We discovered that small-town policewomen did not use any single style or strategy, but they used a variety of them depending on the situation. We were able to identify at least eight different strategies or styles commonly utilized by small-town policewomen, both in the field and on their colleagues in the department. Some were similar to Wexler's categories but many were substantially different, which suggests that a different repertoire of strategies may be necessary for successful performance by women in small-town or rural law enforcement. Moreover, we found that the women who used multiple strategies experienced less stress overall, they seemed to perform more effectively in all areas of policing, and they had the lowest job turnover rate.

Whether this finding for police*women* holds for police*men* is unknown. However, current research suggests that the style of law enforcement used by women as a group may be more effective than styles employed by men as a group. For example, many law enforcement administrators and a large segment of the public believe that female officers are better able than male officers to defuse a potentially dangerous or violent situation (Bell 1982; Balkin 1988; Weisheit and Mahan 1988). Interestingly, the police chief of Madison, Wisconsin was quoted as saying that he believed female officers made his police department a "kinder, gentler organization" (McDowell 1992: 72).

A recent study by Johnson underscores observations that women have a "gentling effect" when dealing with the public and, generally, they experience less stress overall (1991). Johnson looked at gender differences in burnout. Specifically, she examined "internal burnout" that is characterized by feelings of being emotionally depleted on the job, and "external burnout" that is characterized by feelings of being emotionally hardened by the job and lacking compassion for citizens. While there were no significant gender differences in self-described internal burnout, men showed a greater tendency to report feelings of external burnout. Johnson concluded that the relatively low external burnout rate among women officers perhaps was a result of their less aggressive and more gentle policing style. Johnson found in her interviews that policewomen spoke about the compassion they brought to the job, as well as their strong preference for dealing with the public verbally and psychologically, instead of physically.

All of these research discoveries, along with consistent findings that women are perfectly capable of meeting the physical and emotional demands of law enforcement work, suggest that the future for women in law enforcement should be bright. This should be true especially for women working in small-town or rural law enforcement, where the officer must rely on an assortment of interpersonal skills, plus be a "jack-of-all-trades" (Bartol 1982).

CONSTRAINTS
There are four major problems that hamper effective control and reduction of stress in small-town and rural law enforcement: 1) knowledge; 2) resources; 3) politics; 4) the nature of small communities.

Knowledge
One of the overwhelming constraints in successfully dealing with the stress of small-town and rural law enforcement is that we know very little about it. Knowledge about how small-town and rural law enforcement differ from big city, metropolitan or large agency departments is scarce but critical if we are to implement successful programs and effective techniques for stress management. For example, the research literature in industrial/organizational psychology suggests that stress and job performance are inversely related: the higher the stress, the lower the satisfactory job performance. Miner writes: "Performance—whether measured by supervisor ratings, organizational perceptions of effectiveness, or job performance on job-related examinations—has repeatedly been found to decrease with increasing levels of stress" (1992: 156). To date, however, literature on police stress is lacking in assessments of the impact of stress on performance, especially as it pertains to small-town and rural law enforcement (Malloy and Mays 1984; Sewell et al. 1988). Moreover, we do not know what levels of stress are disruptive in law enforcement. It is possible, for instance, that there is a certain amount of stress that increases alertness in officers, and this "optimal" level may be necessary for effective performance.

There are, however, some educated guesses about the nature of the relationships between law enforcement experience, stress and job performance. These hunches may be placed into three major categories based on the relationship between job experience and job stress: 1) the positive linear hunch; 2) the curvilinear hunch; 3) the negative linear hunch. Niederhoffer's research on a large metropolitan department illustrates the positive linear hunch (1967). He supposes that as law enforcement experience increases, self-reports of stress should correspondingly increase, provided that the individual remains a patrol officer as opposed to being promoted to administrator. According to Niederhoffer, therefore, we can expect job performance to decrease with experience.

Violanti's research of several large departments represents the curvilinear hunch (1983). He hypothesizes a curvilinear relationship between stress and experience, with stress increasing during the first 14 years of experience, decreasing after 14 to 20 years of experience (the personalization stage) and increasing again prior to retirement (after 20 to 25 years of experience). Following Violanti's position, we would expect to find an inverted U-shaped function, with job performance low and stress high in an officer's early years, performance at its peak during the middle career years when stress is low, and performance declining while stress increases toward the end of the officer's career.

The negative linear hunch is presented by Ezra Stotland (Stotland 1986, 1991; Stotland et al. 1989). Stotland predicts that as job experience increases job stress will decrease. Consequently, we can expect job performance to increase with experience.

Unfortunately, abundant research examining the relationship between stress, experience and performance is sparse. Our own research over the past 17 years suggests that the negative linear hunch seems to hold for small-town and rural law enforcement. These data identify that job performance (as evaluated by supervisors) increases with experience, while both self-reported and supervisory-reported stress decreases. This relationship may help explain why small-town police officers, on average, are significantly older than officers working in large metropolitan departments. However, we need to know much more before we can advance firm conclusions about the stress-performance relationship.

Another issue related to knowledge constraints is that far too often police psychologists are not specifically trained, suited and knowledgeable about the stressors of small-town or rural law enforcement. While psychologists have clinical skills and knowledge about human behavior in general, frequently they lack the know-how for application to specific areas of law enforcement. This observation especially seems to hold for small-town and rural law enforcement.

Resources

Psychological stress is increasingly recognized as a serious threat to effective performance in law enforcement. It is not surprising, therefore, that large police departments are increasingly hiring full-time police psychologists, or psychological, counseling or psychiatric consultants who are available to consult on cases, and to offer their services to individual officers on an ongoing basis. Delprino and Bahn reported, for example, that 53% of police agencies studied used counseling services for job-related stress (1988). About one-third of these agencies also hired psychologists to provide relevant workshops and seminars on stress management.

Additionally, many family support groups are appearing throughout the country, frequently at the instigation of police spouses who band together to discuss and solve common problems. However, serious monetary constraints prevent small-town police and rural sheriff's departments from hiring full-time police psychologists, and there are further funding limits to retaining psychological consultants to help officers deal with stress, especially by providing meaningful workshops, seminars or training sessions on stress management. Some town or county budgetary constraints even prevent officers from receiving paid release time to attend training sessions, and they do not have the monies to provide counseling for their officers. This trend is likely to continue if the federal government continues to allocate increasingly fewer monies and grants for law enforcement training and services to states, counties and communities.

Politics

In an effort to afford effective law enforcement, there is a discernible shift toward more regional (and larger) agencies and away from small, localized law enforcement departments. Larger regional departments, of course, can pool the limited resources of small communities and, thereby, provide necessary organizational services including stress counseling and management. However, people in small communities continue to want control over local law enforcement and so they resist attempts to create regionalized, perhaps more impersonal, agencies.

Another political constraint is that the small department atmosphere and "the way of doing things" largely is controlled by the police chief or sheriff, sometimes in conjunction with the town manager or chairperson of the town board. Often, these administrators see little need for dealing with stress, and they would rather see their limited resources and personnel funnelled toward providing direct services to the community.

The Nature of the Small Community

The fishbowl factor works against officers going to see a "shrink" within the community. Many residents of small communities expect their officers to be emotionally strong, and they interpret a need for counseling as a sign of weakness. Many police chiefs and sheriffs have similar attitudes, and it is not uncommon for administrators to ask those officers who indicate problems with stress to leave the department. We have found in our longitudinal research that officers who maintain a "stiff upper lip" and manage to hide their emotions, continually receive significantly better performance evaluations over their careers than those who are more willing to admit stress (Bartol 1982, 1991).

SUMMARY

The overwhelming challenge to address stress in small-town and rural law enforcement is to increase the number and quality of research studies examining the problems that they face. We need to learn considerably more about the nature of stress in small law enforcement agencies, and what practical procedures and training are necessary to combat it. A second major challenge is to get more researchers and scholars interested in small-town and rural law enforcement. The area has suffered benign neglect for too long, partly because most of the funding has been directed to large metropolitan departments. Third, we need to get more students interested in pursuing professional careers in small-town and rural police psychology. There is a major shortage of knowledgeable and specifically trained psychologists in this area. One of the challenges for people following a police psychology career is to find ways to get effective and necessary services to the officers without undue strain on the budgets. Finally, we need to educate the public and police supervisors in rural areas about the need for stress management. Related to the challenges of educating the public and law enforcement agencies are the myth and stereotypes about women in law enforcement. It is critical that we educate the police community and the public about the ability and non-violent styles women can bring to small-town and rural law enforcement.

REFERENCES

Appley, M. H., and R. Trumbull. *Psychological Stress*. New York: Appleton-Century-Crofts, 1967.

Balkin, J. "Why Policemen Don't Like Policewomen," *Journal of Police Science and Administration*, 16, 1988: 29-37.

Bartol, C. R. "Psychological Characteristics of Small-Town Police Officers," *Journal of Police Science and Administration*, 10, 1982: 58-63.

_____. "Predictive Validation of the MMPI for Small-Town Police Officers Who Fail," *Professional Psychology: Research and Practice*, 22, 1991: 127-132.

Bartol, C. R., and A. M. Bartol. *Psychology and Law: Research and Applications*. Pacific Grove, CA: Brooks/Cole, 1994.

Bartol, C. R., G. T. Bergen, J. S. Volckens, and K. M. Knoras. "Women in Small-Town Policing: Job Performance and Stress," *Criminal Justice and Behavior*, 19, 1992: 240-259.

Bartol, C. R., and B. A. Urzillo. "Role Styles of Small-Town Policewomen," unpublished manuscript, 1993a.

_____. "Why Do Women Leave Small-Town Law Enforcement?," unpublished manuscript, 1993b.

Bell, D. J. "Policewomen: Myths and Reality," *Journal of Police Science and Administration*, 10, 1982: 112-120.

Berg, B. L., and K. L. Budnick. "Defeminization of Women in Law Enforcement: A New Twist in the Traditional Police Personality," *Journal of Police Science and Administration*, 10, 1986: 180-185.

Chappell, D., and J. C. Meyer. "Cross-Cultural Differences in Police Attitudes: An Exploration in Comparative Research," *Australian and New Zealand Journal of Criminology*, 8, 1975: 5-13.

Cooper, C. L., and J. Marshall. "Occupational Sources of Stress: A Review of the Literature Relating to Coronary Heart Disease and Mental Ill Health," *Journal of Occupational Psychology*, 49, 1976: 11-28.

Crank, J. P., and M. Caldero. "The Production of Occupational Stress in Medium-Sized Police Agencies: A Survey of Line Officers in Eight Municipal Departments," *Journal of Criminal Justice*, 19, 1991: 339-349.

Delprino, R. P., and C. Bahn. "National Survey of the Extent and Nature of Psychological Services in Police Departments," *Professional Psychology: Research and Practice*, 19, 1988: 421-425.

Eisenberg, T. "Labor-Management Relations and Psychological Stress: View from the Bottom," *The Police Chief,* 42, 1975: 54-58.

Feinman, C. *Women in the Criminal Justice System,* 2d ed. New York: Praeger, 1986.

Hilton, J. "Psychology and Police Work," in J. C. Anderson and P. J. Stead, eds., *The Police We Deserve*. London: Wolfe Publishers, 1973.

Jirak, M. "Alienation Among Members of the New York City Police Department of Staten Island," *Journal of Police Science and Administration*, 3, 1975: 149-161.

Johnson, L. B. "Job Strain Among Police Officers: Gender Comparisons," *Police Studies*, 14, 1991: 12-16.

Kroes, W. H. *Society's Victim—The Policemen: An Analysis of Job Stress in Policing*. Springfield, IL: C. C. Thomas, 1976.

Kroes, W. H., B. Margolis, and J. J. Hurrell. "Job Stress in Policemen," *Journal of Police Science and Administration*, 2, 1974: 145-155.

Lazarus, R. S. *Psychological Stress and the Coping Process*. New York: McGraw-Hill, 1966.

Lotz, R., and R. M. Regoli. "Police Cynicism and Professionalism," *Human Relations*, 30, 1977: 175-186.

McDowell, J. "Are Women Better Cops?," *Time*, February 17, 1992: 70-72.

Malloy, T. E., and G. L. Mays. "The Police Stress Hypothesis: A Critical Evaluation," *Criminal Justice and Behavior*, 11, 1984: 197-223.

Margolis, B. L. "Stress Is a Work Hazard Too," *Industrial Medicine, Occupational Health and Surgery*, 42, 1973: 20-23.

Miner, J. B. *Industrial-Organizational Psychology*. New York: McGraw-Hill, 1992.

More, H. W. *Special Topics in Policing*. Cincinnati, OH: Anderson Publishing, 1992.

Niederhoffer, A. *Behind the Shield: The Police in Urban Society*. New York: Doubleday, 1967.

Pendergrass, V. E., and N. M. Ostrove. "A Survey of Stress in Women in Policing," *Journal of Police Science and Administration*, 12, 1984: 303-309.

Rafky, D. M. "My Husband the Cop," *The Police Chief*, 41, 1974: 62-65.

Sandy, J. P., and D. A. Devine. "Four Stress Factors Unique to Rural Patrol," *The Police Chief*, Sept. 1978: 42-44.

Selye, H. *The Stress of Life,* 2d ed. New York: McGraw-Hill, 1976.

Sewell, J. D. "The Development of Critical Life Events Scale for Law Enforcement," *Journal of Police Science and Administration,* 11, 1983: 109-116.

Sewell, J. D., K. W. Ellison, and J. J. Hurrell. "Stress Management in Law Enforcement: Where Do We Go from Here?," *The Police Chief,* October, 1988: 94-99.

Skolnick, J. "A Sketch of the Policemen's Working Personality," in A. Niederhoffer and A. S. Blumberg, eds., *The Ambivalent Force.* San Francisco: Rinehart Press, 1973.

Somodevilla, S. A. "The Role of Psychologists in a Police Department," in W. Taylor and M. Braswell, eds., *Issues in Police and Criminal Psychology.* Washington, DC: University Press of America, 1978.

Stotland, E. "Police Stress and Strain as Influenced by Police Self-Esteem, Time on the Job, Crime Frequency and Interpersonal Relationships," in J. T. Reese and H. A. Goldstein, eds., *Psychological Services for Law Enforcement.* Washington, DC: United States Government Printing Office, 1986.

_____. "The Effects of Police Work and Professional Relationships on Health," *Journal of Criminal Justice,* 19, 1991: 371-379.

Stotland, E., M. Pendleton, and R. Schwartz. "Police Stress, Time on the Job, and Strain," *Journal of Criminal Justice,* 17, 1989: 55-60.

Violanti, J. M. "Stress Patterns in Police Work: A Longitudinal Study," *Journal of Police Science and Administration,* 11, 1983, 211-216.

Weisheit, R., and S. Mahan. *Women, Crime, and Criminal Justice.* Cincinnati, OH: Anderson Publishing, 1988.

Wexler, J. G. "Role Styles of Women Police Officers," *Sex Roles,* 12, 1985: 749-755.

Wexler, J. G., and D. D. Logan. "Sources of Stress Among Women Police Officers," *Journal of Police Science and Administration*, 11, 1983: 46-53.

Wilson, J. Q. *Varieties of Police Behavior: The Management of Law and Order in Eight Communities*. Cambridge, MA: Harvard University Press, 1968.

Witkin, G. "Cops Under Fire," *U.S. News & World Report*, December 3, 1990: 32, 44.

PART III

RURAL COURTS

One of the central features of American justice is the existence of a dual court system; that is, state and federal. The overwhelming majority of all criminal cases are for violation of state statutes, and as a result are tried by state courts. Even though some cases may be appealed and the outcomes ultimately decided in federal courts, these represent only a fraction of those originally heard in the state systems. Within the states themselves, there are a number of historical forces that shape the local legal culture and impact how all criminal justice agencies are structured and how they function despite locale.

The two chapters in this section discuss the impact of these environmental forces as they apply to rural courts, focusing on our three themes of "Conditions, Constraints and Challenges." Anne M. Bartol's "Structures and Roles of Rural Courts" provides a review of the structures and the unique characteristics of rural courts. Using categories that she identifies from the existing literature, Bartol details the consequences of smaller caseloads, interpersonal relationships, inadequate resources, social isolation and the challenge of providing accessible services. As a consequence of these characteristics, she discusses the problems associated with evaluating court performance based on traditional measures. The difficulties and solutions associated with court delay in the rural setting also are analyzed. The author concludes by suggesting that while the unique circumstances of special courts largely have been ignored, they are held to the same expectations as urban courts in terms of performance.

In the second work, "Rural Courts, the Rural Community and the Challenge of Change," Carroll Edmondson discusses the consequences of the environment for the reform of rural courts. He describes the economic, social and political impacts of the rural setting, and concludes that courts in rural America are not strong politically. As a consequence, he identifies resource, ethical and political difficulties that hinder the judiciary's ability to operate independently. The end result is that many have advocated reform of these institutions through implementation of the Unified Court Model. Edmondson observes that while the adoption of such a model may produce benefits, it fails to address the fundamental causes at the root of rural court problems.

CHAPTER 5

Structures and Roles of Rural Courts

by *Anne M. Bartol*

INTRODUCTION

Today, most adults have spent time in a courtroom, if not directly, then through the print media or the magic of broadcasting. We have access to courtrooms via network news and documentaries, and we see court proceedings portrayed in popular entertainment shows. The rural courtroom, however, is seldom adequately represented. The academic study of courts also neglects the rural courtroom. With a few exceptions, almost exclusively, researchers focus on urban and suburban courts.

Although rural courts are guided by the same fundamental principles as those in (sub)urban settings—independence, adversariness and the rule of law—they are confronted with special problems that sometimes constrain their effectiveness such as lack of resources and isolation. However, rural courts have unique features that can make them more effective than urban and suburban courts. For example, a lower volume of cases and closer ties to the community may help rural judges fashion more just and relevant solutions to disputes than can urban judges. A major challenge for rural courts is to maintain this community orientation without ignoring the individual rights of the most powerless citizens who come before them.

This chapter begins with a definition and structural overview of rural courts. Following that, it reviews the distinctive features of rural courts and discusses the challenges that these features create. Incorporated into this discussion is the available research to date. The chapter ends by considering proposals for improving the efficiency of rural courts.

DEFINITION AND COURT STRUCTURE

A rural court may be defined as one with fewer than two full-time general jurisdiction judges, usually located in a county with a population under 60,000 (Fahnestock et al. 1987). Given this definition, just over three-fourths of the state trial courts in the United States, serving about

79

25% of the population, can be classified as rural courts. Here, the term "state trial court" includes the municipal and county courts that serve as the point of entrance to the court system for most citizens.

In the United States, we use the term "dual court system" to refer to the parallel structure of state and federal courts. Under this dual system, state and federal courts operate independently and in tandem, carrying out many of the same functions. While some decisions of state courts may be appealed to the federal courts (e.g., when a constitutional issue is raised), the independence of state courts from the federal judiciary is carefully guarded. Furthermore, although sometimes federal courts are perceived as more prestigious, the decisions rendered by state courts are equally crucial to those who come before them. It is an important principle, therefore, that under the dual system federal and state courts hierarchically are equal (Neubauer 1991).

Sometimes, federal courts are located in rural areas but the average rural resident is far more likely to have direct experience with rural courts in the state system. Traffic law violators, plaintiffs and defendants in civil suits, victims and perpetrators of domestic violence and other crimes, and juvenile law breakers are more likely to appear before the state than federal courts. It is to the state courts that we turn to have our wills probated, guardianships established and custody disputes resolved. We seek restraining orders, injunctions and divorce decrees from the state courts. Because of the high salience of state courts to the average citizen, therefore, this chapter focuses on them.

Although complexity and nomenclature vary widely, state courts usually can be divided into four levels: 1) courts of limited jurisdiction; 2) courts of general jurisdiction; 3) intermediate appellate courts; 4) highest appellate court. Jurisdiction, a critical concept in the judicial process, is defined as the subject matter, persons and geographical areas over which a given court has authority (Abadinsky 1991).

"Limited jurisdiction courts," sometimes referred to as "inferior courts," have carefully prescribed authority over a limited category of cases, such as traffic violations (traffic courts), misdemeanors or minor civil matters. Often, they are not courts of record and may be staffed by non-lawyer judges (authorized in 42 states). These "recordless courts" are seen as an essential component of the state court system since they ease the ever-increasing burdens on courts of general jurisdiction. Because they are unsupervised and unmonitored, however, concerns about deprivations of due process often are raised.

"Courts of general constitutional jurisdiction" have subject matter authority over a wide range of cases including misdemeanors, felonies, and both simple and complex civil suits. Additionally, states have "specialized courts," in which jurisdiction is limited to certain categories of cases but do not qualify as "inferior courts." Examples of these "specialized courts" are family or juvenile courts. The important aspect to remember about these courts is that they are on an equal level to courts of general jurisdiction.

Parties losing a case in either general jurisdiction or specialized courts may appeal the decision to the "intermediate appellate court," and if there is no intermediate court, to the "highest appellate court" in the state, that usually is called the state's supreme court. Because appeals courts tend to be centrally located and have broad geographic jurisdiction, few of them can be classified as rural. This chapter, therefore, focuses on rural courts of limited, general and specialized jurisdiction.

SPECIAL FEATURES OF RURAL COURTS

Theodore J. Fetter, a national expert on rural courts, identifies a number of characteristics that establish special consideration for courts in rural areas (1977). These characteristics include less pressure of volume (smaller caseloads), population density and geographical jurisdiction, wide familiarity of residents, lack of resources, and isolation. Other researchers identify more subtle differences that are not always quickly apparent (see, for example, Stott et al. 1977; Cronk et al. 1982; Fahnestock and Geiger 1982). Using the categories identified so far in the research, we can discuss special features of rural courts in more detail and explain how these offer challenges to judges, clerks, court administrators and citizens.

Caseloads

It is widely recognized that caseloads in rural courts are lighter than those in suburban or urban courts. Often, this is regarded as a positive feature that allows courts to give adequate attention to individual cases and avoid the assembly line justice of urban and suburban courts. Fewer cases do not mean lighter workloads, however. A given court may be in session only one day a week and forced to process all of its cases in that day. Furthermore, rural judges—who sometimes serve as their own clerk and usually are their own court administrator—do not have the time, human resources or technology to operate with maximum efficiency. Rural courts have smaller staffs who often must be generalists capable of performing a vast array of duties from registering deeds to processing complex legal motions. Although rural courts hear fewer cases, therefore, it cannot be assumed that the pressures they face are less intense.

Population Density and Geographical Jurisdiction

Because rural courts are located in less densely populated areas than their urban and suburban counterparts, their geographical reach is far greater. This creates the challenge of making them accessible to the public. States have taken one of two approaches to meet this challenge and sometimes use a combination of both.

Some states have initiated a process of "systematic rotation" of judges among county courthouses. Usually arranged through the court administrator's office, rotation means that a judge will be assigned to one court for a set period of time, usually three or six months, then move to another court while another judge takes his or her place. The rotation has several purposes: to better distribute the presumed burden of working in undesirable courts; to expose the citizenry to a variety of judges, such as would naturally occur in non-rural courts; and to preclude one judge from exercising excessive power in a given courtroom.

Circuit riding is another approach that some states have adopted to deal with problems posed by low population density and wide geographical jurisdiction. This is the practice of having one or more judges travel between court houses, leaving others uncovered. For example, "County A" may not have a judge available during the month of May because the judge is holding court in "County B." Circuit riding, which was the common way of bringing justice to citizens during America's frontier days, is considered necessary and cost efficient in areas where there simply is not enough business to keep a courthouse open at all times.

Both rotation and circuit riding present special problems. The major problems created by rotation are the personal inconvenience to the judges and the inability of one judge to see a case through from beginning to end. This second problem also occurs in non-rural courts, however. Some commentators see rotation as a particularly healthy practice for rural courts (see, for example, Fahnestock et al. 1987). Although it encourages "judge shopping" (waiting for the "right" judge who will be sympathetic with one's case), it precludes the "fiefdom syndrome," in which a court is considered the exclusive province of a given judge. The major problem created by circuit riding is the fact that "emergency justice" must be carried out by non-lawyer staff in the absence of the presiding judge. Additionally, circuit riding takes a heavy personal toll on judges.

Wide Familiarity and "Comity"

Often, it is said of persons living in rural areas that everyone knows everyone else and their business. When citizens appear before rural courts it is likely that the court personnel who deal with them are well aware of their life situations. Frequently, court personnel and the citizenry have grown up attending the same schools, they have gone to each other's weddings, and sometimes they continue to be in the same social circles. In urban courts, judges have a policy of disqualifying themselves when faced with defendants or litigants in a civil suit who they know. Other judges are available to take the cases. In rural areas, such disqualification is impractical. Consequently, rural judges must carefully guard against *ex parte* communication, or efforts to discuss the case or bring information to their attention outside the courtroom.

The wide familiarity with the populace that is characteristic of rural courts has been hailed by some as a way to individualize justice and avoid the assembly line treatment of urban and even suburban courts. Rural courts are seen as more independent than their non-rural counterparts, closer to the community they serve, and more likely to reflect community values and mores. Fetter suggests that communities should be encouraged to make good use of this familiarity and take care of their own (1977). He adds that any strategies for improving justice to rural areas should be based on an effort to strengthen existing communities and their tradition.

If wide familiarity is seen as a positive feature, however, defendants who are not part of the community, either socially or geographically, may be at a disadvantage in the rural courtroom setting. Many a motorist has had the unpleasant experience of appearing in a traffic court before a magistrate who did not take kindly to "out-of-staters." In more serious situations—such as custody disputes where one parent is well known and liked in the community—the stakes for the outsider are much higher. "Fairness in judicial process implies equal *and* individualized treatment, a standard that is hard to maintain in many types of courts" (Stott et al. 1977: 5).

The issue of equal treatment is related closely to the concept of "comity," which Fahnestock and Geiger identify as a subtle, common feature in rural courts (1982). These researchers conducted site visits to 23 rural courts across the country and completed a survey of 25 randomly selected rural court clerks. Comity was defined as "a special type of courtesy wherein the parties continually exchange accommodations for each other's convenience and benefit" (Fahnestock and Geiger 1982: 6).

Fahnestock and Geiger note that because those who participate in rural court systems must work closely together, the adversarial nature of court proceedings may give in to the need to operate with a minimum amount of interpersonal tension (1982). Although comity may work to the advantage of a client when a satisfactory negotiation is needed, comity may be problematic if it prevents an attorney from forcing the opposing side to prove its case beyond a reasonable doubt, which is the essence of the adversarial criminal process. The presence of comity raises important questions about the quality of justice dispensed in rural courts.

Advocates of both criminal defendants and civil litigants charge that in many rural courts, powerless citizens have no neutral arbiter to whom they can turn (Rural Justice Center 1993). These advocates view rural courts as acquiescing to the needs of highly visible decision makers in local communities at the expense of the powerless. "Economic and political pressures, combined with the isolation of the court from any feedback except from the Chamber of Commerce and law enforcement, seriously erode the rule of law in rural counties" (Rural Justice Center 1993).

Lack of Resources

A number of studies of rural courts have documented problems in this area, ranging from low budgets to inadequate referral services (Stott et al. 1977; Cronk et al. 1982; National Center for State Courts 1991). Rural courts routinely receive less federal money and have a lower local tax base than urban and suburban courts, which accounts for the fact that facilities often are outmoded and salaries are low. A shortage of funds and geographical distance often prevent staff from taking advantage of training programs offered in centralized areas. The pool of available attorneys, expert witnesses and even jurors is diminished considerably. Peripheral services, such as the availability of victim's assistants, shelters and services for diverting such special populations as juveniles at risk, substance abusers or the mentally disordered often are lacking (Scheff 1964; Brakel and South 1969; Cronk et al. 1982).

The lack of resources becomes a particular problem in criminal cases, in which criminal defendants have a constitutional right to the assistance of counsel if they are subject to incarceration on conviction of a crime (see, for example, *Gideon* v. *Wainwright* 1963; *Argersinger* v. *Hamlin* 1972). Furthermore, criminal defendants who intend to pursue an insanity defense, constitutionally are entitled to psychiatric assistance in the preparation of that defense (*Ake* v. *Oklahoma* 1985). Howard Eisenberg notes that the *Argersinger* rule, which extends the right to a lawyer to misdemeanor cases, had major impact on rural courts, where the misdemeanor felony ratio often is as high as 30:1 or even 40:1. The requirements may pose both financial and logistical problems (1977). When lawyer's fees come from local budgets instead of state coffers, communities may be hard-pressed to afford the services. Logistically, it may be difficult to find lawyers who are both trained in criminal law and philosophically inclined to represent criminal defendants.

Eisenberg notes that the lack of a sufficient defense pool could lead offenders to challenge their convictions on the basis of inadequate assistance of counsel (1977). Another consideration, given the lack of resources, is that a significant number of criminal defendants may be encouraged to waive their constitutional rights in rural courts. This does not necessarily mean that justice has not been served. Some judges faced with a lawyerless defendant may be especially careful to assure that the person receives a fair hearing. The above is speculative, however, since we do not have "outcome" research specifically focusing on adult rural courts from which to draw conclusions.

Isolation

Another common feature of rural courts is the social isolation experienced by its personnel, particularly judges and court clerks. In a 1987 report, the National Conference of the Judiciary on Rural Courts cited social and professional isolation as recurring negative themes (Fahnestock et al. 1987). That conference, according to its participants, represented the first time an effort had been made to ask rural judges about issues in need of their attention. The judges reported that social isolation was a problem for their families as well as for the judges themselves.

Isolation also refers to a feeling on the part of those associated with rural courts in which centralized court administrators are insensitive to their special needs. The roles of a court administrator's office are to communicate with all courts under its aegis, to allocate resources, to provide technical assistance and information, to prepare reports, and to facilitate education for judges.

The 1987 National Conference Report sharply indicted the judicial administration profession—both national and state—for its neglect of rural courts. Although some state offices were acknowledged as exemplary, the report noted that the majority had an overwhelmingly urban orientation to the detriment of rural courts. Rural courts can ill afford the high costs of education conferences, required forms and computerized record-keeping, particularly when they do not relate to their own pressing needs.

In their survey of rural court clerks, Fahnestock and Geiger also encountered this feeling of isolation and perceived insensitivity, with 60% of the clerks indicating that they did not get their fair share of attention from a centralized state court administrator's office (1982). They further noted that training was inadequate and did not address the particular problems of rural courts. Most significantly, 95% of the clerks found that reports sent to them from the centralized office were useless. The researchers were careful to note that clerks did not display animosity toward the administrative offices; instead, they appeared resigned to living with this inattention.

Despite the constraints placed on them, some rural courts have valiantly embarked on innovative projects and programs to address their own special needs. These innovations range from issuing benchbooks and manuals, and trying to reduce paper flow, to encouraging citizen involvement through volunteer and youth service programs. Without support from state coffers and attention from social science researchers, however, these commendable programs will be successful only on a hit-or-miss basis.

NEED FOR ALTERNATIVE STANDARDS, MODELS AND RESEARCH

In light of the above unique features of rural courts, some court experts question the need to hold rural courts to the same standards of performance as urban and suburban courts. Stott et al., for example, call on those who allocate budgets to recognize the special limitations on rural courts, and to realize that it may cost more to deliver justice in rural areas than urban areas (1977). Fetter notes that although the values related to due process, speedy trial and other constitutional rights clearly need to be applied in rural courts, it is unwarranted to apply nationwide criteria to measure their efficiency (1977). He calls for an alternative rural model that would recognize the strengths of rural courts, and he recommends adapting these strengths to suburban and urban courts.

According to Fetter, rural courts traditionally have emphasized evaluating themselves by looking at final outcomes or products (1977). Their standard of performance is based on whether the decisions make sense within community values. National standards, by contrast, traditionally have emphasized efficiency or looking at how courts work from the inside. These standards have been established by experts whose knowledge has not extended to the operation and needs of rural courts.

The National Conference of the Judiciary on Rural Courts has offered not a model but an agenda for action designed to meet the special—but long ignored—needs of rural courts and the citizens they serve. Their numerous recommendations include: the elimination of local funding; upgrading of the status of clerks; regional instead of statewide, rotation of judges; merit selection, instead of election, of judges; adoption of standards for judicial leadership to be exercised both on and off the bench; accessible training and education for judges and staff; law school recognition of the needs of rural courts; and access to law libraries and legal research facilities for all rural citizens, judges and attorneys.

Taking a slightly different approach, the Vermont-based Center for Rural Justice is an advocate primarily for citizens who are served by rural courts. Established in 1982 as a private, non-profit grassroots group, the center closely works with rural courts, offering education for rural judges in such areas as domestic violence and the adjudication of farm credit disputes.

In a series of studies, these researchers found evidence that minorities and the poor, particularly poor women, fare less well in rural courts than other groups (Sitomer 1985; Rural Justice Center 1991, 1993). The center's research agenda for the immediate future is continuing work in the domestic violence arena, a nationwide study of recordless (limited jurisdiction) courts and a special project to explore the treatment of Native Americans in local and state courts that border reservations.

SPECIAL ISSUE: DELAY

Court delay—whether in urban, suburban or rural courts—long has been a concern of litigants, criminal defendants, the legal profession, advocates of court reform and concerned citizens. Consider the often-heard maxim: "Justice delayed is justice denied."

Courts, legislatures and professional associations have tried to address the issue of court delay. The American Bar Association (ABA) has developed standards for controlling delay or specifically recommending that courts dispose of 90% of all felony criminal cases within 120 days from the date of arrest (ABA 1984). In the matter of civil cases the ABA recommends that 90% be disposed of within 12 months of filing. Additionally, 90% of domestic matters (e.g., divorces, custody disputes) should be resolved within 90 days of filing.

Common sense might suggest that delay is more likely to be a problem in urban than rural areas and some research supports this assumption. Alfini and Doan, for example, found that rural courts disposed of misdemeanor cases faster than urban or suburban courts (1977). This was not necessarily a good thing, however, because attorneys were less likely to be present. The researchers also found that the pressure to dispose of cases quickly came from different sources. Rural judges were pressured by the law enforcement community and local government officials, whereas urban or suburban judges were pressured by the state judicial system. Although research indicates that delay causes substantial harm to litigants and defendants in rural courts (Fahnestock 1990), there is evidence from a two-phase project that significant steps can be taken to reduce that delay (Miller 1990). As one of the few recent extensive projects available on this issue, it deserves discussion in more detail.

In the first phase, researchers studied 10 rural courts over a two-year period. In the second phase, the project was extended to include 19 rural courts over the four-year period, 1984-1988. The researchers used a comparative method of study, combining both quantitative and qualitative research. They analyzed statistical data from court records, they made site visits and observed court proceedings, and they conducted interviews with participants in each of the courts. We will focus on the second and more comprehensive phase, which did not contradict the findings of the first.

Very few courts met the ABA 90th percentile standards. Specifically, only 4 of the 19 courts met the standard for criminal cases, two met the standard for civil cases and none met the standard for domestic cases. In fact, in the domestic context, the closest court to meet the standard completed 90% of its domestic cases within 162 days, almost double the ABA's recommended time frame. When the researchers adopted a 75% criterion, however, they got more success. Nine courts disposed of 75% of their civil cases by the ABA's recommended one-year deadline. Nine also disposed of three-quarters of their criminal cases within 120 days. The researchers noted, however, that 5 of the 19 courts had exceeded 180 days for 75% of their criminal cases. Domestic cases were the most likely to suffer delay beyond ABA standards.

When the researchers correlated case delay with factors that might explain it they found surprising results. The factors related to swift disposition were management related instead of related to features usually associated with rural courts. That is, leadership, clearly established goals and standards, early case control, caseload monitoring and efficient information systems (although not necessarily computerized) were all related to swift disposition. Isolation, geographical distance, size of staff, circuit riding or method of judicial selection did not have a significant relation to disposition time.

Encouraged by this finding, the researchers concluded that rural courts were "fertile ground" for reducing delay. They suggested that relatively inexpensive technological advances—such as facsimile machines and videotapes—should be considered by rural courts wishing to deliver services in a more efficient manner. The need to transport individuals between jails and courts for a variety of pre-trial hearings, for example, can be avoided by allowing a detainee to participate in a court proceeding by conference phone or video. Similarly, judges could use facsimile machines to issue warrants or relief from abuse orders in domestic violence situations. Researchers emphasized that creative approaches to dealing with some of the previously intractable problems faced by rural courts should be encouraged.

Although the above study offers cause for optimism, we should note that it did not measure the quality of court services, only the delay factor. Reduction in delay does not necessarily mean justice has been served in the long run. Nevertheless, it is important to recognize that a creative use of available and inexpensive resources can help hasten the delivery of court services to citizens.

SUMMARY

The special needs of rural courts have long been overlooked by researchers, legal scholars and the legal profession. Although rural courts are under different constraints than suburban and urban courts, the implications of these differences too often are ignored. Rural courts traditionally have been held to the same performance standards and expected to be as efficient as (sub)urban courts without adequate supportive resources. Furthermore, the strengths of rural courts, including their community aspect and the possibility that they can individualize justice better than non-rural courts, have not been recognized.

Documentation of performance outcomes for rural courts is sadly lacking, however. Research on rural courts, despite signs of increasing during the 1960s and 1970s, is very sparse. One reason for this scarcity of research is that the very features that make rural courts problematic for litigants and participants also pose challenges to researchers. Distant locations, shortage of space for on-site research and lack of sophisticated information technology often daunt social scientists who might be interested in this area. Because the research that does exist suggests that we may hold unwarranted assumptions about the rural court process, the dearth of research is extremely disturbing.

There are signs that rural court judges themselves are beginning to speak out in greater numbers about the special needs of their courts. The extensive agenda for action published by The National Conference on the Judiciary on Rural Courts deserves to be considered carefully by both the judiciary as a whole and the court administration profession. Furthermore, the continuing research sponsored by the Rural Justice Center provides an important glimpse into the functioning of rural courts nationwide.

REFERENCES

Abadinsky, H. *Law and Justice,* 2d ed. Chicago: Nelson-Hall Publishers, 1991.

Alfini, J. J., and R. N. Doan. "A New Perspective on Misdemeanor Justice," *Judicature*, 60, No. 9, April 1977: 427-434.

American Bar Association. *Standards Relating to Court Delay Reduction*, Section 2.52, 11-12. Chicago: American Bar Association, 1984.

Brakel, S. J., and G. R. South. "Diversion from the Criminal Process in the Rural Community," *American Criminal Law Quarterly*, 7, No. 3, Spring 1969: 162-168.

Cronk, S. D., J. Jankovic, and R. K. Green. *Criminal Justice in Rural America*. Washington, DC: National Institute of Justice Report, 1982.

Eisenberg, H. B. "Criminal Defense in Rural America," in S. D. Cronk, ed., *A Beginning Assessment of the Justice System in Rural Areas*. Washington, DC: Conference Report, National Rural Center/ American Bar Association, 1977: 159-171.

Fahnestock, K. L. *Time to Justice: Caseflow in Rural General Jurisdiction Courts*. Montpelier, VT: Rural Justice Center, 1990.

Fahnestock, K. L., and M. D. Geiger. "Rural Courts: The Neglected Majority," *Court Management Journal*, 1982: 4-10.

Fahnestock, K., M. D. Geiger, and J. F. Daffron, Jr. *Rural Courts: An Agenda for Action*. The Report of the National Conference of the Judiciary on Rural Courts, 1987.

Fetter, T. "Rural Courts," in S. D. Cronk, ed., *A Beginning Assessment of the Justice System in Rural Areas*. Washington, DC: Joint Conference Report, National Rural Center/American Bar Association, 1977.

Miller, F. G. "Delay in Rural Courts: It Exists, But It Can be Reduced," *State Court Journal*, 14, No. 3, 1990: 23.

National Center for State Courts. *Rural Courts are Fertile Ground for Caseflow Management: The Case Processing and Delay Reduction in Rural Courts Project.* Williamsburg, VA: 1991.

Neubauer, D. W. *Judicial Process.* Pacific Grove, CA: Brooks/Cole Publishing Company, 1991.

Rural Justice Center. *Not in My County: Rural Courts and Victims of Domestic Violence.* Montpelier, VT: Rural Justice Center, 1991.

_____. *Domestic Violence: A Curriculum for Rural Courts.* Rural Justice Center/National Council of Juvenile and Family Court Judges, 1993.

Scheff, T. J. "Social Conditions for Rationality: How Urban and Rural Courts Deal with the Mentally Ill," *American Behavioral Scientist*, 7, No. 7, March 1964: 21-24.

Sitomer, C. J. "Rural Justice Affects Many, but May Serve Few," *The Christian Science Monitor*, May 28, 1985: 23.

Stott, E. K., Jr., T. J. Fetter, and L. L. Crites. *Rural Courts: The Effect of Space and Distance on the Administration of Justice.* Denver, CO: National Center for State Courts, 1977.

CASES CITED

Ake v. *Oklahoma*, 470 U.S. 68 (1985).

Argersinger v. *Hamlin*, 407 U.S. 25 (1972).

Gideon v. *Wainwright*, 372 U.S. 335 (1963).

CHAPTER 6

Rural Courts, the Rural Community and the Challenge of Change

by *Carroll Edmondson*

INTRODUCTION

Historically, the plight of rural courts in this country has been quietly ignored or overshadowed by the escalating and more visible problems of urban courts. There is growing awareness, however, that rural courts deserve greater attention and more consideration than just "low-volume copies of their urban counterparts" (Fahnestock 1991: 19). Rural courts operate under different environmental conditions and constraints, and they have different kinds of problems than urban courts. Their environment reflects economic, social and political influences that shape the way they administer justice, interact with others and maintain their organizational viability as a third branch of government. These environmental influences create substantial challenges for reformers who wish to change the way rural courts operate.

As the conditions and problems of rural courts have surfaced, court reformers have pushed for changes in how rural courts are organized, administered and funded (National Conference 1986a; Goldspiel 1991). Their reform proposals, generally, have remained within the "judicial administration reform consensus" of court unification, which has dominated court reform efforts for nearly 50 years (Gallas 1979: 29). The underlying premise of this court unification consensus is that structural deficiencies constitute the basic problem preventing courts from operating efficiently, effectively and productively. Accordingly, the prescription for reform emphasizes such structural changes as consolidating courts, streamlining procedures, and centralizing authority and funding. This reform focus raises a fundamental question about both the uniqueness of rural court problems and effectiveness of the proposed remedies.

This chapter discusses the conditions, constraints and challenges of rural courts in the context of court reform. It is divided into four sections. The first section briefly delineates the parameters of rural courts. The second section identifies salient features that characterize life in rural communities. Section three examines the impact of the rural community in forging the economic, social and political conditions that shape the character of rural courts. Section four highlights the major tenets of court unification and discusses its implications as an agent for change in rural courts.

DEFINING A RURAL COURT

Despite the growing concern about their future welfare, there is no consensus about what constitutes a "rural court." Fahnestock and Geiger view the number of judges and the type of jurisdiction as the two major criteria that define a rural court (1982). They identify a rural court as any general jurisdiction trial court with no more than two full-time judges (Fahnestock and Geiger 1982: 4). The National Conference of the Judiciary on Rural Courts extends population size to 60,000 or less (National Conference 1986b: iv). Kendall and Shouse define rural courts in terms of the size of the population served by the court: 50,000 or less (1990: 120). Rogers defines rural courts as those with limited jurisdiction (1991: 23-24). Taken alone, each of these definitions is too restrictive to be able to establish what constitutes the operational parameters of a rural court.

This study adopts a definition of "rural court" that synthesizes the major criteria that other studies employ. It identifies a rural court as "any limited or general jurisdiction trial court with no more than three full-time judges, which provides judicial services in a county with a population of less than 60,000 people." In its broadest application, this definition would encompass three-quarters of state trial courts in the United States (National Conference 1986a: ii). Even if the definition were restricted to counties having a population of 20,000 or less, it still would include 51% of all state trial courts in this country (Fahnestock and Geiger 1982: 10). The prevalence of rural courts alone suggests their significance as an important area of inquiry for anyone interested in understanding the administration of justice in American society.

CHARACTERISTICS OF RURAL COMMUNITIES AND THEIR COURTS

While the above definition of "rural court" provides an operational means for objectively delineating the boundaries of a rural court, it fails to address qualitative features of these courts. As Vandiver notes, quantitative measures serve only as surrogates for complex qualitative factors that influence behavior (1991: 51). To capture the full flavor of what constitutes a rural court, it is necessary to identify those distinctive attributes that characterize rural communities, and to distinguish them from urban and suburban communities.

Two factors that distinguish rural communities from urban and suburban communities are population size and density (Stott et al. 1977: 4-7). Rural communities have small populations, which are isolated from large population areas by considerable distances. The combination of these two features produces certain economic, social and political conditions and constraints that pervade rural life. These conditions and constraints establish the milieu in which rural courts must operate.

Economically, the small population of rural communities means that they have a relatively small tax base on which to raise revenue for governmental services. Their tax base further is eroded by a high proportion of poor citizens, especially the elderly (Eisenstein 1982: 32). This erosion will become even more severe in the future if rural communities cannot provide sufficient economic opportunities for young adults to be able to remain in the community, instead of having to move to metropolitan areas. As rural communities are becoming increasingly aware, their shrinking revenue base has economic consequences affecting the quality, availability and delivery of governmental services.

Social life in rural communities places a premium on personal relationships; as a result, it is characterized by intimacy, familiarity and high visibility (Eisenstein 1982: 33; National Conference 1986a). Residents not only know each other but also each other's family history. Active social networks ensure that residents stay attuned to local activities and events. Unlike urban areas, the populations of rural communities are relatively homogeneous. This homogeneity reinforces social cohesion, and it places a high degree of consensus on core values. Together with the emphasis on personal relationships, social homogeneity explains why rural communities favor informal legal and socio-political processes over formal ones.

The political characteristics of rural communities largely are a byproduct of their economic and social environment. Dominant economic interests in the community exert tremendous influence on governmental leaders, as well as political outcomes (Jacob 1978: 7). The community's emphasis on personal relationships and cohesion keeps political conflict within certain boundaries. Rural communities discourage the divisive and acrimonious political battles often found in metropolitan areas. They accent the necessity of "going along to get along" (Fahnestock and Geiger 1993).

Environmental Impact

The nature and limitations of rural communities have important consequences for courts that must operate in them. Understanding these effects is essential to grasping the challenges confronting court reformers' efforts to change the way rural courts operate. To shed some light on these outcomes, it is helpful to examine the economic, social and political impact of the rural environment on rural courts.

Economic Impact

Whether a community is rural or urban, economics play a significant role, which includes: the recruitment and utilization of court personnel; the adequacy and availability of facilities and services; and a judge's decision-making options. For rural communities, however, these issues are crucial particularly because of their impact on judicial independence.

Due to their small population base, rural communities must recruit judges, court personnel, prosecutors and public defenders from a very restricted pool of candidates. Other factors relate to economics such as: low salaries, poor facilities, limited cultural opportunities, and the amount of required travel. These factors limit the available pool of candidates within the community as well as discouraging outsiders from seeking positions in rural areas (Stott et al. 1977: 13, 21-22).

Although rural circumstances do not necessarily produce less qualified judges or court personnel, they do diminish the chances that the overall quality will be as high as it is in urban or suburban communities (Gradwohl 1987). In those communities where attracting and retaining high caliber candidates is a problem, judicial competency and confidence in the judiciary often become problems.

In rural communities, economics often dictate the use of job sharing and part-time personnel. Rural courts are much more likely than urban or suburban courts to have part-time judges, non-attorney judges, part-time prosecutors, and court personnel who split their time between the court and another government agency (Stott et al. 1977: 15-21). One study estimates that over 50% of the rural counties in the United States use part-time prosecutors (Fahnestock 1991: 14). Many of these counties and the cities within them are served by part-time judges, especially in limited jurisdiction courts. Workload volumes do not justify full-time personnel. Local budget priorities favor other types of services. Part-time judicial and prosecutorial personnel, therefore, provide rural communities with cost effective and readily available personnel for performing essential governmental functions.

There is a critical trade-off for the judicial system in the accommodation to the rural community's financial resources and economic priorities. Part-time judges who are attorneys and part-time prosecutors who have their own private practices invariably become entangled in either actual or perceived conflict of interest problems. A prosecutor who has represented a litigant in civil court as a privately retained attorney, and then later has prosecuted the litigant as a criminal defendant, cannot escape public suspicion that the defendant received favored treatment. Similarly, a part-time judge who presides over court one day, and appears in court the next day as an advocate for his client, creates concerns about the integrity of the judicial process. Such practices undermine the role of courts as fair and impartial arbiters, and they foster perceptions of courts as pawns of attorneys promoting their own economic self-interest.

Job sharing arrangements also have significant political implications for rural courts. In numerous rural jurisdictions across the country, the clerk of court works part-time for the court and part-time for another city or county agency (Vandiver 1991: 53). If this second agency happens to be a police or sheriff's department, the job sharing blurs the distinction between the court's role and law enforcement's role in the criminal justice system. Whatever the economic necessity, job sharing reinforces a common perception by many county commissioners and city councils that the court is just another agency of county or city government instead of a separate and co-equal branch of government. More importantly, it directly threatens the institutional identity and organizational independence of rural courts at the local level.

The use of non-attorney judges in rural courts, mainly in limited jurisdiction courts, is another economic issue with serious political overtones. Rural communities utilize non-attorney judges for two primary reasons: 1) they cost less than attorney judges; 2) there are no available attorneys in the community, or available attorneys are not willing to take the job (Stott et al. 1977: 15). In rural communities that lack judges who have legal training, their lay judges tend to be less inclined to challenge lawyers appearing before them. As former law enforcement officers, many lay judges bring to the bench that orientation. On disputed issues, they often defer to the prosecutor more than to the defense counsel (Stott et al. 1977: 62). Consequently, rural courts staffed by lay judges generally exhibit a strong prosecutorial bias, which often is shared by the community as a whole.

Economic conditions and constraints in rural areas also affect the quality and availability of facilities and court support services. Judges and court personnel often are squeezed into insufficient quarters because the county lacks sufficient funds to expand the court house or replace it with a new one. Few rural communities have adequate drug treatment services, detoxification centers, juvenile detention centers, shelters for battered women or facilities for the mentally ill (Stott et al. 1977: 57). In some rural areas, residents have to travel to regional centers or urban areas for these facilities. If the community has a jail, it often becomes a multi-purpose facility serving as a juvenile detention center, a detoxification facility, as well as a jail (National Conference 1986b: 22). Similarly, distance and economics affect the availability and delivery of court services in rural communities. Services provided by probation officers, pre-trial release and diversion programs, family counseling or mental health and alcohol rehabilitation programs, often are not conveniently available in rural communities. If they are available, either the staff has to travel extensively to deliver the services or clients have to travel a lengthy distance to receive them. Thus, logistical constraints in the rural environment reduce cost efficiency and restrict the accessibility of court and social services.

Perhaps the most important consequence of the constraints for the rural judiciary is that they limit decision-making options for rural judges. For instance, rural judges in communities without alcohol treatment facilities or counseling services must decide between requiring the DUI (driving under the influence) offender to travel a substantial distance to obtain treatment or some other sentencing option that may only address symptoms and not the problem itself. Similarly, a rural judge in a community without a jail may be reluctant to incarcerate defendants due to the expense of housing them in another community's jail. If a community lacks temporary shelters for juveniles, a judge may be forced to place the juvenile in the county jail or a juvenile detention center because a more suitable option is not available.

To a certain extent, rural judges can meet these challenges by becoming more creative in their sentencing behavior, and by developing alternatives to traditional methods of delivering court services (Cody 1991). Creativity alone, however, cannot supplant resources that are needed to provide judges with a full range of sentencing alternatives that meet social needs.

Social Impact

Unlike most other public officials, judges must adhere to a rigorous code of ethics designed to promote an impartial, independent and fair judiciary. This judicial code of ethics places severe restraints on a judge's social, civic, professional and financial activities (Dilweg 1991). Many judges contend that strict adherence to the judicial code creates professional and social isolation for both them and their families. However, few judges ignore the code because violations may lead to disciplinary actions or removal from office by the state supreme court. Yet, the code creates tension between normative standards of conduct and practical standards moderated by social and political needs.

The tension between normative and practical standards of conduct especially is evident in rural communities because of the emphasis placed on social cohesiveness and harmony. Most residents of rural communities expect the judge to be as accessible as other public officials. When they want to talk about their court case on the street or at a social event they do not realize that judges cannot engage in this type of *ex parte*, or one sided, communication without violating ethical standards (National Conference 1986b: 4). As part of the rural community elite, judges are expected to participate in social events, and to promote values important to the community (Fahnestock 1991: 19). Yet, their role as a neutral arbiter often requires them to weigh constitutional dictates more heavily than community values. Even if rural judges are willing to isolate themselves socially from their communities in order to strictly adhere to the legal code of ethics, doing so probably would have serious political consequences. Most rural judgeships are elected positions. Any rural judge who loses close contact with the community jeopardizes his or her job at the next election. To survive politically, therefore, rural judges have to perform a balancing act between normative legal standards and the social demands of their community.

The rural community's emphasis on social cohesion and harmony also exerts a potent influence on the way rural courts process their cases. Although the adjudication process generally is portrayed as an adversarial system, it is characterized more by bargaining and accommodation than conflict (Dubois 1982b: 3; Holland 1982: 17; Kendall and Shouse 1990: 122; Fahnestock and Geiger 1993). Except for a few highly visible exceptions, most cases are resolved between the parties, and not by a trial before a judge and jury. Often in criminal cases, the prosecutor and defense attorney reach an agreeable plea bargain to present to the judge for approval and legitimization. In civil cases, attorneys for the plaintiff and defendant use the discovery process, in which both attorneys must show each other their respective evidence, to assess the strengths and weaknesses of their cases before compromising on a mutually agreeable monetary award.

The transformation of the judicial process into a bargaining and negotiating arena is not unique to rural courts; it is typical also of most urban courts (Jacob 1973: 102). The forces promoting the change, however, are quite different between the rural and urban settings. In urban courts, a high caseload volume without a corresponding increase in resources provided the impetus for the transformation from an adversarial to a bargaining system. The urban courts' need for enhanced productivity and efficiency to cope with burgeoning caseloads facilitated the shift from conflict to comity; that is mutual accommodation. By contrast, in rural courts the caseloads are much more manageable so that caseload volume does not exert the same pressures for enhanced productivity and efficiency. Comity developed as a natural outgrowth of a social environment that stressed social harmony and personal relationships. Social norms in the rural community have reinforced expectations that judges, attorneys, prosecutors and law enforcement officials should accommodate each other whenever possible (National Conference 1986a: 3-7; Fahnestock 1991: 19). As a result, comity in rural courts carries with it a social imprimatur, or sanction, that is not found in urban courts.

One of the consequences of comity is that it strengthens the local character of courts to the disadvantage of outsiders. Attorneys from outside the community often find it difficult to break through the informal norms that influence local practices and procedures. Local procedural rules generally reflect the customs and preferences of the specific community, as well as the style of the resident judge. Outsiders may not be fully cognizant of these local nuances and their impact on decisions, unless outside attorneys practice regularly in the court. They also do not have the advantage of knowing the strengths and weaknesses of their local opponent so well as local attorneys do. Such disadvantages may not be severe enough to prevent outside attorneys from prevailing in rural courts but they definitely provide handicaps that must be overcome.

By eroding the adversary system, comity weakens procedural safeguards designed to ensure the impartiality and fairness of courts, and to protect constitutional rights of litigants. For example, speedy trial guarantees often fall prey to a judge's willingness to continue cases for an attorney's convenience or because the client has not paid the attorney. Similarly, the police may arrest a person without sufficient evidence so as to avoid offending a prominent citizen, and the prosecutor may try weak cases to stay on good terms with law enforcement. Because interpersonal accommodation supersedes prescribed procedural safeguards, adjudication becomes "a ritual that validates the law enforcement accusation rather than a fact-finding activity" (Fahnestock and Geiger 1982: 8). Courts become legitimizers instead of decision makers.

Comity also impacts the administration of justice in rural courts by fostering delay. Although rural courts' workloads are substantially lighter than those of urban courts, their processing times are only marginally better (Fahnestock and Geiger 1990; Miller 1990). To a certain extent, the slower-than-anticipated pace of litigation in rural courts may reflect their lower resource levels or their reduced court schedules because of circuit riding. However, primarily it reflects local expectations and norms that attorneys should control the pace of litigation to fit their convenience and needs (Church et al. 1978). Rural courts remain attorney controlled, although nearly every study of court delay in the last 15 years has found considerable empirical evidence to substantiate the American Bar Association's position that "the court, not the lawyers or litigants, should control the pace of litigation" (Solomon and Somerlot 1987: 77).

As products of the rural community and local bar association, generally rural judges have been programmed to acquiesce to the bar's control of the docket. For them to challenge this control would mean a challenge to comity itself. Thus, as one study concluded, "It is not surprising that moving cases through the system expeditiously is the exception rather than the rule in many courts" (Fahnestock and Geiger 1990: 10).

Undeniably, social influences reinforce the local character of rural courts, and they often neutralize procedural safeguards designed to strengthen judicial functions and control. Social influences help to shape the political forces that impact rural courts.

Political Impact

The economic and social influences of rural communities impose political constraints on rural courts that challenge their institutional identity and viability as a separate branch of government. Perhaps this interplay is demonstrated most vividly by the way local executives and legislative bodies view courts. City and county officials view courts less as institutions of justice and more as economic institutions that should contribute to the local coffers (Stott et al. 1977: 61; Rogers 1991: 24). Despite constitutional doctrine to the contrary, these officials subtly may inform rural judges that increases in salaries or court budgets will be in direct proportion to revenues generated by the court. To them, the court is just another local governmental agency and not a distinguishable branch of government with a distinct constitutional function. While rural judges may resist this interpretation of the court as an economic institution, frequently their challenges are stifled by pressure for comity and weak political resources. Re-election concerns may mitigate in favor of quiet acquiescence instead of institutional conflict over abstract principles that may not be fully understood by the electorate. The result is a court that lacks the political strength to function properly as a countervailing force to legislative and executive abuses.

Cost effectiveness concerns and the "coziness" of a rural community also may blur a rural court's identity and purpose. As mentioned previously, in some communities the clerk or some other court personnel may work part-time for the court and the remainder of the time for the police department or a local official. Such job-sharing arrangements create the impression that the court's function is indistinguishable from any other local agency. Even without job-sharing to muddle the picture, rural court personnel sometimes tend to view themselves as an extension of law enforcement and not as part of an independent organization that functions as an arbiter (Fahnestock and Geiger 1982: 6). A typical comment like "We arrested so and so last night" vividly illustrates this orientation (National Judicial College 1990: 78).

In their political struggle to maintain their identity and independence, rural courts have a potentially powerful ally in their state supreme court and the administrative office of the courts. However, state supreme courts and their administrative offices historically have focused their primary attention and resources on urban courts instead of on rural courts. Generally, they eschew involvement in local political battles for either urban or rural courts. Typically, in instances where state supreme courts have established minimal statewide standards for locally controlled courts, they have lacked the political will to enforce them (Rogers 1991: 25). Additionally, they have exhibited a reluctance to become entangled in local political controversies by narrowly limiting the application of the inherent power to modify court orders as a legal tool for enhancing a court's resources (Cratsley 1980). The state judiciary, therefore, has provided little support to strengthen the rural court's political resources vis-à-vis local executives and legislative bodies.

Finally, the political impact of the rural environment on rural courts is demonstrated by the limited accessibility of the judicial system to disenfranchised groups or unpopular causes. Rural communities often lack public defenders, legal aid societies or other legal groups that champion controversial issues and represent indigent litigants at little or no cost. Unpopular groups or indigent litigants must rely on local attorneys for legal services. However, few local attorneys in small rural communities are inclined to forcefully adjudicate controversial cases for fear of community antagonism (Kendall and Shouse 1990: 123-124). As part of the community elite, they tend to support the underlying socio-economic structure and value system of the community (Eisenstein 1982: 36). When controversial issues are raised, usually these cases involve an outside attorney representing the party challenging the status quo. As a consequence of such circumscribed accessibility to legal representation, rural courts rarely become agents of socio-political change unless the impetus for change is imposed from outside of the rural community.

In summary, rural courts are weak political institutions. They commonly lack the political support and resources to safeguard their institutional identity and preserve their autonomy. Overcoming this weakness has become the focal point for court reformers who seek to strengthen rural courts and enable them to cope more effectively with their environmental conditions and constraints.

IMPLICATIONS OF COURT REFORM FOR RURAL COURTS

Most calls for court reform in this country are based on a court unification model formulated by Roscoe Pound over 50 years ago. Although there are numerous variants to the model in both practice and theory, the basic Pound Model constitutes what Gallas calls "the now dominant paradigm of judicial administration" (1979: 29). It is no surprise, therefore, that rural court reformers also have embraced the major tenets of court unification in their efforts to strengthen the independence and efficiency of rural courts.

In its purest form, the court unification model creates a highly centralized hierarchical court system administered by the state supreme court and financed primarily by state funds. Trial courts are consolidated into a single tier: they are hierarchically structured with appellate courts to make the judicial system more understandable and accessible to the public, more efficient and cost effective, and more accountable to the state supreme court. Efficiency and accountability are enhanced by vesting administrative rule-making authority, management authority and budgeting authority with the state supreme court. State funding of trial courts completes the cycle by drastically reducing local political control over courts, and by strengthening the effectiveness of the judiciary as a unified and coherent institution in the political arena. Thus, court unification focuses on the reorganization of structure, authority and resources within the judiciary to remedy problems associated with fragmentation and local control of trial courts (Berkson 1977; Berkson et al. 1978: 4; Dubois 1982a: 1).

Unification offers several potential benefits for rural courts. State funding provides greater opportunities for channeling more resources to rural areas. These resources could alleviate some of the problems in rural areas caused by distance and population sparcity, especially if they are employed to harness new technology to the needs of rural courts. A unified court system also may reduce the sense of isolationism of rural judges and reduce ethical conflicts since the supreme court could assign rural judges outside their home districts on a regular basis.

The greatest advantage of unification for rural courts, however, is to strengthen the independence of rural courts vis-à-vis the local community. When rural courts become state funded and administered by the supreme court, their political orientation shifts from the local community to the judicial bureaucracy. As part of a coherent state network of trial courts, they develop greater resistance to political pressures at the local level. A reallocation of political power takes place whereby local communities lose power to a newly formed bureaucracy within the judiciary. That rural communities recognize this shift in political power is evidenced by their usually vehement opposition to court unification legislation in state legislatures (Glick 1982: 25).

Despite potential benefits, court unification is not likely to alter significantly the conditions and constraints that shape the behavior of rural courts. Its emphasis is on organizational changes, whereas the rural court environment is deeply rooted in a social system that transcends formal organizational structures (Glick 1982: 30). Comity, for instance, remains largely unaffected by court unification in many rural areas. It still exerts a potent influence in rural North Carolina, for example, even though its courts have been unified for two decades. Moreover, while unification may ameliorate the professional isolation of rural judges through periodic reassignments, it cannot eliminate the problem. Rural judges and their families must still live in their local communities, and they must adhere to a code of judicial ethics that stresses professional values of impartiality and judicial independence over social values.

In practice, the economic and political benefits of court unification for rural courts have rarely lived up to expectations. Although rural courts have a much greater revenue base with state funding, they must compete with high-volume urban courts for these resources. Thus, their resource levels may change little as they move from local funding to state funding. More importantly, unification does not sever rural courts' political ties to the community; it only loosens them. The predominance of elections as the primary means of selecting judges and clerks-of-court in this country allows local communities to retain significant influence in the courthouse, even in unified court systems. State funding does not eliminate the continued involvement of rural judges and clerks in local politics because no state court system is completely funded by the state. All state-funded court systems still require local governments to finance and maintain courthouses and other court facilities. Consequently, state-funded rural courts must still battle local governing bodies for resources that significantly affect their operations.

Court unification exemplifies the pitfalls of universal prescriptions for change. Although it offers benefits for rural courts, its focus is broader and more generic than rural courts. Rural reformers only need to look at the application of court unification in several states to ascertain its limitations in addressing the specific problems of rural courts. By emphasizing structural solutions as the means to increase efficiency and enhance judicial independence, unification largely ignores sociological undercurrents at work, particularly in rural courts. Most importantly, it addresses performance issues only indirectly instead of directly. The assumption is that courts will perform to their fullest capabilities once they have been organized along the lines proposed by the unification model.

The basic challenge for rural courts is to attain greater control over their environment. Court unification may assist in this process but it is not a panacea. In the final analysis, the structure of courts is less important than their performance. The need to recognize performance as a central issue for trial courts has gained momentum in recent years (Commission on Trial Court Performance Standards 1990: 1).

For rural courts, emphasizing performance will direct greater attention to critical issues for rural reform such as changing norms and expectations about institutional relationships, and the court's managerial role. It should assist rural judges and court managers in developing reform goals and strategies better tailored to their operating environment by forcing them to examine their specific needs, resources, strengths and weaknesses. To succeed, however, rural judges and court managers must take the leadership role at the local level and be supported in critical ways by the administrative office of courts. Without a focus on performance and a leadership strategy that utilizes the social and political systems in rural communities to effect changes, rural courts will remain passive institutions controlled by an overbearing environment.

SUMMARY

The rural environment molds the economic, social and political conditions that shape the character of rural courts. It creates constraints that undermine the rural judiciary's capacity and capabilities to function properly as a viable, independent branch of government. Concerns about the resource, ethical and political problems created by these constraints have precipitated calls for court reform.

In searching for solutions to rural court problems, reformers have united behind the court unification model. This model of court reform emphasizes reorganization of structure, authority and resources within the state judiciary as a whole to strengthen the courts' political powers and improve their efficiency. While unification may assist rural courts in reaching these goals, it fails to address the sociological underpinnings of rural court problems. To make progress toward substantial change, rural reformers will need to shift their focus from a structuralist to a performance orientation. Such a shift should provide them with a better means for addressing their fundamental challenge—harnessing the rural environment.

REFERENCES

Berkson, L. "The Emerging Ideal of Court Unification," *Judicature*, 60, 1977: 372-382.

Berkson, L., S. Carbon, and J. Rosenbaum. *Court Unification: History, Politics and Implementation*. Washington, DC: National Institute of Law Enforcement and Criminal Justice, 1978.

Church, T., A. Carlson, J. Lee, and T. Tan. *Justice Delayed: The Pace of Litigation in Urban Trial Courts*. Williamsburg, VA: The National Center for State Courts, 1978.

Cody, M. D. "Rural Courts in America—Their Secret Weapon: Volunteer Help," *Judges Journal*, 30, 1991: 56-63.

Commission on Trial Court Performance Standards. *Trial Court Performance Standards*. Williamsburg, VA: National Center for State Courts and the Bureau of Justice Assistance, United States Department of Justice, 1990.

Cratsley, J. C. *Inherent Powers of the Court*. Reno, NV: The National Judicial College, 1980.

Dilweg, V. L. "Balancing Right from Wrong: What the New A.B.A. Code of Judicial Conduct Says," *Judges Journal*, 30, 1991: 26-29; 70-71.

Dubois, P., ed. *The Politics of Judicial Reform*. Lexington, MA: D. C. Heath and Company, 1982a.

Dubois, P., ed. *The Analysis of Judicial Reform*. Lexington, MA: D. C. Heath and Company, 1982b.

Eisenstein, J. "Research on Rural Criminal Justice: A Summary," (original publication 1982), reprinted in *Rural Courts Manual: A Course Module*. Reno, NV: The National Judicial College, 1990: 32-39.

Fahnestock, K. "The Loneliness of Command: One Perspective of Judicial Isolation," *Judges Journal*, 30, 1991: 13-19; 65-66.

Fahnestock, K., and M. Geiger. "Rural Courts: The Neglected Majority," *Court Management Journal*, 1982: 4-10.

_____. *Time to Justice: Caseflow in Rural General Jurisdiction Courts*. Montpelier, VT: The Rural Justice Center, 1990.

_____. "We All Get Along Here: Caseflow in Rural Courts," *Judicature*, 76, No. 5, 1993: 258-263.

Gallas, G. "Court Reform: Has it Been Built on an Adequate Foundation?," *Judicature*, 63, 1979: 28-38.

Glick, H. R. "The Politics of State Court Reform," in P. Dubois, ed., *The Politics of Judicial Reform*. Lexington, MA: D. C. Heath and Company, 1982.

Goldspiel, S. "Planning for Change: What Rural Judges Want," *Judges Journal*, 30, 1991: 20-21.

Gradwohl, J. "The Rural Judges of America," *Judges Journal*, 26, 1987: 21, 41.

Holland, K. M. "The Twilight of Adversariness: Trends in Civil Justice," in P. Dubois, ed., *The Analysis of Judicial Reform*. Lexington, MA: D. C. Heath and Company, 1982.

Jacob, H. *Urban Justice: Law and Order in American Cities*. Englewood Cliffs, NJ: Prentice-Hall, Inc., 1973.

Jacob, H. *Justice in America: Courts, Lawyers, and the Judicial Process*. Boston, MA: Little, Brown and Company, 1978.

Kendall, M. C., and R. R. Shouse. "The Role of Rural Lawyers in Denying the Adversarial Legal System to Rural Americans: Problems, Causes, and Solutions," reprinted in *Rural Courts Manual: A Course Module*. Reno, NV: The National Judicial College, 1990: 118-137.

Miller, F. "Delay in Rural Courts: It Exists, but It Can Be Reduced," *State Court Journal*, 14, 1990: 23-40.

National Conference of the Judiciary on Rural Courts. *The Rural Courts: An Agenda for Action*. Co-sponsored by The National Judicial College, American Bar Association Conference of Special Court Judges and The Rural Justice Center, 1986a.

_____. *Report of the National Conference of the Judiciary on Rural Courts*. Co-sponsored by The National Judicial College, American Bar Association Conference of Special Court Judges and The Rural Justice Center, 1986b.

National Judicial College. "Rural Court Staffs," in *Rural Courts Manual: A Course Module*. Reno, NV: The National Judicial College, 1990: 77-81.

Rogers, F. B. "The Problem Courts: What's Wrong?," *Judges Journal*, 30, 1991: 22-25; 68-69.

Solomon, M., and D. Somerlot. *Caseflow Management in the Trial Court: Now and for the Future*. Chicago: American Bar Association, 1987.

Stott, E. K., T. Fetter, and L. L. Crites. *Rural Courts: The Effect of Space and Distance on the Administration of Justice*. Denver, CO: The National Center for State Courts, 1977.

Vandiver, R. "Get the Best: How the Court Administrator Can Work for You," *Judges Journal*, 30, 1991: 50-55.

PART IV

CORRECTIONS

The next two articles primarily explore facilities that oversee the incarceration of those who are convicted of crimes. "County and Municipal Jails," by Lois A. Guyon, discusses selected issues in jail management and some of the conditions in modern rural jails. The author reviews the history of rural jails and describes their inhabitants as inebriates, tramps, travelers who needed shelter and those who violated the law. Additionally, the reader is given an account of life in these early lockups and is presented with an overview of the physical setting. Constraints and challenges facing many rural county and municipal jails today are described as being essentially the same as they were historically.

The work by Herman Wood and Stanford Schwartz, "Structure of Rural Corrections," concentrates on how two major divisions of rural corrections are organized and operated. First, jails mainly are custodial in character and become low economic and political priorities for sheriffs who view their primary function as law enforcement. These constraints lead to such challenges as a lack of rehabilitation and counseling services. The authors also discuss suggestions for establishing regional jails by the state, through several counties working together, or by private companies. Some contend that these arrangements provide solutions to many of the difficulties associated with rural corrections. Wood and Schwartz present the views of both the advocates and opponents of these proposals. Second, probation and parole are discussed; as with other aspects of rural criminal justice, many aspects of these functions are handled informally by actors who perform multiple roles.

CHAPTER 7

History of County and Municipal Jails

by *Lois A. Guyon*

INTRODUCTION

County and municipal jails may be large urban institutions holding hundreds or thousands of inmates, or they may be small rural facilities with one or two cells that remain unoccupied on occasion. The modern definition of a small jail includes those with 50 beds or less (Washington 1988). This chapter specifically focuses on rural jails that historically have been small in size. First, the history and role of rural jails is reviewed. Second, modern rural jails are described. Additionally, current issues in jail management are discussed, which include: the use of regional jails; jail inmate services; modern physical plants; and jail community relations.

Much of what has been written about the development of jails focuses on large county or city jails. Recent awareness of the needs of small jails has led to the development of information and services for use by administrators of small jails. Information on jails may be found in the literature on architecture, correctional institutions, criminal justice, sociology, criminology, psychology and social work.

HISTORY OF SMALL-TOWN JAILS

The earliest jails in the United States were simple structures, either adapted facilities such as mines converted to secure prisoners or built for the express purpose of locking up people. Small rural jails in incorporated towns with populations under 2,000 generally were built for the purpose of housing prisoners. These small jails often were called a "jug" or "calaboose." Guyon and Green researched early small town jails, described the unique architectural characteristics, and reported on the staff and inmates who worked in, and inhabited, the calaboose (1990). They found these jails were constructed as one of the necessary public services instituted to serve the citizens of the community at the time the town was founded. While these jails commonly are not used

113

today, they are still in existence in many rural towns. The sturdy construction of the buildings, as well as their small size, has resulted in their preservation. In some cases, original hardware may be attached, making their identification certain.

The size of the jail building usually was about 10 feet x 14 feet. These buildings were placed on public land designated in the original plat of the town. Moved buildings are generally close to the first location. If original hardware does not identify a building as a former jail, a close look at windows and doors may show where metal bars or locks once were placed. A review of town council proceedings and financial records also may give clues to the existence of a calaboose. Additionally, some restored jails are listed on the National Register of Historic Buildings.

INHABITANTS OF EARLY RURAL JAILS

In the mid-1800s, when many towns were establishing their first jails, the buildings were required by necessity instead of by legal dictate or convention. The inhabitants of the calaboose, who required a secure housing arrangement, were of four types. The first and most common type was the inebriate. Local oral histories are rich with stories about the night that the town drunk was locked in the jail. Release from the jail usually occurred within a few hours when sobriety was attained.

A second visitor to the calaboose was the tramp. Tramps were transient males with no visible means of support, and who had committed no violation of the criminal codes. These men were housed in jails due to lack of hotel rooms or lack of funds to pay for such if they did exist. The tramps were looked on with suspicion by local citizens, and generally, they were closely watched by marshals who had no trouble identifying them as strangers. In small towns, the marshal knew all local inhabitants. Tramps usually were encouraged to move on to another town after being given one night free lodging at the jail.

Travelers made up a third type of resident in the calaboose. In towns with no temporary public rooms for rent or where locals were unwilling to rent, the jail was used as an occasional low-cost bed.

The fourth category of jail resident included those confined because of criminal acts. Criminal offenders were held only until transportation could be arranged to the county jail or until a local magistrate was available to hold court.

Once an inmate was transferred to the county jail, the inmate would be held until trial or until the sentence of the court had been carried out. The sentence of the court might include a fine, a jail sentence, a penitentiary sentence or death.

In the case of a death sentence, the hanging or shooting of the convict was carried out at the county jail. It was common to move the prisoner several counties away to reduce the chance of his falling into the hands of hostile vigilante groups who wanted to prematurely kill him. Vigilante groups wanting speedy revenge of a murder commonly were controlled by state military forces that would be authorized by the governor of the state to guard the prisoner. It was common to walk a convict, flanked by soldiers, to the trial or to an execution. Today, prisoners are executed by the state instead of the county.

Counties wanting to hang a prisoner might borrow a gallows from a neighboring county, which reduced the cost of the hanging. In contrast to the 8 to 12 years that a modern inmate might spend on death row, the death row inmates of the early rural jails generally would be executed within six months of the time of the crime. Statutes allotted time between sentence and execution so that hasty executions did not contribute to a miscarriage of justice. However, the time was measured in weeks, not the years that are now elapsing.

Both women and children were held in early county jails. Children were separated by gender instead of age, and often they would be in contact with older criminals. Women were housed in areas separate from men only when such areas were available. Women generally were jailed because of crimes so serious they could not be overlooked. Early law enforcement personnel were reluctant to lock up women unless there appeared to be no reasonable alternative.

THE NEED FOR RURAL JAILS

The limits of transportation technology dictated the need for a local jail. In many rural areas of the United States, roads were not paved or even graveled until after World War I. In winter or when there were frequent rains the roads became impassable. Prisoners could not be transported until the snow was removed or the roads dried.

Two developments made major changes in when prisoners could be transported in rural areas of the country. The first was the availability of the automobile, which reduced the amount of time required to transport prisoners. By horse, transporting a prisoner to the county jail could be a two-day event. Use of the automobile reduced the time to no more than half a day. A second development was the paving or placing of gravel and cinders on roads. Gravel or cinder roads could be traveled even after heavy rains.

ADMINISTRATION OF EARLY RURAL JAILS

The policing function of the small town either was accomplished by a marshal who was appointed or by a constable who was elected. The statutes of the state of Iowa in 1888 made provision for both. In some small towns such as Toronto, Iowa, the town first used a constable and then dropped that plan in favor of the marshal system (M. St. John, personal communication, August 4, 1989).

When using the marshal system, staffing the calaboose was the responsibility of the town council. A marshal was hired and given authority to arrest, guard, care for and transport prisoners. The marshal of Grand Mound, Iowa was paid $150 a year, according to Council Minutes of 1895. He was paid quarterly. He was expected to light the street lamps, janitor the City Hall and watch the town at night. In the 1930s, the marshal sold marriage, hunting and fishing licenses, as well as permits for new cars. He also served as an insurance agent and was the manager of the scale where crops were brought to be weighed (R. H. Green, personal communication, January 15, 1989).

Being a marshal also required supervision of part-time police. These temporary "special marshals" were paid $5.00 (day and night) for policing special occasions, such as Fourth of July celebrations when extra manpower was needed.

The marshal was expected to use his own clothing, and when transportation was needed, to supply the horses, carriage or automobile. The town would provide a badge on occasion but it was not uncommon for marshals to provide their own badge and gun.

Training of the marshal consisted of on-the-job experience, and after World War II, an occasional one-day meeting at the state capital. The meeting was not required, and generally, was attended by those invited by the county sheriff. The meeting would consist of a speaker, and it provided opportunities for social interactions with others in law enforcement.

After fiscal constraints caused the disappearance of the local small-town marshal, the calaboose fell into disuse. Small towns found it increasingly difficult to financially support 24-hour policing and dropped the local marshal in favor of area or county-wide policing. When transporting prisoners to the county jail became practical, the calaboose was seldom used, and with the marshal gone, jails were no longer needed; so ending a chapter in our nation's criminal justice history.

CONSTRUCTION METHODS OF EARLY JAILS

The physical structure of the calaboose varied depending on local resources. Generally, local materials were used in construction. One common building material was the rough hewn log. An example of the log jail existed at Nashville, in Brown County, Indiana (*Corrections Today* 1989). This jail was built in 1837. There were two stories, the upper cell being reached from an outside stairway. The entrance was protected by two strong iron doors. Two small windows were covered with heavy iron grating and solid iron coverings that were locked with padlocks. Each entrance had a heavy solid iron door, with a grated iron door to provide additional restraint. Locks consisted of heavy padlocks; the middle door was locked by two lever locks. The key for the large lever lock measured 36" in length and weighed about five pounds. A wood-burning stove in the lower cell provided heat for both the upper and lower compartments of the jail. The walls, consisting of three tiers of logs, were three feet thick. The inner and outer tiers were horizontal, while the center tier was perpendicular. In September 1919 the last inmate was removed from this old log jail.

A second construction method was that of the common 2" x 4" board structural member laid one on top of the other so that the 4" dimension created a 4" thick wall. The Coal Valley, Illinois jail was a one story 2" x 4" construction building that has been restored. The 12' x 16' structure had two cells in the rear, the rooms being created by a 2" x 4" wall extending between the cells. Iron barred doors were used to secure the cells. A small 6" x 8" opening was located over each cell door. The floor and ceiling were both 2" x 4" construction. A jailer's office was in front of the cells. It contained two windows on the front of the building. A wood-burning stove faced the door and sat along the wall between the cells. This stove was used to heat both the cells and the office space. The outside door to the jail was constructed with two layers of 1" thick boards. The doors of some wooden jails were made of three layers of 1" x 6" boards. The layers alternated between vertical, horizontal and diagonal.

Concrete block also was used in some small-town jails. This third type of building material was available prior to 1900 and was used to construct the Welton, Iowa jail. This single story, 13 1/2' x 15 1/2' building had a metal ceiling with metal braces. The floor was of poured concrete. The one room jail was built in 1908 and contained a two-cell iron cellblock. A small narrow window was on one side of the building and a large window was on the front, to the left of the door. A brick chimney provided evidence that a wood-burning stove was placed on the left wall outside the cell area. It would have been used to heat the jailer's area as well as the cells.

Fourth, some jails were made of stone. A restored example is at Delmar, Iowa where the jail had an arched roof made of stone. The door of the 10' x 12' calaboose was of solid iron with a small metal grate at eye level. Two small windows, 26 1/2" x 34 1/2", centered on each side of the building provided scant light and ventilation. Metal mesh covered the windows on the outside; this mesh covered iron bars located outside glass windows. The glass windows were hinged at the top. According to local lore, this one-room lockup once held 21 drunk and brawling railroad workers (M. Maltas, personal communication, November 29, 1988).

Adobe is a fifth construction material used to construct rural jails. This method proved less than desirable, as escapes easily were accomplished by digging through the walls (Harrison 1968). Adobe is mud, and sometimes grass, pressed into bricks that are dried in the sun. Iron bars could be sunk into the adobe to form cells. This type of construction was not limited to small jails but also was used in the construction of Utah's first penitentiary.

A sixth method of construction was the frame building. Wooden siding was placed over wood studs, with wood shingles placed on the roof. Generally, this form of construction was not secure, so iron cages soon were introduced inside the frame structure. Iron cells also were placed in concrete, brick and stone buildings for additional security and as a means of separating inmates from each other.

Brick was used as a seventh construction mode. The jail of DeWitt, Iowa contained six cells and once was used as a county jail. While larger than some small town calabooses (48' 4" x 38' 4"), the brick structure served as a rural town jail when the county seat was moved to Clinton, Iowa. This jail was built in 1856.

The flooring of the DeWitt, Iowa jail was of 2" oak planking placed in two layers. The second layer was laid across the first, and both layers were spiked into the joists. Ten-penny fencing nails were then driven into these planks about an inch apart, with several kegs of nails used in the flooring. Newspaper accounts describe the floor as "an ugly impediment in the way of even the most accomplished diggers" (Wilkinson 1974).

In some jails, concrete was used as a flooring surface. The wooden 2" x 4" board construction was used in floors, as well as in ceilings and walls. When used as flooring, the 2" x 4" resulted in a 4" thick wooden floor.

Walls of many early small jails were covered with plaster or masonry. Plaster walls were whitewashed with calcimine paint that was made from lime. The lime coating acted as a disinfectant, deodorizer and light reflector in the often dimly lit cells. The white surface was used, as in modern jails, as a giant palette for scribbling obscenities, names and sometimes art work by the inmates.

LIFE IN EARLY RURAL JAILS

Security in small jails consisted of a combination of physical structure and supervision by the jailer. Small-town marshals reported using the jail as an overnight holding cell only when absolutely necessary. When prisoners were in the jail, the marshal was expected to sleep at the jail or at least to provide continuous intermittent supervision in case of fire, suicide or escape attempt (M. St. John, personal communication, May 13, 1989).

Food for prisoners generally was not a consideration. Prisoners were released after a few hours in jail to "sober up" or were transferred to county jails if longer-term jailing was indicated by the condition of the prisoner or the offense. In county jails, food was prepared in the jail. Heat was provided by burning wood or coal in small stoves that were vented through the walls. The town provided fuel. Generally, stoves were outside the cell area but in some cases the stove was accessible to the prisoners.

Toilet facilities consisted of what was called a "vault" or bucket that would be emptied outside the jail. The vault was a hole dug in the ground through the floor of the jail. Wooden benches with four holes over the vault were seen in some jails. Inmates would use this "outhouse convenience" instead of having to empty what was called the "slop bucket." There was no running water or plumbing in the early small town jails. When indoor plumbing became common in rural homes it was installed in rural jails. The standard of living in rural jails has generally reflected the lifestyle of the poor people in the society of the day.

Additional living conditions in the calaboose included the fact that beds were cots or metal frames with wire to sleep on. Blankets were provided. Clothing worn by the prisoners was the property of the inmate. No effort was made to alter clothing or other personal property, with the exception of checking the prisoner for knives and other weapons. Although sanctioned by statutes in the 1800s, prisoners seldom were held long enough in small jails to be put to hard labor. Prisoners had little to occupy their time. Typically, no programs of rehabilitation, work or treatment were used.

CONDITIONS IN RURAL JAILS TODAY

With urbanization, the availability of fast convenient transportation and rural communities' desire to divest themselves of the responsibility to supervise prisoners, local lockups closed in towns of under several thousand persons. The county jail became the primary holding facility for those being held prior to trial, and for those serving short sentences. Conditions in rural county jails vary according to the size of the jail, architectural design, community interest and financial resources.

Responsibility for the operation of jails, in most states, is the duty of the county sheriff. Alternate forms of statutory authorization allow for special, elected jail administrators or control of the local jails by a state's department of corrections. In communities where local lockups are maintained, the lockups are given direct supervision by the chief of police by authorization of the mayor and city council or by the city manager. Many states provide jail and lockup inspections, which measure current jail conditions against published standards. In some cases, there is no provision for enforcement of standards if violations are found.

Today, some "mom and pop" jails still exist on the county level. These jails, such as the Gilmer County Jail in West Virginia, have the jailer and his family living in the jail while supervising and caring for a small number of inmates (*Pantograph* [Bloomington, IL], 1990). Some of these jails have as few as two cells; the Gilmer County Jail may hold as many as nine inmates on an average day.

In the evenings, prisoners play table tennis and watch television in a recreation room. They may make local calls on the jailer's telephone and eat the same food as the jailer and his family.

REGIONAL JAILS

Cost effectiveness and inability to meet state standards have closed many small rural county jails. Some have been replaced by regional jails where several, as many as 12, counties cooperate in the construction of a new, modern jail. These jails are operated in a similar manner to jails in urban areas, and they contend with the same operational problems, which include: overcrowding with little capacity to expand; predatory inmates; staffing shortages; transportation issues; community (in)acceptance; failure to comply with statutory, professional or legal standards; physical plant design limitations; and financial constraints.

Not all new jails are regional. Since 1974, as many as 500 counties across the United States have opened new jails with 50 beds or less (Kime 1986). Of 3,316 jails in the United States in 1988, 2,219 had an average daily population of under 50 inmates. These small jails held 38,934 of 336,017 inmates in custody (United States Department of Justice 1991). Many insufficient, old and small jails are in operation. The small jail is supplemented by local lockups in some towns with populations large enough to warrant a local law enforcement agency. Rural communities continue to be in the corrections business. In addition to rural lockups and jails, rural communities also are the site of many of the nation's prisons. Urban communities, with growing economies and sufficient jobs, reject the placement of prisons near dense population centers. Rural communities needing employment opportunities generated by the existence of a prison, and lacking in political power, become the site for many prisons that house perpetrators of urban as well as rural crimes.

INHABITANTS OF TODAY'S RURAL JAILS

Both urban and rural jails simultaneously house male and female prisoners. Jails hold convicted criminals and those accused of crimes who are awaiting trial. Until threatened by withdrawal of federal funds, many jails also held juveniles. Juveniles now are required to be held in special detention centers, separated from adults.

The drunk continues to occupy a prominent role in the life of today's rural jails. Despite the decriminalization of alcoholism in many jurisdictions, the lack of treatment centers results in police charging the inebriate with criminal offenses so that the disorderly person may be detained "for his or her own good."

A second non-criminal who occupies the local jail is the mentally ill person (Kerle 1983). The philosophy of deinstitutionalizing the mentally ill resulted in moving many mental hospital patients into the community. Lack of local community mental health services places the mentally ill in a situation comparable to the alcoholic, who is arrested to provide shelter, if not treatment. Staffs of rural jails are not generally trained in treating or handling the mentally ill. Instead of treatment, custody and control of the mentally ill person becomes the jail's objective.

Historically, a feature of small rural jails has been their informality. Administering a jail with a small number of inmates allowed for individualized treatment of prisoners. Drunks could be released without formal processing and a "paper trail" of forms sent to every level of government. Those accused of crimes deemed serious enough for longer term incarceration or treatment were retained, and formal record keeping and processing occurred. Today, this informality is being replaced in most rural jails by a formal process that is not unlike that of urban counties and cities.

DIFFERENCES BETWEEN LARGE AND SMALL JAILS

Mays and Thompson note differences between small and large jails (1988). Small jails tend to be older than large jails, have smaller cells, lack ability to segregate inmates from each other and lack economy of scale in providing necessary services to inmates. Lack of economy of scale results in high costs per inmate when, for example, a doctor must be called to evaluate or treat an inmate. In staffing around-the-clock positions, with an employee working a 40-hour week—given sick leave and vacation days, as well as days off—five persons are needed. These five people are required if there is one inmate to supervise or many.

Additional constraints on small jails include their staff having little division of labor. Staff members do not have the luxury of being a specialist doing one function. They may be required to keep records, do booking, clean, answer the phone, function as a receptionist for visitors or serve food. These activities must be accomplished while supervising inmates. The result is that inmates in small jails spend much time in lock-down. Additional constraints include the fact that time away from the jail to train small-jail staff seldom is available. Costs involved in acquiring substitute workers limit the amount of training possible. Limited staff also increases the risk of inmate-to-inmate and inmate-to-staff violence. Without constant visual supervision, suicide risk also is increased.

ASSISTANCE TO SMALL JAILS

The federal government recognized the limitations of, and need for, services to jails of all sizes. In 1977, the National Institute of Corrections (NIC) was funded to assist jails throughout the country. The NIC provides special consultation and services to managers of small jails. Literature, seminars and training are available for a number of areas: legal issues; staffing; security; inmate management; classification; overcrowding; architectural design; treatment programs; food service; jail industries; and health services. NIC services also include technical assistance for specific problems and grant money to obtain expertise, resources and services necessary to address jail problems.

SMALL-JAIL ARCHITECTURAL DESIGN

Small old jails still used today were built on a linear model that employed a square or rectangular building in which small cells were constructed. Iron bars and other construction materials were selected to prevent escape and property damage, and to facilitate cleaning. Supervision of inmates by staff in these jails was intermittent and led to opportunities for suicide and violence.

With the introduction of the New Generation philosophy, many newly constructed jails use a podular design to allow for direct supervision of inmates (Zupan 1991). Inmates are housed in groups of less than 50 persons in areas called modules. Furnishings are designed for noise reduction, attractiveness and privacy. Staff are trained in interpersonal skills and are expected to interact with inmates to become knowledgeable about what is happening within the group.

Research has not shown the New Generation jail to be problem-free. Overcrowding has forced double celling in some new facilities and providing trained staff is not always possible even in large jails. So long as constraints on resources prevent the building of new jails in rural areas, and staffing shortages or limitations continue, the rural small jail will tend to be bypassed by the innovations of the New Generation jail philosophy. Challenges facing rural county or municipal jails, as they move toward the twenty-first century, include many of the same problems that were seen in early rural jails and lockups. Descriptions of conditions in today's jails read as though they were written when the jail system of the United States first was developed.

Lack of suitable space with adequate light and ventilation, as well as lack of inmate services, are still concerns of modern jail administrators. Clean jails, with nutritious food and activities for inmates, remain difficult to provide.

Community apathy toward jails results in lack of funding. Some small-jail administrators recognize the value of bringing community residents into the jail for tours, or as volunteers in recreational, educational or religious programs. Traditionally, however, the public has been viewed with suspicion by many jail administrators. This suspicion continues today. It is the public who criticize the jail at the time of a suicide or escape, and who resist attempts to raise taxes to support correctional facilities and programs (Handberg 1982).

SUMMARY

Rural jails were built for the temporary detention of persons who represented the following types: inebriates, tramps, travelers, criminals. Construction methods included: log, 2" x 4" lumber, concrete block, stone, adobe, frame, and brick.

Small-town jails were administered by appointed marshals, by elected constables or by an elected sheriff. No professional training was needed to hold these positions.

The death sentence once was carried out at rural county jails. This function now is performed at the state level.

Life in rural jails has been characterized by lack of activity. Food, clothing and sanitary conditions generally have been at a standard equal to that of the poor people of the society at any time in our history.

Many rural jails are being replaced by modern central facilities called regional jails. Some of these new jails are based on the New Generation philosophy. Cost effectiveness and inability to meet standards have caused this centralization. Problems associated with large jails now are being introduced to the inmates from rural communities.

REFERENCES

Guyon, L. A., and H. F. Green. "Calaboose: Small-Town Lockup," *Federal Probation*, 2, 1990: 58-62.

Handberg, R. "Jails and Correctional Farms: The Neglected Half of Rural Law Enforcement," *Journal of Correctional Education*, 32, No. 4, 1982: 20-23.

Harrison, F. *Hell Holes and Hangings*. Clarendon, TX: Clarendon Press, 1968.

Kerle, K. "The Rural Jail: Its People, Problems and Solutions," *Human Services in the Rural Environment*, 8, No. 1, 1983: 9-17.

Kime Planning & Architecture. *Small Jail: Special Issues*. Kime, DA: Author, 1986.

Mays, G. L., and J. A. Thompson. "Mayberry Revisited: The Characteristics and Operations of America's Small Jails," *Justice Quarterly*, 5, No. 3, 1988: 421-440.

"Mom, Pop Jail Reminiscent of Mayberry," *Pantagraph* [Bloomington, IL], April 29, 1990: 3.

"Old Log Jail," *Corrections Today*, 50, 1989: 70.

United States Department of Justice. *Correctional Populations in the United States, 1988* (NCJ-124280). Rockville, MD: Bureau of Justice Statistics, 1991.

Washington, J. "ACA's Standards: Tailoring the Process to Fit Small Jails," *Corrections Today*, 50, No. 7, 1988: 42-43.

Wilkinson, H. "Of All Things," *The Dewitt Observer*, September 30, 1974.

Zupan, L. L. *Jails: Reform and the New Generation Philosophy*. Cincinnati, OH: Anderson Publishing Company, 1991.

CHAPTER 8

Structure of Rural Corrections

by *Herman Wood* and *Sanford Schwartz*

INTRODUCTION

Corrections in rural America reflect many of the same problems that are evident in other fields, such as rural medical service. The manner in which we have gone about solving the problems or adjusting to them reflects the diversity of culture in the various regions of the country. In this chapter, we discuss some of the more common organizational adaptations, along with some of the more innovative attempts at finding solutions to common problems.

A difficulty that we encountered in developing this chapter was one of definitions. "Rural" has been a neglected area in the correctional field. Even when research does apply, "rural" often comes under the heading of size rather than location. For instance, the National Institute of Corrections and the American Corrections Association define "small" jails as those with 50 or fewer inmates. Standards were developed for large jails, all of which are in metropolitan areas, and then the process was tailored to fit small jails (Washington 1988). This definition is applicable to rural America in many aspects, such as economy of scale calculations in food and medical services. However, generally, it ignores the fact that a 30-bed city jail in the midst of a metropolitan area faces far different problems than a 30-bed county jail in a more remote area. For instance, the judicial system served by the rural jail might be limited to a choice between probation or incarceration, while an urban jail of the same size would be able to take advantage of many programs and assets available in the urban area (Ralph et al. 1994).

Correctional agencies face another set of problems in transitional areas. These areas are unique in that formerly they were "rural" areas but now are on the outskirts of an expanding metropolis. They still have the budget and fiscal policies of the rural areas, while the population base is swollen by people moving out of "the big city." This migration brings with it many of the problems that these new residents hope to escape. With improvement in transportation systems, in some areas, not just bedroom communities but entire bedroom counties, face the issue of not yet having the industrial base to generate large amounts of tax money. The highway and rapid transit networks are permitting families to move out to more rural settings for better places to raise children and escape high-density living. However, they bring with them a demand for services that presents new challenges to the local governments whose tax bases often lag behind, and whose political systems often resist adjusting to the new realities. These areas eventually adapt; they become intertwined with the metropolitan complex and begin contributing to the sprawl into the bordering rural areas.

In non-metropolitan or rural sectors not adjacent to urban centers, economic conditions vary considerably. Some counties are sites of intergenerational poverty and a disproportionate percentage of working poor, the very young and elderly, and those dependent on public assistance (Cook and Mizer 1994). These areas see their high school graduates go away to college or jobs in the cities and never return to their original homes where opportunities are limited. This leaves less working age people to make up a vital labor force, which in turn impacts the entire community (see, for example, Lasley 1994). This drain in resources affects corrections just as it does other services.

Data show that 85% of rural juveniles live with both parents, while only 67% of urban juveniles do so (North Dakota Census Data Center, personal communication). A juvenile justice study reveals that juveniles in rural areas not only have more two-parent families but they also have more parental involvement in the correctional process when compared to those in urban centers (Kempf et al. 1990). Rural juveniles are more likely to be placed outside a detention facility and their cases handled on a more informal basis. This informality appears to be part of a tradition of self-reliance and assistance by family members and neighbors which has marked the rural areas. These factors contribute to the attraction that rural areas have of low-population density, less crime, a cleaner and quieter lifestyle, and a sense of independence from government or other outside control.

RURAL CORRECTIONS IN PERSPECTIVE

The criminal justice system reflects the community of which it is a part and operates in rural areas in a much more personal way. Elements in the rural settings, such as pre-trial release and sentencing decisions, often can be made based on personal knowledge of the defendant or his/her family, and on the community support that s/he might have outside the formal referral system.

Corrections, for example, in rural communities readily is divided into confinement or jails on the one hand, and probation and parole or (minimal) rehabilitative services on the other. This is the case because from an organizational standpoint jails and parole, generally, are quite separate, with jails being operated by the most local-level political subdivision, and the parole system and probation services commonly being operated and financed by the state.

To be able to appreciate some of the constraints and challenges associated with rural corrections, let us begin to put it in perspective by looking at a metropolitan system. At one time, the authors of this chapter operated a county jail system with 300 beds, with a social service staff of about 12 professionals, and with a county misdemeanant probation system staffed by up to 39 probation and parole officers who supervised combined caseloads of over 3,000. In addition to this county-funded jail and misdemeanant system, the state Board of Probation and Parole operated from three offices with dozens of officers to serve the felony system in the county. There was a separate county juvenile court that had its own detention system with numerous deputy officers to handle the juvenile caseload in the community. The state operated a separate office to supervise those juveniles who had been released from state detention facilities. This urban county corrections system was in a Justice Service Department that was organized separately from the county police and the county sheriff who performed only civil and court duties.

Contrast the metropolitan system described above with rural counties found only a few miles away: these rural counties have an elected sheriff, with a handful of deputies to patrol the county and who operate the jail as an additional, low-priority duty. There is a state probation office that handles only felony cases, and which operates over a number of counties with sometimes less than one officer per county. A juvenile officer is available for the judicial circuit covering several counties. Few correctional services other than confinement exist for minor offenders, who comprise the majority of arrested persons. We will discuss other systems with a variety of sizes and organizational structures but this description should serve as a framework of extremes on which to build a better understanding of the constraints that present a series of challenges to rural jurisdictions.

To further put rural corrections in perspective, it is instructive to review briefly some data associated with jails in the United States. Allen and Simonsen note that statistics in this area are hard to obtain and national surveys are rare (1995). Every half decade since 1970 the United States Department of Justice has conducted a census that includes all of the nation's jails. One such survey was performed in 1988 and made available in 1990. The latest full tabulation was in 1993 but will not be released until late 1995. This information has been supplemented by periodic surveys that provide a sampling of jurisdictions. Based on these reports, there are approximately 3,316 locally administered jails in the United States, not counting holdovers and drunk tanks (United States Department of Justice 1990). The 10 largest facilities (only 0.3% of the total), each of which is part of a large metropolitan system, accounted for 20% of the jail population (Cole 1995). The other 80% of jail inmates are spread over the remaining 3,006 facilities, which are located predominantly in rural areas. In a 1992 survey of 795 jurisdictions, it was found that the largest 25 (3%) housed a full one-third of those incarcerated in jails (United States Department of Justice 1995). Indeed, most jails are small; 63% are designed to hold fewer than 50 inmates (Cole 1995).

RURAL CORRECTIONS: CONDITIONS AND CONSTRAINTS

Rural jail administration and the corrections organization of rural systems are usually very passive in nature, dealing with custody instead of services. Historically, this focus goes back to our English legal heritage. In the Old English system, law enforcement was geographically the responsibility of an earl or count in his county or shire. He discharged his responsibility by appointing a chief law enforcement officer who was given the title of county, or shire, reeve ("shire reeve" = sheriff). Originally, the jail, or English gaol, was not a place for punishment. Like the dungeon, it was a place to initially confine prisoners awaiting trial, sentence, ransom or payment of debts. Sentences themselves either were death; corporal punishment such as flogging; or public embarrassment like the stocks, pillory or branding. Later, the English jails became places to hold prisoners who were awaiting a ship to carry out the sentence of "transportation beyond the seas." It was left to the American colonists to "invent" the idea that a person could repent their "sins" if they were confined to a penitentiary or for minor crimes to a jail.

It seems logical that the official charged with arresting a suspect and presenting him for trial (see, for example, the sheriff) should be the person responsible for holding the prisoner until trial. This holding function became even more important under the American system of justice, where a single "circuit" judge physically would ride a circuit of several county seats. Trials might not have been as speedy as some would have liked since prisoners had to be held until the judge arrived. An extension of this holding function was the idea of using confinement to jail as punishment for minor offenders who did not merit a long term penitentiary sentence. Jail confinement rose to even higher levels as American society began to abandon the practices of branding, flogging or public scorn as punishment for misdemeanor-level crimes in favor of short jail sentences.

Enforcement of the law has remained the primary function of most rural sheriff's departments (Allen and Simonsen 1995; Cole 1995) despite the increase in requirements for jail operations. Most often, sheriffs have experience and training in police functions, are elected on that basis, and view the jail as a place for custody functions only. It would be a very unusual sheriff who would run for election on the basis of being a good jailer and as one who would work to incorporate better rehabilitation programs. Most sheriffs regard the jail as "an invisible political issue" until such time as there is an escape or a suicide that comes to public attention (Kalinich and Klofas 1986: 115).

The jail takes the back seat in budget allocations; for example, typically when it is a choice between a new patrol car or a new heating system for the jail, budgetary preference is given to the car. The elected sheriff can be expected to spend money on the jail to eliminate the threat of fire or escape, or to ward off the threat of being accused of running an unsanitary facility. But the sheriff cannot be expected to recommend expenditures for such corrections functions as rehabilitation, education, counseling or to professionalize jail staff if such actions would detract from his primary peace-keeping functions. The jail also comes in last when personnel assignments are made. Most sheriffs begin their new, inexperienced staff in the jail and then promote them to law enforcement functions at a later time.

There are many more jails than any other type of correctional institution, yet the small jail remains outside the professional corrections community. A look at the membership of state correctional associations reveals that such professional groups primarily are made up of probation and parole officers, state prison staff and a very few employees from the largest metropolitan jails. Seldom are the sheriff's deputies and jailers represented. This leaves the jailers to concentrate on custody without involvement in the professional rehabilitation community, and without the training and technical assistance required to bring rural jails into the corrections mainstream. At least in part, this is a reflection of the situation discussed above where many small jails are not given priority by the communities in which they are located.

In 45 states, there is statutory authority or a requirement, for the sheriff to serve as jailer. Kentucky is the only state where its constitution provides for a separate, elected jailer. In that case, s/he is an officer of the court, not a law enforcement officer in the sense of having a police function. In Pennsylvania, a sheriff runs the jail in each of the 36 small rural counties. In New Jersey, county freeholders operate the jail in eight counties through appointed jailers, while the sheriff operates the jail in the other counties (Kerle 1983). In Missouri, there is authority for civil service appointment of the jail operator in the large metropolitan areas, while elected sheriffs retain that function in the other 103 counties. Only Alaska, Vermont, Connecticut, Rhode Island, Delaware and Hawaii have their jails operated on a regional basis by the state (Cole 1995).

As a general rule, smaller jails are older, cells are smaller, and many cannot provide sight or sound separation between juvenile and adult, or between male and female prisoners. Some states, such as Maryland, New Jersey and Massachusetts, no longer mix juveniles with adults. Other states still do so in rural jails. Champion notes that "segregation is a luxury and cannot be accomplished effectively" in many smaller jails because of space limitations (1991: 199). One of the unfortunate problems is that many juveniles are being detained for what would not be classified as a crime if they were an adult (status offenders). A study in Minnesota, for example, found that 17% of youths were in jails because of such "status offenses" as running away from home, truancy or incorrigibility (Schwartz et al. 1988). Although a larger jail might make classifications of prisoners easier, size does not guarantee effective separation. While operating a 100-bed jail, with 20 of the beds in a women's section and 80 in the men's wing, one of the authors of this chapter was faced with days when the jail would have held over 90 men and only one or two women prisoners. A few days later, cots might have been set up to accommodate an overflow in the women's section. This same problem exists in smaller jails, where the jail may be overcrowded on one day but soon thereafter may be completely vacant. When considering new construction, the "average daily inmate count" becomes a statistic that cannot be relied on, particularly in the smaller jail.

PROPOSALS TO RESTRUCTURE RURAL CORRECTIONS

One way in which some observers have suggested we deal with the difficulties discussed above is to modify the structure of rural corrections. As noted earlier, several states have established, and are operating, jails on a regional basis. Others favor a local, cooperative arrangement whereby several counties could band together to build and operate one jail on a more efficient scale. Even if it were possible to find contiguous counties whose residents could put aside their rivalries and political differences, always there would be counties left out of the system unless some other agency drew the boundaries. Essentially this would require a state mandate to force counties into regions, possibly against their will, and to mandate expenditure of county funds. If this occurred, then the state could proceed to the next step and actually finance, build and operate a state jail system, as is done in six states.

Advantages of Regionalization

Regional jails would provide an economy of scale in such areas as food and medical services, and from a correctional standpoint, it permits the introduction of social workers and other rehabilitation specialists into the rural picture. One possible advantage of regionalization is that the social service staff of such a facility could use pre-trial release and parole recommendations as jail population control, and it would be able to marshall community alternatives on a larger scale. Those who have done their research on larger jails rightfully infer that larger jails could provide: mental health and suicide screening; less per-inmate cost for food and medical service; crisis intervention programs to help solve pressing inmate problems and to provide short-term counseling; pre-trial release screening; and assistance to families of inmates.

Opportunities for suicides and homicides are reduced in larger jails because there is a greater likelihood for around-the-clock inmate supervision. In smaller jails, it is not highly unusual to have one employee who is required to function as turn-key, dispatcher, booking officer, janitor, transporter of prisoners and the like. It is even possible for that person to be called out in an emergency, leaving the jail locked and unsupervised. In some rural jails, the lack of 24-hour supervision appears to be routine. This condition of one staff member performing multiple functions, and thus divided alertness levels, increases the chances for suicides and homicides in small jails.

Advocates of state operated regional jails point to the administrative advantage of being able to promote and transfer staff as the need arises. They also support transfer of inmates as a means of population control between the various regional institutions. As we shall see when we discuss objections to regional arrangements, not only would this increase transportation problems but it brings immediate objections from communities to outside inmates being transferred into their midst.

Those who are proponents of regional jails designed to serve several counties also point out that while jailers in small jails receive lower salaries, the average cost per inmate is over twice that of the larger jail (Mays and Thompson 1988). They also identify the almost complete lack of recreation facilities, the poor design, the old age, and the likelihood of local politics and the tax base precluding small, rural jails being replaced by safe, modern facilities. These advocates further highlight the large number of rural areas where the tax base depends on agriculture, which consequently have a declining population. Despite problems with a sufficient tax base, jails remain at the low end of the priority list at all levels of government but particularly at the rural level where we have jails in counties with a population of less than 5,000 (Kerle 1983).

A centralized state jail administration could set and enforce standards for custody, care and correctional functions. Presently, the quality of jail administration varies widely from county to county, and from one election to the next. The American Correctional Association, National Sheriffs Association and the National Jail Association have promulgated sets of jail standards and made herculean efforts to have them adopted. Other organizations, such as the American Bar Association and the American Medical Association, have published specialized standards in the legal and medical areas. Thirty-eight of the 44 states that have locally administered facilities have adopted their own jail standards. However, in six states they are voluntary, and in seven cases, implementation has not taken place. Only 14 states have included direct enforcement power; six states have provided for jail inspectors with advisory duties only. Others must petition the courts or as in North Dakota, the attorney general, to gain compliance (Mays and Thompson 1991).

Objections to Regionalization

Clear and Cole observe that the adoption of the regional jail concept has been hindered by several groups who would lose influence (1994). For instance, many sheriffs see significant problems in regionalization, regardless of who operates the regional facility. The sheriffs would have to give up control of patronage jobs in many cases, and they would lose a source of local political influence and clout. The local government would give up a measure of societal regulation in that they no longer would be able to determine who was to be incarcerated. The jails have become a repository for society's problem people (Zupan 1991; Cole 1995). This is true in all areas, but even more so in rural areas where alternative programs do not exist. A survey taken of Missouri institutions by the Special Offender Council, with the participation of both authors, revealed that in excess of 10% of the inmates were mentally retarded (Wood and Schwartz 1976). A range of 20% to 50% of pre-trial prisoners were held in lieu of very small bonds, possibly indicating an inordinate number of poverty-level defendants or persons with a lack of support in the community.

Another very real objection to regionalization involves time, distance and transportation. It should be noted that four of the states operating regional jails are very small geographically, and that although the other two, Alaska and Hawaii, involve vast geographic distances, they readily divide into population centers, with sparse or no populations in between. In many other geographically larger states, the local sheriff would encounter significant prisoner transportation difficulties. While they no longer would require a jail or jailer, they still would be required to staff and operate a temporary holding facility, and would now have to take an officer and, sometimes more important, a patrol car off the road to transport prisoners. This would be true not only at the times of arrest and release but also for bail hearings, trials, sentencings, various motions and the like. Groups interested in the reform of the judicial system frequently object to relocating individuals to a different community (Clear and Cole 1994). Also, some local bar associations have voiced objections to moving defendants out of the local courthouse area on the grounds that the distance involved makes it difficult for them to confer with their client and prepare a case. Last, distance must be considered for family visitation purposes.

Local communities also express fear that the rural jails could become a means for the state to control state penitentiary populations by housing serious offenders in these jails. They see this as creating problems caused by inner city inmates being put out into their community on such programs as work release. The NIMBY syndrome ("Not in my back yard") rears its ugly head in some areas (Clear and Cole 1994), while others actively seek such institutions as they create badly needed jobs.

Other Proposals for Change

Another restructuring proposal calls for removing jail control from the hands of law enforcement agencies and placing responsibility in the hands of corrections professionals hired to operate the jail for the county. Whether this practice would decrease costs awaits research from across the nation. Additionally, finding qualified correctional personnel in sufficient numbers would seem to be a challenge.

While most correctional facilities and programs of all kinds are operated by public agencies, some individuals recommend that non-governmental organizations oversee these functions. Allen and Simonsen highlight the fact that suggestions typically take one of four forms: 1) operation of correctional industries; 2) contracting for such items as health care or food services; 3) financing of construction projects; 4) operation of institutions themselves (1995). The most controversial developments have been in the last area. Under these arrangements, private parties are obligated to provide security, safeguards, medical needs and counseling that a state or county would be expected to administer. Expenses such as food, clothing, heat, light and other overhead costs would also be the responsibility of the commercial enterprise.

By mid-1993, at least 18 companies operated some 70 correctional institutions of various types such as jails, prisons and units for juvenile offenders in 17 states. Precise figures are difficult to obtain because it is not always easy to classify all facilities, and contracts may be created or dissolved rapidly. Advocates of such arrangements contend that the private sector can deliver needed services more inexpensively and flexibly when compared to governmental agencies such as counties. They perceive fewer problems with governmental "red tape," and an ability to hire, train and dismiss staff more efficiently (Cole 1994; Allen and Simonsen 1995).

Those who object to these compacts raise several concerns. First, some question whether corrections should be delegated from a governmental entity to a private business. Second, others ask how a private agency would be able to operate more inexpensively than the county or state. For example, labor unions have expressed doubts over wages, benefit packages and pensions. Third, some have focused on issues of accountability and supervision. They worry that such agreements will be difficult to monitor by state officials. Finally, accurate estimates of the costs associated with privatization do not always include elements such as federal grants. Because many of the private organizations that supervise these facilities are relatively new, studies that evaluate their degree of effectiveness and limitations are few. Whether the supporters or detractors of privatization are proved correct remains an issue for further research; despite this qualification, some initial reactions from those doing assessments have been positive (Cole 1994; Allen and Simonsen 1995). At a minimum, the same objections previously noted regarding time and transportation issues for law enforcement as they relate to regionalization will continue to exist.

PROBATION AND PAROLE

The administration of probation and parole systems is rich in diversity. Juvenile probation systems were developed largely in the juvenile courts, so normally they are administered locally. Adult parole systems are a responsibility of the state, with felony probation being added on to existing parole systems in many jurisdictions. There are jurisdictions, such as Illinois, that have a state-administered adult parole system but a probation system administered by the local circuit courts. California has a probation system that is administered locally but is subsidized by the state on a per diem basis with some built-in controls. These controls include a prohibition against using the subsidy to increase salaries; instead, subsidy dollars must be used to expand or enhance the probation system, thereby reducing the reliance on incarceration and its higher cost. These varied methods raise a major question of organization: whether or not a probation system should be controlled by the court it serves, or by some other umbrella agency.

The judge, whose training usually is legal and not administrative, may find in a rural system that s/he can readily become familiar with community assets, such as group homes, foster care, detoxification and chemical dependency treatment, along with self-help groups such as Alcoholics Anonymous. With only a handful of deputies and perhaps only one probation officer, s/he quickly may develop a working relationship that puts him/her in direct contact with the limited assets in the community. Each person in the rural system must become a "jack-of-all-trades" or a corrections generalist. Additionally, in some rural jurisdictions, such as Minnesota, probation officers may handle case loads with both adult and juvenile offenders. An urban system may have a specialist in employment, one for sexual offenses, another for spouse or child abuse cases, several officers specializing in substance abuse and the like. Rural arresting officers must be better trained in alternatives to arrest in order to divert some persons out of the system at the earliest stages, and to get them into the mental health system, detoxification centers and other services.

As mentioned, judges in rural areas must establish a relationship with community resources in order to move cases more rapidly and on an informal basis. In keeping with community preferences for informality and personal contact, the rural courts and police long ago developed a system of diversion, referral and "bench" probation where the judges use unsupervised release into the community or release to the "custody" of family, friends or employers. Informal corrections becomes less possible as an area increases in population density, as transportation networks bring in outsiders or state statutes begin mandating arrest and confinement for such offenses as spousal abuse or driving while intoxicated. Smaller systems remain more free from bureaucratic constraint with the abilities to remain flexible and tailor their correctional decisions to what is possible given the community assets available. In areas where the judge, sheriff and probation officer can present a united front, they can be extremely effective in organizing and even creating the community support they need for rehabilitation programming.

Studies of juvenile courts clearly show two distinct juvenile justice systems with differential processing between the urban and rural courts (Aday 1986; Kempf et al. 1990; Lockhart et al. 1990; Feld 1993). Aday describes this difference as centralized operation in the rural courts and decentralized operation in the urban system (1986). In urban areas, the systems have separate detention facilities, a chief juvenile officer with numerous deputies, and juvenile judges who rotate on and off the juvenile bench. Decisions are made by different staff members at each stage of the process, with their decisions frequently being based on strict written guidelines developed by the bureaucracy. They tend to process cases based on the category of offenses, and to dispose of the cases along legalistic lines.

Rural systems, on the other hand, usually are supervised by a single judge who is more likely to retain those duties for longer periods of time. Decisions tend to be made by the judge in concert with one juvenile officer. Frequently, they do not have a detention option other than the adult jail, and they do not have the broad range of placement facilities available to urban systems. They tend to make decisions strictly on the basis of what they see as the good of the community and child, instead of on legalistic or bureaucratic directives. Kempf et al. call for recognition of this "justice by geography," and for a redistribution of resources to create a single system (1990). This, of course, first would require decisions as to which system would best serve society, not only in the categories of adult/juvenile but also in the jail/probation areas.

SUMMARY

In this chapter we have discussed several aspects of the structure of rural corrections. First, we described conditions associated with small jails which are found in many rural areas and the constraints and challenges that must be overcome with limited resources and within existing social and political considerations. Next, we explained several proposals that have been made to restructure rural corrections under the supervision of the state, a number of counties working together or private companies. The advantages and disadvantages associated with each of these arrangements were provided. We also briefly reviewed the nature of probation and parole in the rural context. Several seemingly contra- dictory trends exist in this regard. Judges in rural areas are more familiar with local resources and can place offenders into service agencies more rapidly where they do exist. Rural criminal justice agencies are less formal and in a relative sense, they are both more efficient and effective in providing services. On the other hand, fewer resources usually exist when compared to urban centers, and judges are more constrained in trying to help offenders.

REFERENCES

Aday, D. "Court Structure, Defense Use and Juvenile Court Decisions," *The Sociological Quarterly*, 27, No. 1, 1986: 107-119.

Allen, H. E., and C. E. Simonsen. *Corrections in America: An Introduction*. Englewood Cliffs, NJ: Prentice Hall, 1995.

Champion, D. J. "Jail Inmate Litigation in the 1990s," in J. A. Thompson and G. L. Mays, eds., *American Jails: Public Policy Issues*. Chicago: Nelson-Hall, 1991.

Clear, T. R., and G. F. Cole. *American Corrections*. Belmont, CA: Wadsworth, 1994.

Cole, G. F. *The American System of Justice*. New York: Wadsworth, 1995.

Cook, P., and K. L. Mizer. *The Revised ERS County Typology: An Overview*. Washington, DC: United States Department of Agriculture, Economic Research Service, 1994.

Feld, B. C. *Justice for Children: The Right to Counsel and the Juvenile Courts*. Boston: Northeastern University Press, 1993.

Kalinich, D. F., and J. Klofas. *Sneaking Inmates Down the Alley*. Springfield, IL: Charles C. Thomas, 1986.

Kempf, K. L., S. H. Decker, and R. L. Bing. *An Analysis of Apparent Disparities in the Handling of Black Youth Within Missouri's Juvenile Justice System*. St. Louis, MO: University of Missouri-St. Louis Press, 1990.

Kerle, K. "The Rural Jail: Its People, Problems and Solutions," *Human Services in the Rural Environment*, 8, No. 1, 1983: 9-17.

Lasley, P. "Rural Economic and Social Trends" in R. D. Conger and G. H. Elder, eds., *Families in Troubled Times: Adapting to Change in Rural America*. Hawthorne, NY: Aldine DeGruyter, 1994.

Lockhart, L. Z., P. D. Kurtz, R. Sutphen, and D. Gauger. *Georgia's Juvenile System*. Athens, GA: School of Social Work, University of Georgia, 1990.

Mays, G. L., and J. A. Thompson. "Mayberry Revisited: The Characteristics and Operations of America's Small Jails," *Justice Quarterly*, 5, No. 3, September, 1988: 421-440.

_____. "The Political and Organizational Context of American Jails," in J. A. Thompson and G. L. Mays, eds., *American Jails: Public Policy Issues*. Chicago: Nelson-Hall, 1991.

Ralph, P. H., R. M. Hoekstra, and T. R. Brehm. "Community Corrections in Rural States: Reinvolving the Community," in J. Smykla and W. S. Selke, eds., *Intermediate Sanctions: Sentencing in the 1990s*. Cincinnati, OH: Anderson, 1994.

Schwartz, I. M., L. Harris, and L. Levi. "The Jailing of Juveniles in Minnesota: A Case Study" *Crime and Delinquency*, 34, 1988: 133-149.

United States Department of Justice, Bureau of Justice Statistics. *Census of Local Jails, 1988*. Washington, DC: U. S. Government Printing Office, 1990.

_____. *Correctional Populations in the United States, 1992*. Washington, DC: U. S. Government Printing Office, 1995.

Washington, J. "ACA Standards, Tailoring the Process to Fit Small Jails," *Corrections Today*, 50, No. 7, December, 1988: 42-43.

Wood, H., and S. Schwartz. *Recognition and Handling of the Mentally Retarded Offender*. Special Offender Council: St. Louis, MO, 1976.

Zupan, L. *Jails: Reform and the New Generation Philosophy*. Cincinnati, OH: Anderson Publishing Company, 1991.

PART V

SPECIAL ISSUES IN RURAL CRIMINAL JUSTICE

In a monograph published by the National Institute of Justice, Weisheit et al. discuss several "special issues and emerging problems" for rural criminal justice (1994). They cite the following topics that they believe deserve further investigation by researchers, and which are becoming of increasing importance to rural police: gangs, substance abuse, vice and organized crime, violence, hate crimes, arson, and special crimes such as those related to wildlife and agriculture. There are four readings in this section of the text, and several of the issues that are raised by the pieces touch on a number of the categories listed above.

We begin with Chapter 9 by Nanci Koser Wilson, which is titled "The Industrialization of Wilderness: Women, Crime and Rurality." The author combines several themes in her presentation. First, she argues that there has been a rise in crimes by rural women, in rural areas in general and by individuals against the environment ("green crime"). Second, the industrialization of rural areas has had an impact on all three of the above categories. Last, the author presents predictions for the future, especially concerning the role of rural women.

In regard to "ordinary crime" rates, Wilson relies on data from the FBI's Uniform Crime Reports (UCR) to demonstrate that there are different kinds of crime that typically are committed by rural women when contrasted with rural men, and to make the point that rural women commit fewer crimes. She explains recent rises in the rates for women on the basis of a modern division of labor between the sexes and finds differences based on gender in rates of sexual crimes, income producing crimes and violent crimes.

Wilson also reviews the effects of the industrialization of rural areas, which she believes impacts crime; generally, those violations involving women and acts against the environment. She also contends that the decline of the family farm, and the advent of agribusiness and their accompanying practices, have influenced rates of crime. A loss of family and community unity also are cited as contributing to rises in crime generally, and in rural areas particularly.

Last, the author focuses on the future concerning patterns of crime for rural women. She concludes that both the sexual hierarchy that exists in contemporary society, and the lag in the industrialization of the work of women, make their patterns of crime different from those of men. However, due to industrialization, she predicts that the role of women in ordinary crime is likely to be similar to that of men, especially as it relates to illegal activities that produce cash income.

The second special issue given attention in this section is "Rural Juvenile Courts: A Structural Assessment" by Randall R. Beger. As with previous pieces, one major area of focus is a comparison of rural and urban criminal justice agencies. Several conditions relating to the structure of rural courts are reviewed: how the principal reforms that were implemented in the juvenile justice system in the late 1960s have been applied; the various roles that actors within the system perform; the chief procedures that are involved in the screening of cases; and the span of services that are available. These factors lead to several important constraints and challenges. The author details the difficulties of limited personnel, inadequate budgets, the problems associated with informal procedures and policies, and the relative isolation of the rural environment. Beger analyzes the difficulties of maintaining adequate support services for those who are diverted from the system, for the mentally ill, and for families. He argues for more coordination with agencies outside of the system, more creative use of regional sites, and the increased recruitment and instruction of volunteers to serve as lay counselors. Lastly, he takes the position that court members must take greater responsibility for educating the local public concerning the role of their organizations.

The third special issue addressed in the special topics section is "American Indian Justice Systems and Tribal Courts in Rural 'Indian Country'," by Melissa A. Pflüg. The piece focuses on three main areas: how United States federal Indian policy and statutes have established, conditioned and constrained traditional justice systems among rural Indian communities; what are the structures, concerns and characteristics of tribal courts; and future challenges facing tribal justice systems. Pflüg analyzes the philosophical and ideological clash between U.S. law and American Indian systems of justice, especially by underscoring that traditional Indian systems were "places of relationships" that maintained

144

justice through methods of decision-making by a council of elders. Today, U.S. law, with its emphasis on adversarial arbitration, has put conditions and constraints on justice as a matter of collective consensus aimed at healing disrupted relationships between parties that threaten entire communities. The author highlights that Indian "sovereignty" and traditional ways of doing things have been conditioned by U.S. federal Indian policy as it has evolved over the past 200 years, and by court decisions that have constrained the status of tribes to being "domestic dependents" under the legal and political dominion of both the federal and state governments, so establishing a guardian-ward relationship. Thus, although federally recognized Indian tribes in rural Indian country have tribal courts, they do not enjoy sole jurisdiction over cases but often face cases involving cross-jurisdiction between their own, and state and federal court authority.

The final selection, authored by Robert A. Wood, is titled "Right-Wing Extremism and the Problem of Rural Unrest." The work describes the role of the Christian Identity Movement in providing basic doctrines and a philosophical rationale for the beliefs of many of the radical groups in rural areas. Typically, they embrace ideas associated with racial superiority, patriotism, an anti-federal government agenda and anti-Semitism. A socio-economic profile and information concerning the membership and recruitment of individuals into these groups also is presented. Despite the basic similarity of beliefs, the actions of the far Right differ greatly. Ted Gurr has noted that the activities of these groups can be described as legal, of borderline legality, illegal but non-violent and violent (1988). All of these behaviors present major challenges to law enforcement officials. Future trends also are reviewed, and the author predicts that right-wing violence will not subside in the near future because of the fundamental conditions of the rural setting.

REFERENCES

Gurr, T. "Political Terrorism in the United States: Historical Antecedents and Contemporary Trends," in M. Stohl, ed., *The Politics of Terrorism*. New York: Marcel Dekker, 1988.

Weisheit, R. A., D. N. Falcone, and L. E. Wells. *Rural Crime and Rural Policing*. National Institute of Justice, Washington, DC: United States Government Printing Office, 1994b.

CHAPTER 9

The Industrialization of Wilderness:
Women, Crime and Rurality

by *Nanci Koser Wilson*

INTRODUCTION

To redeem an untamed wilderness through cultivation and human habitation has been a central theme in the American experience. E. F. Schumacher identified a resulting problem: "In our time, the main danger to the soil, and therewith not only to agriculture but to civilization as a whole, stems from the townsman's determination to apply to agriculture the principles of industry" (1973: 109). Today, some 500 years after Columbus "discovered" the prime American wilderness, the stress points in this "dream of the earth"[1] have begun to issue forth in debts to nature we hardly know how to repay. Not the least sufferer has been human nature. Male, urban, human nature felt these stresses first—now female, rural, human nature experiences these stresses as well. We see this reflected in their crime rates. And, intimately related to problems of "ordinary crime" are the emerging issues of "green crime," which are very serious in rural America. Both types of crimes have a single source in the industrialization of wilderness.

Rural women, long the possessors of the lowest crime rates of any American, appear to be "catching up" with the rest of us. Similarly, the rural countryside, long the most pristine of environments, now is experiencing serious environmental degradation and even producing poisonous food.

In what follows, we first trace the course of rural female "ordinary" crime, and of rural environmental crime over several recent decades.

---

[1] This is Thomas Berry's phrase. He suggests that we now have a choice between two guiding mythologies or "dreams"—the industrial versus the ecological "dream of the earth." The industrial dream is "the most powerful dream that has ever taken possession of the human imagination" but dream visions "can be destructive as well as creative," and currently we seem to have an "inability to awaken out of this cultural pathology" (Berry 1988: 202-205).

Next, an argument is presented regarding the effects of industrialization on these two types of crime. The essay closes with a discussion of the implications for the rural future, especially with reference to the role of women.

CRIME DATA

Ordinary Crime[2]

The facts regarding ordinary crime include lower rates, different kinds of crime and recent increases. First, rural people have lower crime rates than do urbanites, women have lower rates than do men and rural *women* have the lowest rates of anyone: see Table 1.

---

[2] The data for "ordinary crime" are derived from the FBI *Uniform Crime Reports*. As reported, these data are recalculated to produce three main categories of crime and four subcategories. Sex crimes include rape, prostitution and the FBI category "sex offenses" (except forcible rape and prostitution). Violent crime includes: murder; rape; aggravated assault; other assaults; carrying/possessing weapons. Income-productive crimes are the total of the following four subcategories.

  a. Career theft: robbery; burglary; motor-vehicle theft; fencing (buying/receiving/possessing stolen property). These offenses, while sometimes committed by amateurs, most usually involve the offender in a criminal subculture and give to her/him a criminal self-image. They require geographical mobility and long working hours.

  b. Amateur theft: larceny-theft; forgery and counterfeiting; fraud and embezzlement. These offenses are easy for an amateur without ties to a criminal subculture to engage in. They do not require mobility or long working hours away from home.

  c. Prostitution.

  d. Drugs.

Together these four subcategories include most of the ways that crime can be made to produce cash income for the criminal.

Sex-specific rates are calculated from tables giving rural and urban arrests by sex. The population given in the table is halved in calculating these rates. Thus, for example, Table 47 on page 155 of the UCR for 1970 gives the rural population reporting areas as 19,366,000. Sex-specific rates are then calculated by the formula:

$$\frac{\text{\# female (or male) arrests} \times 100,000}{9,683,000}$$

The reader should note that these data refer to arrests, so that they do not represent all crimes committed, only crime where police made an arrest. (Obviously the gender of the perpetrator cannot be determined when no arrest is made.)

TABLE 1: 1990 Crime Rates for Urban and Rural Contexts According to Gender

	I-P Crime[*]	Violent Crime	Sexual Crime
Urban Males	3054.48	1442.50	166.51
Rural Males	1295.59	729.56	86.13
Urban Females	1011.23	234.76	91.52
Rural Females	411.51	108.55	3.63

[*]Income-Productive

Second, rural women are similar to their urban counterparts in that the type of crimes they commit are very different from men's crime (see Tables 2, 3 and 4). Income-productive crimes predominate, and among these, career theft is low, while amateur theft is significantly higher and coming steadily closer to the male rates. Additionally, women are much less violent than men. Female crime is inter-sexual, instead of intra-sexual—there is very little female-on-female crime—in stark contrast to male crime, which is highly intra-sexual (this fact is not evident from the data presented here; see Wilson 1992). There is very little sex crime among women, instead women are its victims.

TABLE 2: Percent of Crime Committed by Females in Rural and Urban Contexts

RURAL	1970	1975	1980	1985	1990
Violent Crime	6.82%	8.99%	10.27%	11.97%	12.95%
Career Theft	5.18%	5.96%	6.79%	7.12%	8.77%
Amateur Theft	13.88%	20.80%	28.63%	33.87%	34.99%
Prostitution	65.80%	67.10%	63.09%	52.26%	39.78%
Drugs	13.71%	11.22%	11.99%	14.04%	16.38%
Total I-P[*] Crime	10.63%	13.82%	19.35%	22.81%	24.11%
Sex Crimes	9.15%	7.94%	5.53%	4.12%	4.05%

URBAN	1970	1975	1980	1985	1990
Violent Crime	11.75%	12.68%	12.22%	13.42%	14.00%
Career Theft	5.52%	6.70%	7.33%	8.64%	9.68%
Amateur Theft	28.62%	32.60%	31.39%	32.80%	33.93%
Prostitution	79.13%	74.25%	69.28%	70.03%	65.12%
Drugs	15.69%	14.07%	13.24%	13.52%	16.69%
Total I-P* Crime	20.18%	21.92%	22.53%	24.26%	24.87%
Sex Crimes	42.47%	36.56%	39.59%	39.36%	35.47%

*Income-Productive

TABLE 3: Rural Crime Rates for Females and Males: 1970 through 1990

	1970	1975	1980	1985	1990
FEMALE RATES					
Sex Crime	3.79	3.82	2.68	3.13	3.63
Violent Crime	18.84	47.46	59.34	76.16	108.55
I-P* Crime	93.9	234.90	332.39	376.90	411.51
Career Theft	17.72	33.02	32.68	28.83	35.93
Amateur Theft	56.88	154.84	258.57	294.08	305.61
Prostitution	1.61	2.44	1.37	1.10	.91
Drugs	17.69	44.59	39.75	52.96	69.04
MALE RATES					
Sexual Crime	37.62	44.28	45.82	73.08	86.13
Violent Crime	257.63	480.36	518.32	560.35	729.56
I-P* Crime	789.46	1464.42	1385.82	1275.42	1295.59
Career Theft	324.26	520.77	448.62	376.07	373.83
Amateur Theft	353.04	589.74	644.69	574.10	567.86
Prostitution	.83	1.19	.80	.92	1.39
Drugs	111.31	352.70	291.70	324.31	352.51

*Income-Productive

**TABLE 4: Urban Crime Rates for Females
and Males: 1970 through 1990**

	1970	1975	1980	1985	1990
FEMALE RATES					
Sex Crime	79.96	60.47	86.36	104.95	91.52
Violent Crime	99.38	114.80	122.46	151.75	234.76
I-P* Crime	528.27	689.26	727.86	850.54	1011.23
Career Theft	46.85	65.98	68.64	70.45	90.78
Amateur Theft	331.79	482.51	501.97	575.67	662.82
Prostitution	67.32	55.43	80.73	96.60	82.86
Drugs	82.29	85.32	76.51	107.80	174.75
MALE RATES					
Sexual Crime	104.26	104.91	131.77	161.70	166.51
Violent Crime	746.21	790.30	879.89	978.95	1442.50
I-P* Crime	2089.84	2458.86	2502.74	2655.97	3054.48
Career Theft	802.55	918.26	868.30	745.22	847.32
Amateur Theft	827.38	997.44	1097.31	1179.61	1290.49
Prostitution	17.75	19.22	35.80	41.34	44.37
Drugs	442.15	520.93	501.32	689.78	872.28

*Income-Productive

Third, there have been recent increases (see Tables 3 and 4). Just as the rural countryside is becoming more like the urban areas, with an increase in crime (see Table 5), so too the rural woman, who we may see as perhaps the last hold-out, is catching up both to her rural brothers and her urban sisters. Importantly, however, there is little change in the types of crimes she commits. These still distinguish her from both men and urban women.

TABLE 5: Rural Rates as a Percentage of Urban
Crime Rates According to Gender

FEMALES	1970	1975	1980	1985	1990
Violent Crime	18.96%	41.34%	48.46%	50.19%	46.24%
I-P*	17.38%	59.63%	45.67%	44.31%	40.69%
Sex Crimes	4.74%	6.32%	3.10%	2.98%	3.97%
MALES					
Violent Crime	34.53%	60.78%	58.90%	57.24%	50.58%
I-P*	37.38%	59.63%	55.37%	48.02%	42.42%
Sex Crimes	36.00%	42.49%	34.77%	45.19%	51.73%

*Income-Productive

These facts about the crime of rural women are explicable in terms of the contemporary division of labor, which may be described as both elaborate and hierarchical. The highly elaborate division of labor typical of industrial societies promotes crime for specific reasons, which will be advanced later. Here, it is enough to note that rural areas are affected by industrialization in two ways. First, rural people emigrate to cities where industrialization raises the urban crime rates, leaving rural rates lower for some decades. Then, as industrialization begins to affect the countryside, rural crime rates climb as well.

The hierarchical form of the division of labor is marked especially in the sexual differentiations it makes—women's work is radically different from men's and also less well remunerated. In the commercial labor market, women still make about 60 cents to the male dollar and do most of their work under the supervision of men. They are responsible also for most of the domestic labor—the care of children and the elderly, and the housework associated with such care. For domestic labor, women are not remunerated at all—housework is unpaid work.

For these reasons, we see in the data lower but increasing rates of ordinary crime in rural versus urban areas. We also note strong sexual differences in crime. First, sexual crime in itself reinforces the hierarchical sexual division of labor. Rape is a crime that almost always features male offenders and female victims (as do wife battery and sexual harassment for which the FBI does not provide data). As for prostitution, while the criminal justice system treats the prostitute (typically female) as offender, and rarely prosecutes pimps and customers (typically males), it makes much more sense to see the prostitute as a victim. The woman typically is forced into prostitution either literally or through overwhelming economic need. The objectification and commodification of sexuality is similar in all sexual crime (Barry 1984).

Income-productive crimes show less strong, but still marked, differences between men and women. The recent increases in income-productive crime among women, and especially rural women, reflect the increasing need for cash resulting from movement into an industrial world; a trend that affected women later than men, as we shall see in our discussion. But even in income-productive crime, women's participation is different from men's. Women are more likely to engage in amateur theft than career theft, as the latter requires immersion in a criminal subculture and does not mesh well with domestic labor (see Wilson 1983).

Violent crimes typically are the provenance of men, and as we have seen, women rarely are violent against one another. It has been suggested that this too is the result of a sexual division of labor that places men in situations where violence becomes the solution to problems (see Wilson 1992). For example, in illegal businesses such as drug dealing, disputes cannot be resolved through recourse to the formal social control system of the courts. While violence is a poor solution to disputes, it may sometimes be the only solution.

Green Crime[3]

In agriculture we see effects of environmental degradation in the two major areas of cultivation and animal husbandry. In the cultivation of land, damaging effects are felt from monoculture farming, from the use

---

[3] Many of the ecologically damaging practices described here have not yet been criminalized—there is very little effective environmental law. Some pesticides are prohibited under FIFRA, and laws like the Clean Water Act, the Clean Air Act and RCRA can be applied to damaging farming practices. Most of these are regulatory laws but do have criminal sanctions attached.

of chemicals (fertilizers, pesticides and herbicides)[4], and from the use of heavy machinery for tillage. These features of post WWII agriculture have caused degradation and depletion of both soil and water. Soils are full of excess nitrogen, phosphorous and potassium from overuse of fertilizers (Jenny 1984; PA Wildlife Federation 1988). Similarly, water is contaminated with nitrogen and pesticide residue (PA Wildlife Federation 1988). Depletion is a very serious problem. For example, Iowa farmers now use up to six bushels of topsoil for every bushel of corn they grow, and Kansas corn farmers have depleted the Ogallala aquifer below replacement levels through irrigation on prairie land unsuited to corn farming (Jackson 1987: 34-35).

Post-modern animal husbandry features confinement feeding and drug dependence, which are damaging to the animals themselves, sometimes to the soil and water and, additionally, produce toxic food dangerous for human consumption (Mickley 1985). Even as early as the mid-1970s, the USDA had found illegally high levels of drugs and pesticides in 14% of the meat and poultry they inspected (Unsigned 1985: 13). By 1991, the USDA was warning consumers to cook all meat (beef, as well as pork and chicken) to the well-done state, since it cannot guarantee the purity of the meat it inspects (Eames 1991: 11). This can be noted too in the recent infamous and unpopular decision by New Jersey health authorities to require all restaurants to cook eggs to the hard yolk stage, thus denying New Jersey restaurant patrons soft boiled, soft poached, sunny-side up and easy-over breakfast eggs, Caesar salad dressing, and egg-based French sauces such as hollandaise and bearnaise. Mickley reports that government studies implicate food-producing animals as the source of resistant strains of salmonella responsible for human deaths and illnesses (1985: 7-8). The antibiotics, growth hormones and appetite stimulants fed to stock create antibiotic resistant organisms that transfer to humans and have led to, among other problems, ovarian tumors in pubescent girls who eat poultry frequently (Mickley 1985: 7-8). Almost 9000 Americans die of food poisoning each year (McGraw and Taylor 1991: 8).

Finally, contemporary agriculture uses long distribution chains that require refrigerated transportation, usually by truck, thus adding to fossil

---

[4] From 1964-1982, cultivated acres remained stable, yet pesticide use climbed 170%, while from 1960-1982 chemical fertilizer use tripled, and from 1972-1982 herbicide use doubled (Mansur 1991: 21).

fuel depletion and air pollution. For example, in 1979, New Yorkers spent $6 million to move 24,000 tons of broccoli from California, in the process consuming 950,000 gallons of fuel for transport (Unsigned 1985: 12). The refrigeration used for such transportation, of course, contributes to ozone depletion, since it contains CFCs.

INDUSTRIALIZATION AS THE KEY

The major effect of industrialization is the dissolution and reformation of unities. Localized unities are dissolved and unity is re-established on a broader scale. Industrialism specializes as it creates finer and finer divisions of labor. Production and consumption of goods, and even the production of sub-parts of a single product are ripped apart—these are dispersed in space, time and creatures (we include both humans and non-humans, and consider them as both producers and consumers). The result is that exchange networks lengthen, information is lost, response time is lengthened and control is dispersed. And, for the former unities, each is transformed into one part in a larger unity so that: diversity is lessened; options are narrowed; the capacity to respond to problems and to meet emergency needs is lessened or lost; internal control is lost or lessened, as each local unit becomes less and less autonomous; and hence, vulnerability increases in proportion as diversity decreases.[5]

FARM, FAMILY AND VILLAGE: SPECIFIC EFFECTS OF INDUSTRIALIZATION ON FORMER UNITIES

Farm

"What is happening to the farmer and the farm is a faint foreshadowing of what is to come to the culture at large.... Vulnerability and helplessness [only] begin with the fields" (Jackson 1987: 74-75). A specific series of events has altered the nature of farming in America. Instead of many small, family-run farms we have the postmodern, industrial farming system of agribusiness, which may be described as a

---

[5] But, see Wes Jackson who notes that there are limits to diversity. "Even species diversity within an eco-system has its limits...there can be too much" (1987: 134-135). Complementarity, he observes, is as important as diversity.

vertically integrated, automated food production and distribution system (Hightower and DeMarco 1987).

The first event was a shift to fewer, but larger farms. In 1935, there were 6.8 million American farms with a mean acreage of 155. In 1964, 1.8 million farms were responsible for 90% of farm sales, but by 1974, only 825,000 farms were responsible for 90% of farm sales. By 1982, there were 2.4 million farms with a mean acreage of 433. Farming has thus become "more productive,[6] more concentrated and more centralized" (Rosenfeld 1985: 12).

The second event has been a shift toward monocultures (the planting of one crop in extensive acreage) and toward single species animal production (see Mickley 1985; Jackson 1987: 148). Here we see the decreased diversity typical of industrialism.

Third, there has been a shift toward large-scale mechanization, which includes tilling and harvesting equipment used on the land. It also involves the machinery used for animal husbandry, such as milking machines, and giant "hen houses" holding 100,000 chickens that depend on automated feeding and machine run temperature controls.

The fourth event has been a trend toward vertical integration. Corporations that previously had *sold to* farmers (such inputs as seed, fertilizers, pesticides, feed and machinery), or *bought from* farmers (corporations that process, market and retail products, such as Del Monte that alone controls 16% of the canned fruit market in the United States), decide to become farmers themselves. "In most cases, vertical integration is accomplished through contracts with farmers; the corporation does not become a farmer, it rents one...but farmers are forced into signing contracts that promise a corporate middleman a certain amount at a given

---

[6] Productivity's meaning (more output per man-hour of labor) often is forgotten, so that even with high unemployment we seem to desire more productivity, as if it were an end in itself. Or, if by productivity we mean more output per acre of land, we must figure in the long-term costs of soil erosion, water depletion and toxicity. If we mean more productivity in animal husbandry, then we must figure in the costs of poor health and misery in dairy cattle, veal calves and battery chickens. Quite curiously, this is something that proponents of factory farming never seem to do. Other productivity figures also may be misleading. Again, Wes Jackson puts the point well. Citing the roadside signs that read "One farmer feeds 68 people + you," he notes that this *should* read "One farmer + lots of fossil fuel + John Deere etc. + suppliers of inputs and feeds" (1987: 103). My own observation suggests that by 1991 these signs boasted a figure of 98!

price.... Through the market power of the corporate integrator... corporations can lock up an entire market, forcing farmers either to sign contracts or go under. Vertical and contractual integration is increasing, affecting nearly a fourth of total farm output" (Hightower 1987: 206).

Thus, the former American agriculture—a series of small, diversified family farms that integrated fodder and animal production and, additionally, included small production units for family use and local exchange (vegetable gardens, a few dairy animals, a flock of poultry, perhaps some pigs) has been replaced by agribusiness. Farms have become large, mechanized monocultures. The industrial model applied to agriculture has centralized production and created far-flung distribution networks.

In the process, much farm work has moved off the farm, and on the farm there is a greater reliance on off-farm inputs. The latter would include seed, energy and fertilizer. The exchange networks have, of course, lengthened. Generally, postmodern agribusiness may be described as less labor- and more capital-intensive than traditional farming.

Therefore, there also is increasing economic vulnerability. From 1970 to 1980, nationally the number of farmers declined from 2.4 million to 2.2 million. In Iowa, the numbers of farms declined from 140,000 in 1969 to 115,000 in 1982; a 27% decline (Lasley 1987: 104). In 1950, there were 4.3 million hired farm workers in America; in 1970 only 3.5 million (Hightower and DeMarco 1987: 140). At the end of WWI, 27% of the nation's workers were in agriculture; at the end of WWII, 14%; and in 1971 just 4.4% (Schumacher 1973: 113). As a result of this job displacement, unemployment rises not just in rural areas, but also in the cities where former rural people have fled. In fact, "Each year about a million of these people pour out of rural America into the cities" (Hightower and DeMarco 1987: 135). The link between unemployment and ordinary crime is known so well as to not require documentation here.

Another source of economic vulnerability inheres in agribusiness itself. This style of food production has created enormous surpluses, driving prices down. In its nature, agriculture cannot expand as rapidly as other sectors of the economy. Demand for food does not increase at the same rate as does real income, since people can consume only so much food (Schumacher 1973: 112). Some demand is created by federal policies, such as the food stamp program (currently almost 25 million, or 1 in 10, Americans use food stamps, [*Indiana Gazette* 2-29-92]), and international agreements on trade and foreign aid. Yet, these markets for farm goods are highly unstable, as the electorate is unwilling to support aid programs during recessionary or depressionary economic cycles, and currently is becoming more isolationist on trade.

The need for off-farm inputs is yet another source of economic vulnerability. Since 1952, farm costs have risen 122%, while farm prices have increased only 6% (Hightower 1987: 202). In 1985, as many as one-third of Iowa farms were too highly leveraged for safety, having debt/asset ratios from 41% to 70% (Lasley 1987: 105). Thus, economic instability in this sector has not only increased street crime through displacement of workers but also has had an impact on white-collar crimes, such as bank fraud. This is especially because during the 1970s, farmers borrowed more and more from banks and S&Ls too willing to make shaky loans.

The advent of factory farming also has meant a loss of information, a lengthened response time to problems, and a loss of control. It is these effects of industrialization, together with the loss of diversity, which result in "green" crime.

On the small, diverse family farm, more information is available regarding ecologically damaging farm practices. When the farm becomes too large in relation to its workers, and when the farmer purchases chemical additives, instead of using the traditional farming practices of animal fertilization, plus crop rotation and naturally disease- and pest-resistant seeds, he creates soil erosion, water pollution, animal disease and sometimes toxic food. In part, this is because of loss of information. For example, lessened individual attention to dairy cattle has led to disorders such as ketosis (where the cow breaks down her own body to produce milk) and laminitis (a painful foot inflammation) not being diagnosed and treated in time (Mickley 1985: 5). And, when Ortho recently contaminated a supposedly organic product (soap for plants) with the man-made chemical oxyfluofen, it killed vegetables in users' gardens. But, information regarding the product was not widely dispersed—until it was too late (McGrath 1992: 6ff). When the farmer uses such off-farm inputs, he is dependent on a producer who has no interest in the health of his farm, but only in his own profit margin.

Similarly, capacity to respond to problems locally is less possible. For example, large machines are ruinous to soil because they compact it, decreasing its fertility and creating erosion problems. They require the off-farm input of petroleum, but they do not provide the on-farm solution to fertilization that draft animals and food stock would. Instead, another problem is created: when food animals are raised in the confinement feedlot style, their manure—a useful fertilizer on the small farm—creates dangerous methane and water pollution problems.

Generally, the farmer loses much control. The small, diversified farm was a relatively autonomous and closed eco-system, which united production and consumption, producing little, if any "waste," and it relied on its own internal resources for soil fertility and animal health. Industrial, or factory farming, the agribusiness model, opens up the loop of food production and consumption. The producer has less interest in, and less knowledge of, the consumer of his products. The farm wife who raised a flock of chickens for her family, and sold excess eggs or meat to her neighbors, had a natural interest in the purity of her products. The farmer who raises 100,000 battery chickens for sale to a large supermarket chain will never meet the consumers of his poultry. It is reported, in fact, that many agribusinessmen refuse to eat their own products themselves (Schumacher 1973: 106). Similarly, the farmer who fed his beefstock on grain raised by himself had a natural interest in the health of his soil, he had a natural interest in using the manure from his cattle to fertilize these fields—it was cheap, it often spread itself on the fields,[7] and it created no waste. The corporate owners of Pampered Beef have no similar interest in soil fertility and must be forced by law to control the water pollution caused by run-off. Because they "treat" the manure before returning it to the waterways, a valuable source for soil fertility is lost and the grain producer, not without cattle, must buy chemical fertilizers that damage soil, water and the food grown with them.

Here we see that the natural controls on "green crime" have vanished in the move from farming to agribusiness—and also that these controls are largely *social* controls. They arise naturally when production and consumption are close in time and space, and when the same decision maker is in charge of both production and consumption. The ripping apart of this natural unity of production and consumption, so characteristic of agribusiness, lessens diversity, lengthens exchange networks, results in lost information and lengthened response time to problems. The individual producer has less autonomy, and as control is

---

[7] One farmer calls his beefstock "walking fertilizers" (Mansur 1991: 21).

dispersed, much of it is actually lost. We see the results in biological terms. For example, the monoculture farm, because it is less diverse, is less naturally fertile and must rely on off-farm inputs—chemical fertilizers and gasoline powered tractors are two examples. Both are dangerous to the biosphere, but their producers do not have an immediate, natural economic interest in that. This latter effect is a loss of social control, instead of a strictly biological matter. Again, the lengthened exchange networks are less biologically healthy because they create air pollution (when produce is trucked from California to New York, for example, and because of an insistent push for less healthy food that is now designed to "look good," instead of taste good, after machine picking and lengthy transport (for example, tomatoes are designed for thick skins that mechanical pickers will not damage, oranges are designed to be picked green and ripen during transport, and dyes are added to apple skins, [Hightower and DeMarco 1987: 139-145]). At each stage of this process, producers, processors and sellers operate as they do because they have no natural, immediate, economic interest in the health of their products. Consumer revolt, if it happens at all, comes in the form of an organized "Alar scare" for instance, but it often does not occur at all since the consumer does not have the information about what is damaging his health.[8] So, the industrialization of farming means that we lose natural biological control, but it also implies that the motoring force is the loss of natural social control. The rules promulgated and enforced by regulatory agencies such as The Food and Drug Administration (FDA), the EPA and USDA are a poor substitute (see Wilson 1991).

Family

Industrialization also has affected the family unit and, similarly, led to crime. It is an old observation that many family functions have been moved outside the family: for example, education, religion and economic production have been allocated to large institutions outside the control of

---

[8] "When cancer rates climb this is not associated with soil mismanagement. Instead, the chosen approach is to use chemical warfare and surgery on the tumor (cf. to chemical farming) and to attempt to find a 'cure' [which will] kill the patient's tumors" (Drengson 1985: 30). Similarly, when consumers learned that Merkt cheese would recall cold-pack cheese contaminated with Listeria, they also were advised that "It would be difficult to say what the source of the bacteria was" (*Indiana Gazette* 3-9-92). This AP story failed to alert the consumer that drug dependence of animals was a likely source.

the family. Because the family is now less diverse, more exchange is necessary. This includes both economic exchange and social control. As economic exchange increases, the family becomes more and more dependent on cash, and family members begin to work outside the family.

> The question of the survival of...the farm family is one version of the question of who will own the country.... If many people do not own the usable property, then they must submit to the few who do own it. They cannot eat or be sheltered or clothed except in submission. They will find themselves entirely dependent on money; they will find costs always higher and money always harder to get.
>
> —Berry 1987: 349

As to social control, information about family members is lost as each spends much of his/her working and socializing day outside the family unit. This lessens the capacity of the family to respond to problems, lengthening response time and dispersing control so widely that much of it is simply lost. The vulnerability of individual family members is increased and this, together with loss of familial controls, increases crime. As the family performs fewer functions for its individual members, it is less able to meet the needs of its members. Thus, the family commands less loyalty and is less able to exercise control over individual members.

Village

In a study of a rural community in New York conducted during the last half of the 1980s, Janet Fitchen found that "The community is [still] seen as composed of families, as an aggregate of its constituent families," but "loss or alteration of some of the economically productive aspects of the community" has lessened community identity (1991: 254ff). "Many villages have become decoupled from local farming [and have lost] their agriculture-related businesses, as surrounding farm people began to reorient toward a larger town, where they deal with merchants, take out bank loans and attend field days" (Fitchen 1991: 254ff). As Wes Jackson puts the issue, "The farm family cannot exist in any dignified way without farm community" (Jackson 1987: 94).

In Iowa, for example, between 1970 and 1980, "32% of the communities with less than 2,500 people lost population; 22% of the 95 small Iowa cities with populations between 2,500 and 25,000 people also saw their populations decline" (Lasley 1987: 104). As the unity of the village dissolves, exchange networks lengthen and interaction with strangers increases. This, of course, leads to crime vulnerability (Hindelang et al. 1978).

Further, there is information loss and a lengthened response time to "trouble," as it can no longer be handled locally. Wilkins describes the village social system as a "very effective information network" in which "support and correction is immediate upon any deviation owing to the ready flow of information and a general knowledge of individual norms" (1965: 98).

The village also exhibits more tolerance for such minor deviance as does arise. Dinitz reports that police in Lincoln are encouraged "to wink and turn their heads at much verbally deplored 'deviant behavior'.... Offenders are defined not as revolutionaries or as 'hard-core criminals,' but as boys ('who will be boys') or as 'good people who just got into little scrapes'" (1973: 15). Gibbons describes rural offenders as situational offenders (1972: 189), and Clinard reports that rural offenders "do not see themselves as criminal social types" (1944: 45). It appears that villagers seek reconciliation of the community with the offender. Certainly, small towns rely very heavily on informal familial and village controls (Dinitz 1973: 11-13).

When villages dissolve, however, informal social control dissipates. Control is now dispersed. Dispute resolution becomes more formalized, tending to rely more on outside agents. Family problems require outside-the-family and outside-the-village solutions (such as juvenile court, family court, etc.). Decisions about how to handle deviance are removed from the victim-offender relationship. Attempts to replace this with victim compensation programs, victim input in sentencing, and offender restitution are awkward and not localized. Moreover, there is less imperative for reconciliation with a deviant because he is not now experienced as *needed* to keep the village functioning.

INDUSTRIALISM AND WOMEN'S CRIMINALITY

Let us summarize what we know about industrialism's effects on both ordinary and green crime, and discuss the ways in which these affect women's crime.

As the former unities of the farm, the family and the village dissolve, the vulnerability of each increases because each becomes merely a link in a larger chain, and lacking diversity, each lacks resources to solve problems internally. Tolerance for deviance decreases, as does the capacity to control deviance through punishment and reward—now beyond the control of the farmer, the family, the neighborhood and the village.

As to green crime problems, the farmer loses significant control when he acquiesces to monoculture. The problems of the farm as a unity no longer can be solved on the farm. Moreover, the farmer feels less loyalty, or allegiance, to the constituent members of his own farm because he experiences himself as needing them less. Why does he need to treat his poultry correctly if all they do is lay eggs and die, and if neither he, his family, nor his neighbors eat the eggs? Why does he need to ensure the health of feed-lot cattle, or of his soil, if fertilizer and energy are off-farm inputs? Increasingly, he cannot solve problems of soil fertility, animal health and "waste" on the farm itself. He even needs to work off-farm to provide income for farm inputs such as mortgages, equipment loans and so forth. Farm income increased from $25 billion in 1967, to $60 billion in 1983 mainly due to off-farm earnings (Lasley 1987: 102). For the farm population, farm income as a percentage of total income moved from 69% in 1950 to 38% in 1982 (Rosenfeld 1985: 17).

The vulnerability of the factory farm is enormous, tolerance for deviance is less. A large poultry ranch can lose 100,000 hens at once if the air conditioning fails—a circumstance almost entirely outside the control of the rancher. The consumer looses significant control in factory farming as well. First, s/he is less likely to have the information. Then, s/he must go through layers of bureaucracy and cross-cut political units to complain about the salmonella in her eggs or the dioxin in cow's milk. Because consumer pressure on producers is diffused in time and space, it has much less effect as a natural control on unhealthy production decisions.

As to ordinary crime, it appears that under industrialism, people are as dependent on others as ever, but have less control in their relationships with them. Those upon whom they are dependent are strangers or faceless bureaucrats. These strangers owe each other no personal allegiance. The fewer functions the family, the neighborhood, and the village perform for the individual, the less able each of these is to fulfill the needs of its members. So, the less loyalty they command, the less control over individual behavior they are able to exercise. This probably led to Adler's conclusion that in the few industrialized countries she studied which had little crime, "There appears to be a steady effort on the part of most of the ten countries to maintain the involvement of the citizens in the affairs which concern their own destiny" (1983: 132).

Industrialization affected men first, taking their work out of the family and moving them into factories and paid work. This effect is seen most dramatically in farming whose industrialization did not occur until after WWII. The time period from 1970-1990 represents the most expansionary phase in agribusiness, and the crime rates reported here reflect the concomitant dislocations.

The industrialization of housework is similarly a phenomenon of the post-WWII period. But, the industrialization of women's work still lags behind that of men even in rural areas, largely because of female responsibility for child care. Child care keeps the worker close to home; hence women have been woven more tightly into the web of family.

When women spend large blocks of time within the home, the domestic economy they establish within the family is a unit capable of meeting needs, solving problems and exercising control internally. Traditionally, women's work always could be used within the family, where women tended to cope with crisis through expansion of housework. If times got hard, women could make a garden, sell eggs, take in ironing, or take on the care of others' children or boarders. Often their home-based labor was used simply to improve the family's standard of living (Bernard 1981: 393ff). This contrasts with men's work, which has always been to produce income, even on the farm (Rosenfeld 1985: 22, 185). So, the natural male response to crisis often is income productive crime. But, because women's work could be used most effectively in the household, they were less likely to become independent as the result of wage labor and so were less likely to respond to economic crisis with income productive crime.

Women's work, however, is increasingly being taken out of the household. Factory-made goods often are cheaper and legal restrictions have limited cottage industry (Rosenfeld 1985: 20ff). As women's work becomes increasingly cash work outside the home, the domestic economy weakens and crises are less capable of household solution. So, for women too, crime is a solution to economic crisis because family solutions are blocked or less available.

Industrialism also has effects on women's victimization. It makes them more vulnerable to stranger crime, but perhaps less vulnerable to intimate crime. This is because women's vulnerability to intimate crime was always dependent on luck in having a good father and/or finding a good husband. If a woman's male protector subjected her to rape or battery, she had little recourse, since the formal social control system would not come to her aid. Perhaps a "good" village, or a "good" neighbor or family, would intervene on her behalf, but this seems to have been unlikely (see, for example, Dobash and Dobash 1979). The formal social control typical under industrialism has been more helpful to women victims of intimate crime, probably because by the time it arose, women had gained some power in the public arena and were able to institute change.

SUMMARY

If we make predictions based on what we have learned from the past, we may wish to make the same predictions for urban and rural women because, as we have seen, their rates are converging (with the important exception of sexual crime [mainly prostitution], which remains an urban phenomenon for women). As to predictions about the future of sexual differences in crime, the past has taught us that the patterns of difference between men and women remain similar, even when rates climb.

Two things have made women's crime different from men's: sexual hierarchy, and the delayed industrialization of women's work. Sexual hierarchy meant, among other things, very little, if any, sexual crime among women. And that women were more tied into the pre-industrial economy of the household than were men meant that women were more engaged in non-paid work and had shorter exchange networks for their goods, which were often traded or bartered. Hence, women were kept out of contact with strangers. All of the factors associated with home-based labor mean less criminogenic circumstances, as we have seen above. Also, because of their capacity to meet economic crises through household work and home-based production, women had less need to commit income-productive crimes. Their lesser need of cash also may have contributed to a lower rate of violent crime, because violence often arises with income-productive crime work, such as drug dealing. Violence is, of course, inherent in agribusiness too—chemical farming is far more dangerous, ultimately, than cocaine use. It would appear that violence is a solution to certain problems of large-scale production and distribution.

Women's roles in ordinary crime are likely to follow the path of men's crime insofar as industrialization has inflated these rates, especially for crimes that produce cash income. With the advent of industrialized child-care, processed food, fast food restaurants and oil-based clothing that requires little care, much housework is simply disappearing. This is occurring concomitant with increasing poverty among women, as the number of female-headed households increase. We may expect, as the domestic economy of women breaks down, that their income-productive crime rates will soar, as will perhaps that portion of violent crime related to illegal income production (Wilson unpublished paper).

It is unlikely that sexual crime among rural women will increase. Prostitution appears sensitive to male demand, instead of female need. The data indicate that as the feminization of poverty proceeds, the "new female criminal" turns to crimes of theft, not to prostitution (Wilson 1981-82). Rape, wife-battery and sexual harassment are not crimes women commit, as their very function is to reinforce sexual hierarchy. If this hierarchy dissolves, women's rates of victimization will, of course, decline.

If we consider women's role in green crime, we may make the following notations:

1. Women typically do not make large-scale production decisions, rather men do. Rosenfeld (1985: 24) notes this is true of contemporary farm production; it may be said of non-farm industrial production as well.

2. Many small-scale production decisions have been transformed into large ones, as small home-based or "cottage" industries (such as poultry and egg production) were removed from the home and, thus, taken out of women's hands. This change in farmwifery means that farm women no longer are solely responsible for any production unity; instead they keep the books, that is, records on men's production decisions (Rosenfeld 1985: 24). Because of these two factors, women are unlikely to contribute substantially to a change in the nature of large-scale production in this country, except through the attenuated power of their vote.

3. Women do, however, make most of the consumption decisions related to buying out-of-family inputs such as food, clothing, home furnishings, cleaning agents, and the like. Thus, women have a chance to affect production decisions through their consumptive behavior.

4. Women still do the nurturant work for the family—including large identifiable blocks of time in caring for young children and elderly family members. Smaller, or at least less identifiable, "blocks" of time are devoted to the "stroking" function. Thus, women literally have less time for crime and, importantly, more time to do traditional housework while they are "there anyway" caring for others. Even working mothers, then, are less likely to switch to industrial housekeeping featuring pre-processed foods and other ecologically dangerous housekeeping practices. And, too, their psychology remains more "pre-industrial," so that they are more open to a reversal of industrial values and cultural themes.

Our questions about the future thus become: "Will sexual hierarchy dissolve?" and "Will the industrial model be abandoned or altered?" The two questions are not unrelated, for under industrialism women have had less power than in any earlier economic arrangement. Further, poll data show that women are more ecologically conscious than are men (Howe 1990; Hueber 1991). Perhaps these two revolutions will interact, helping one another to succeed, as ecofeminists hope (Warren 1990).

While it may not be necessary to abandon completely the industrial model, we surely must heal it. Our production at least must be smaller scale. We must seek appropriate technologies. Appropriate technology would, for example, keep many farm products on the farm and require few off-farm inputs. It would not insert into the biosphere man-made chemicals with which "our bodies have no evolutionary experience" (as Wes Jackson so felicitously phrases it: 1984). And, we must return biological and social control to the individual, the farm, the family, the neighborhood and the village. These are not "idealistic desires" for a utopian future but requirements for ordinary living—demands that the planet makes on us if we are to remain here. A healing of the industrial model is a necessity insofar as halting the damage of green crime; and because ordinary crime has the same source, such healing should also reduce it.

REFERENCES

Adler, F. *Nations Not Obsessed with Crime*. Littleton, CO: Fred B. Rothman and Company, 1983.

Barry, K. *Female Sexual Slavery*. New York University Press, 1984.

Bernard, J. *The Female World*. New York: The Free Press, 1981.

Berry, T. *The Dream of the Earth*. San Francisco: Sierra Club Books, 1988.

Berry, W. "A Defense of the Family Farm," in G. Comstock, ed., *Is There a Moral Obligation to Save the Family Farm?* Ames, IA: Iowa State University Press, 1987.

Clinard, M. B. "Rural Criminal Offenders," *American Journal of Sociology*, 50, 1944: 38-43.

Dinitz, S. "Progress, Crime and the Folk Ethic: Portrait of a Small Town," *Criminology*, May 1973: 3-21.

Dobash, R. E., and R. Dobash. *Violence Against Wives*. New York: The Free Press, 1979.

Drengson, A., Jr. "Agriculture and the Staff of Life," *The Trumpeter*, 2, No. 3, Summer, 1985.

Eames, D. "Cooking It Right," *Kansas City Star*, Dec 8-14, 1991: 11.

Federal Bureau of Investigation. *Uniform Crime Reports*, annually.

Fitchen, J. M. *Endangered Spaces, Enduring Places: Change, Identity and Survival in Rural America*. Boulder, CO: Westview Press, 1991.

Gibbons, D. C. "Crime in the Hinterland," *Criminology*, August, 1972: 177-191.

Hightower, J. "The Case for the Family Farm," in G. Comstock, ed., *Is There a Moral Obligation to Save the Family Farm?* Ames, IA: Iowa State University Press, 1987.

Hightower, J., and S. DeMarco. "Hard Tomatoes, Hard Times," in Gary Comstock, ed., *Is There a Moral Obligation to Save the Family Farm?* Ames, IA: Iowa State University Press, 1987.

Hindelang, M., M. Gottfredson, and J. Garofalo. *Victims of Personal Crime: An Empirical Foundation for a Theory of Personal Victimization.* Cambridge, MA: Ballinger, 1978.

Howe, H. "Public Concern about Chemicals in the Environment," *Public Health Reports*, 102, No. 2, March-April, 1990.

Hueber, G. "Americans Report High Levels of Environmental Concern, Activity," *Gallup Poll Monthly*, April, 1991.

Indiana Gazette. "Almost 25 Million in U.S. Use Food Stamps," February 29, 1992, Indiana, PA.

_____. "Firm Recalling Cold-Pack Cheeses," March 9, 1992, Indiana, PA.

Jackson, W. *Altars of Unhewn Stone*. San Francisco: North Point Press, 1987.

Jackson, W., W. Berry, and B. Coleman. *Meeting the Expectations of the Land*. San Francisco: North Point Press, 1984.

Jenny, H. "The Making and Unmaking of a Fertile Soil," in Jackson, Berry, and Coleman, *Meeting the Expectations of the Land*. San Francisco: North Point Press, 1984.

Lasley, P. "The Crisis in Iowa," in G. Comstock, ed., *Is There a Moral Obligation to Save the Family Farm?* Ames, IA: Iowa State University Press, 1987.

Mansur, M. "One Farmer's Solution to USDA," *Kansas City Star*, December 8-14, 1991.

McGrath, M. Editorial comment, *Organic Gardening*, 39, No. 2, February, 1992.

McGraw, M., and J. Taylor. "Deadly Meat," *The Kansas City Star*, December 8-14, 1991.

Mickley, L. D. "Trends in Agriculture," *The Trumpeter*, 2, No. 3, 1985.

Pennsylvania Wildlife Federation. *First Environmental Quality Index*. Harrisburg, PA, 1988.

Rosenfeld, R. A. *Farm Women: Work, Farm and Family in the United States*. Chapel Hill, NC: University of North Carolina Press, 1985.

Schumacher, E. F. *Small Is Beautiful: Economics as if People Mattered*. Harper and Row, 1973.

Unsigned. "Further Observation and Facts About Agriculture," *The Trumpeter*, 2, No. 3, Summer, 1985.

Warren, K. J. "The Power and Promise of Ecological Feminism," *Environmental Ethics*, 12, No. 2, Summer, 1990: 125-146.

Wilkins, L. T. *Social Deviance*. Englewood Cliffs, NJ, 1965.

Wilson, A. V. "Prostitution, Theft, and Occupational Choice in Crime," *LAE Journal of the American Criminal Justice Association*, 43, No. 1 & No. 2, 1981-82: 7-17.

_____. "Making a Living at Crime: Differences in Male and Female Criminal 'Work'." Paper presented at the annual meeting of the American Society of Criminology, Denver, CO, November, 1983.

Wilson, A. V. "Shame and the Sacred." Paper presented at the annual meeting of the American Society of Criminology, San Francisco, November, 1991.

_____. "Gendered Interaction in Criminal Homicide," in A. V. Wilson, ed., *The Dynamics of the Victim/Offender Relationship*. Cincinnati, OH: Anderson Press, 1992.

Wilson, N. K. *Crime, Gender and Work*. Unpublished manuscript, n.d.

CHAPTER 10

Rural Juvenile Courts: A Structural Assessment

by *Randall R. Beger*

INTRODUCTION

This chapter examines several aspects of the rural juvenile court system. First, it looks at the organizational structure of rural juvenile courts. Second, it discusses how rural juvenile courts have responded to major juvenile justice reforms that were introduced in the late 1960s. Third, it examines the major decision-making steps within the rural juvenile justice system.

Although the purpose, language and scope of most states' juvenile court acts are similar, their application is different between urban and rural courts. Juvenile courts in urban areas routinely handle large numbers of cases and are structured to respond to heavy demands for service. Normally, a full-time professional staff performs specialized functions such as legal screening, intake adjustment interviewing, and psychological testing and evaluation. The work of probation officers is evaluated according to written rules and published standards. Structurally, urban juvenile courts separate legal and treatment functions, and they have the resources to provide youth with legal counsel. Checks and balances are built into the court system to protect the rights of juveniles and their families. Judges in urban juvenile courts devote their day to hearing juvenile cases exclusively, and court hearings are formal and regularly attended by private or court appointed attorneys.

In contrast, informality characterizes the rural juvenile court system. Rural juvenile court officials know each other on a more personal level and may travel together to outlying counties on designated court days. A network of close-working relationships makes adherence to statutes and written rules less practical. The day-to-day procedures for handling cases are based more on mutual understandings and verbal agreements.

The varied resources that urban juvenile courts take for granted are in short supply in the rural juvenile justice system. Rural courts often function without a full-time judge and probation staff. The services of psychologists and child care specialists are unavailable in most juvenile

173

cases. A part-time rural court staff is forced to perform a variety of services involving different roles for which they may have no professional training.

Apart from these problems, rural juvenile courts have many inherent strengths. The preferred approach in the rural juvenile justice system is to find solutions to problems without the necessity of court intervention. Instead of the formal system of services that exists in the urban setting, rural justice officials take advantage of local churches, civic groups, neighbors and other types of helping networks to assist youths and their families (Waltman 1986). The structural characteristics of the rural juvenile court system, together with lighter caseloads, permit greater personal attention to each case.

STRUCTURAL CHARACTERISTICS

A major factor distinguishing rural juvenile courts from their urban counterparts is staff size and relative operating scope. Rural juvenile courts are small-scale institutions organized within a single judicial circuit that includes several counties within its geographical boundary. Typically, a rural juvenile court staff includes only two persons: 1) a judge who hears all civil, criminal and juvenile cases; and 2) one full-time probation officer who handles both adult and juvenile cases.

Although rural juvenile courts are not structured identically, generally, it is true that the volume of referrals is low. Pawlak surveyed urban and rural courts in an unnamed eastern state and found that "Several of the largest urban courts individually had more referrals in one month than many of the rural courts combined had in three years" (1980: 38). Because of lighter caseloads, less task differentiation among staff is common. Probation officers negotiate directly with victims, help police with investigations, interview parents and youths, file petitions and supervise juveniles placed on court-ordered probation. As generalists, these rural probation officers perform functions normally handled in urban settings by prosecutors and judges. Due to the smaller scale of operations and limited probation staff, there is no need for bureaucratic methods to coordinate activities.

Other structural features of rural juvenile courts include procedural informality and high discretion. In urban juvenile courts, all hearings are formal and conducted with attorneys present. The adjudication (trial) and dispositional (sentencing) hearings are held separately. Rural juvenile courts do not have the staff to "bifurcate" hearings. The absence of attorneys in rural juvenile courts, combined with procedural informality, maximizes the discretionary powers of rural justice officials.

JUVENILE COURT RE-ORGANIZATION UNDER THE FOUR-D'S

During the late 1960s, government task force commissions initiated a series of reforms in juvenile justice standards and practices. These reforms were known as the "Four-D's": diversion, deinstitutionalization, decriminalization, and due process.

Diversion, as defined by A. R. Roberts, is "any process that is used by components of the criminal justice system (police, prosecution, courts, corrections) whereby youths avoid formal juvenile court processing and adjudication" (1989: 78). This first reform has two applications: 1) "true diversion," which means that a child is released by police or court officials with "no strings attached" (Klein 1979: 152); or 2) diversion that minimizes introduction into the juvenile court system. The latter type diverts youths away from the formal court process by referral to a community social service agency for counseling and treatment, or by informal supervision that may include restitution or community service. If a minor refuses to obey the terms of informal supervision, a petition may be filed to compel cooperation through court action. Most juvenile courts reserve diversion for status offenders and youths charged with petty misdemeanor acts (e.g., disorderly conduct, retail theft).

The second reform, deinstitutionalization, applies to removing abused and neglected children and juvenile status offenders from secure institutions and detention facilities in favor of community-based alternatives. Deinstitutionalization of status offenders (DOS) was the first real federal commitment to juvenile justice reform. Under the 1974 Juvenile Justice and Delinquency Prevention Act, formula and discretionary grants became available to assist states in developing and financing alternatives to institutionalizing juvenile status offenders and non-criminal youth (abused and neglected children). Massachusetts, Vermont, Pennsylvania and Utah spearheaded the drive to deinstitutionalize status offenders, and have taken the lead in developing smaller group homes and non-secure residential centers to replace larger custodial institutions (Coates 1989).

The third reform, decriminalization, refers to alternative means of classifying status offenders. Historically, youths charged with status offenses were handled in the same manner as serious delinquent offenders. During the 1960s, states began to classify status offenders differently from delinquent offenders by using the terms CHINS (*child* in need of supervision) or PINS (*person* in need of supervision).

Prior to the 1960s, youths entering the juvenile court system were denied the procedural safeguards of constitutional due process of law. The justification for this practice derived from the English common law doctrine known as *parens patriae*. This doctrine gave court officials wide-ranging and unchecked discretionary powers over juveniles. Procedural due process of law finally was extended to juveniles in three United States Supreme Court rulings: 1) *Kent* v. *United States* (1966); 2) *In re Gault* (1967); 3) *In re Winship* (1970).

In the *Kent* decision, the Court held that children must be afforded the protection of a full hearing before a judge to determine whether the juvenile court should transfer jurisdiction to a criminal court. The *Gault* decision entitled juveniles to the following rights: adequate and timely notice of charges; the privilege against self-incrimination; the right to legal counsel; and the right to confront and cross-examine witnesses. The *Winship* case extended the standard of "proof beyond a reasonable doubt" to juvenile court delinquency proceedings. Prior to the *Winship* decision, juveniles could be declared delinquent minors under the lower standard of proof traditionally used in civil cases, known as "preponderance of the evidence." The impact of all the "Four-D's" has resulted in different applications in rural settings.

RURAL APPLICATIONS

In rural areas, families, schools and the community play an active role in diversion. Rural families prefer dealing directly with their children's problems instead of seeking assistance from juvenile court professionals. Compared with urban youth, rural adolescents spend more time with their parents and extended family members, and they are under tighter family control and supervision (Farley et al. 1982). Schools in rural settings reluctantly refer students to the juvenile justice system because it generates negative publicity and creates the possibility of out-of-home placement by the court (Kurtz and Lindsey 1987). Social welfare expert, Beverly Hagen, contends that one of the advantages of growing up in a rural environment is that community members "feel a kind of personal investment in adolescents and their behavior; such support may result in immediate feedback and, at times, in informal reprimands rather than legal action" (1987: 26). Rural sociologist, Joseph DeJames, observes that "many of today's 'reforms' in the juvenile justice system such as nonintervention, restitution and dispute settlement have been time-honored practices in rural America" (1980: 12). The existence and widespread use of helping networks in rural communities such as churches, local charity groups and indigenous people who act as problem solvers is well documented (Weber 1980; Heyman 1982; Melton 1983).

Contrary to these informal methods in the rural setting, major metropolitan areas offer a wide range of formal diversion services aimed at keeping youngsters out of the juvenile justice system. Police officers in urban areas have their own diversion programs, and juvenile court intake officials have the authority to divert youths into programs such as family crisis intervention and substance abuse counseling. The entire urban pre-court diversion process operates according to clearly defined formal goals, uniform and objective decision-making criteria, and it offers a wide range of support services. Rural diversion programs are less sophisticated and generally experience three problems: 1) inadequate resources; 2) limited ties and coordination with outside agencies; 3) no objective diversion guidelines.

Rural areas lack professional support services for emotionally disturbed and runaway children who are diverted from the juvenile court (Libertoff 1980). Very few family support services exist and the absence of licensed mental health professionals reduces the availability of psychological assessment services. Local drug and alcohol treatment programs are underfunded and insufficient to serve the population in need. Between 1984 and 1988, arrests for drug abuse violations in rural areas increased by more than 54% (Office for Substance Abuse Prevention 1991). Due to limited community resources and staffing problems in rural juvenile courts, "true diversion" occurs by default, not by choice.

Today, many youths entering the juvenile justice system are exhibiting complex personal problems, including dysfunctional family relationships, emotional disorders, and cross addiction to drugs and alcohol (Elliot et al. 1985). These youths require the help of more than one agency. However, in rural areas, multi-agency coordination is handicapped by greater travel distances and isolation. Diversion to minimize court penetration often is based on informal ties and communication with local service providers, not clear or explicit referral guidelines. This absence of clear juvenile diversion guidelines results in a system where the length and conditions of informal supervision are not fixed or clearly defined. The inherent dangers are that rights of youths will not be adequately protected and officials will use their own personal criteria to decide which juveniles should be diverted from the juvenile court system.

The informality of rural juvenile courts makes it difficult to objectively evaluate the effectiveness of diversion projects. Brakel and South encountered this problem in rural areas of Illinois:

> Because officials did not keep records of the informal types of disposition, it was impossible to determine which manner of handling was most or least prominent. Nor was it feasible to ascertain precisely which types of cases were most likely to be handled formally or informally.
>
> —1969: 161

The lack of local, community-based programs for status offenders and non-offenders such as foster care, counseling services and group homes, have impeded deinstitutionalization efforts in rural communities. In the urban juvenile justice setting, children who refuse to return home are released to a social service agency that offers crisis intervention counseling and temporary shelter care. In the rural juvenile justice system, runaway youths are sent home with no follow up assistance or they are placed temporarily in a secure detention facility, or jail, to "cool off." Despite federal and state efforts to decriminalize status offenses, rural youths who skip school, stay out all night or disobey their parents, still are exclusively handled by the "police-correctional network" (Libertoff 1980: 100). This police intervention, by definition, means that some juveniles become subjects of the juvenile court system.

ENTERING THE SYSTEM

Although police are the major source of court referrals (Roche 1985), youths also enter the rural juvenile justice system through the actions of parents, social service agencies and schools. Procedurally, when a referral is made, the first step is to determine if the court has jurisdiction. The juvenile court's jurisdiction extends to five basic categories of cases: 1) delinquency; 2) neglect; 3) dependency; 4) abuse; 5) juvenile status offenses. Delinquency cases are those that pertain to youths who are accused of violating a federal or state criminal statute, or a municipal ordinance. Neglect and dependency cases usually involve parents or guardians who have failed to provide proper care for, or support of, their children. Abuse cases involve the infliction of physical or psychological harm by a parent or guardian. Status offenses refer to behaviors that are illegal only for minors, such as underage drinking, being beyond parental control, violating curfew and truancy. All of these behaviors render the minor subject to a possible court petition for remedial action.

Most state juvenile codes permit court personnel to place delinquent youth temporarily in a detention facility. Detention is defined as the short-term custody and care of a minor in a physically secure setting pending court disposition (National Council on Crime and Delinquency 1961). In urban areas, prosecutors determine if the appropriate criteria for detention have been met (Rubin 1980). The decision to detain a youth in the rural juvenile court system is made by a probation officer. Generally, minors are placed in a secure detention facility for one or more of the following reasons: to protect the community from further law violations; to protect the child from self-inflicted harm or injury; and/or to insure appearance for a court hearing.

Critics of the juvenile justice system charge that far too many detention placements are made. They estimate that only 10% of all juveniles need to be held in a juvenile detention facility (Community Research Associates 1980). A survey of state variations in detention rates found that admissions were determined by the availability of beds and not by the needs of youths or the seriousness of their offenses (Krisberg et al. 1984).

In rural areas, minors often are detained in jails and adult lockups even though state and federal regulations prohibit this practice. During the mid-1970s, 10 predominately rural states—Idaho, Kentucky, Minnesota, New Mexico, Illinois, Oregon, Wisconsin, Ohio, Texas and Virginia—accounted for over 50% of the juveniles held in jails (Community Research Associates 1980). Several factors are responsible for the continued flow of rural youth into adult jails: lack of adequate secure and non-secure alternative placement facilities; opposition to jail reform legislation from rural law enforcement officials who object to the time and costs involved in transporting youths to a regional detention center; and the mistaken belief held by some rural justice officials that putting juveniles in jails and adult lockups is a valuable "learning experience."

The deplorable conditions of jails that house juveniles are well documented (Children's Defense Fund 1976; Cottle 1977). A federally sponsored study found that youths placed in adult jails are eight times more likely to commit suicide than those in juvenile detention centers (National Coalition of State Juvenile Justice Advisory Groups 1986). Female youths placed in adult jails are extremely vulnerable to physical and sexual assaults (Chesney-Lind 1988).

Schwartz et al. found that almost 50% of the 4,000 juveniles held in jails and lockups in Minnesota had committed either minor property offenses (e.g., vandalism, receiving stolen property) or status offenses (e.g., running away, truancy, curfew violations) (1988). This study also identified that the average length of confinement was longer in rural county jails as compared to urban municipal lockups.

In 1980, Congress amended the 1974 Juvenile Justice and Delinquency Prevention Act (JJDP) to include jail removal as one of its key mandates. The language of the amended Act required 75% removal of juveniles from adult jails by 1985, with 100% removal by 1988.

Although compliance with the JJDP Act across all states was slow to be achieved, some states made significant progress relatively quickly. Officials in Pennsylvania, for example, reduced jail admissions by expanding intensive probation services, foster homes and group homes (Keve 1984). In 1980, there were 396 juveniles confined in jails in the Upper Peninsula of Michigan. The Michigan Department of Social Services used federal grant funds to develop "holdover centers" in the state's rural Upper Peninsula. A holdover center is a non-secure setting such as an empty office, a motel room or a county building lobby, where a youth may be detained up to 24 hours. By 1985, the total number of jailed youth had dropped to 71, largely because of state funding to expand non-secure holdover centers (Community Research Associates 1987). Similarly, several counties in North Dakota have established "attendant care" sites, which offer a safe alternative to jail or secure detention (North Dakota Division of Juvenile Services 1991). Viable alternatives to jailing juveniles that were developed in Pennsylvania, Michigan, North Dakota and other states, include: home detention programs, which permit youths to live at home while meeting with probation officers on a regular basis; crisis foster care; proctor programs; and emergency shelter care facilities. These and other options in the rural judicial system suggest fundamental differences from the urban setting, especially in screening cases of juvenile offenses.

RURAL-URBAN CASE SCREENING DIFFERENCES

Nationwide, approximately 50% of the case referrals to juvenile courts do not progress beyond the intake stage (Rubin 1989). A significant percentage are dismissed due to the petty nature of the charge. Others are diverted from the juvenile court system to community social service agencies. The remaining juvenile cases are evaluated by court staff with an eye toward filing court petitions. In urban areas, prosecutors are responsible for determining whether there is sufficient evidence to file a juvenile court petition. In rural courts, the decision is made by probation officers who have no formal legal training. Rural probation officers must try to establish a relationship of trust with the same youths they have petitioned to court.

A recent study of case screening in Minnesota's juvenile courts uncovered a system of "justice by geography" (Feld 1991). The intensity of court intervention as measured by rates of non-judicial handling, placements in detention and severity of sentence varied by court location. Feld gives the following description of his findings:

> Urban courts sweep a broader, more inclusive net and encompass proportionately more and younger youths than do suburban or rural courts.... The more formal, urban courts place over twice as many youths in pre-trial detention and sentence similarly-charged offenders more severely than do suburban or rural courts. As a result, where youths live affects how their cases are processed and the severity of the sentences they receive.
>
> —1991: 157-158

In urban juvenile courts, pre-court intake screening and pre-trail detention are formal and due process oriented. Case screening in rural juvenile courts is more informal and less sensitive to procedural due process requirements (Feld 1993).

Kempf et al. tracked the flow of cases through Missouri's juvenile courts (1990). Like Feld, they found two very different systems of juvenile justice:

> Rural courts typically are guided by one judge who holds the
> position for several years and the majority of decisions are
> made by one juvenile officer.... In urban courts the judge
> rotates to other types of courts frequently. Different staff are
> responsible at different stages of the process.... The two types
> of courts function by different standards as well. Rural courts
> adhere to traditional...juvenile court *parens patriae* criteria in
> their handling of youths. Urban courts are more legalistic in
> orientation and process cases more according to offense
> criteria.
>
> —1990: 19

This study also discovered that in the urban courts, petitions were filed
in over 60% of juvenile delinquency referrals and detention placement
occurred in 26% of the referrals. In the rural juvenile courts, petitions
were filed in only 27% of all delinquency referrals and 10% of youths
accused of criminal acts were placed in a detention facility.

The limited availability of court time is a major factor that explains
why rural juvenile courts handle most referrals informally. Generally,
judges in rural circuits set aside only one or two days at the end of each
month to hear juvenile cases, which has the effect of placing only the
most pressing cases before the court. Socio-ecological characteristics of
rural areas such as lower population density, overlapping interpersonal
relationships, shared values and the lack of anonymity also may
contribute to greater informality in dispositioning rural youth (Polk 1963;
Gibbons and Jolin 1982). Michael Roche believes that resource
inadequacies in the rural juvenile justice system explain the desire for
informal dispositioning: "the notion that local and informal is better is
influenced greatly by the awareness of the minimal number of viable
options available in the rural justice system" (1985: 67). Fewer court
resources include, for example, limited access to legal counsel despite
such constitutional guarantees.

RIGHT TO COUNSEL IN JUVENILE COURT CASES
In 1967, the U.S. Supreme Court decision in the case of *In re Gault*
extended the Sixth Amendment right to legal counsel to juveniles accused
of crimes for which they could be institutionalized. Although the *Gault*
decision only mandated counsel for juveniles facing possible
institutionalization, in most urban jurisdictions legal counsel now is

considered a non-waivable right (Sarri and Hasenfeld 1976). If parents or guardians in urban settings are indigent and cannot hire an attorney for the juvenile, the court must locate a public defender or appoint private counsel at the county's expense. Rural courts cannot afford this practice.

Four years after the *Gault* decision, Cannon and Kolson conducted a study of legal representation in Kentucky's rural juvenile courts (1971). They found that in approximately one-third of the courts surveyed, the frequency of legal representation was no higher than 10%; in less than two-fifths of the courts, such counsel was 50%.

A comprehensive study of legal representation for juveniles in Minnesota revealed that only 45.3% of all juveniles appearing in juvenile courts had legal counsel (Feld 1989). Significantly, this study showed that in urban counties, 63% of all minors had counsel, compared to just 25.1% of rural minors. In a few rural counties, less than 5% of juveniles had attorneys. These data suggest that the vast majority of youths in the rural court system—even those who face possible institutionalization—are adjudicated and dispositioned without legal representation.

ADJUDICATION AND DISPOSITION
In large urban-based juvenile courts, cases referred to court are scheduled for an initial appearance, commonly known as an "arraignment hearing." At this first court appearance, legal counsel for the minor is appointed, a plea is entered responding to the petition and a hearing date is set for adjudication on the merits of the petition.

Court adjudication is somewhat similar to the trial stage in a criminal proceeding. During this hearing, the prosecuting attorney, usually the state's attorney for the county, presents evidence to support the allegations in the petition and counsel for the juvenile has the right to cross-examine witnesses. In a delinquency hearing, the state has the burden to prove the allegations "beyond a reasonable doubt" before the minor can be found guilty. Based on the decision in *Mckeiver* v. *Pennsylvania* (1971), however, juveniles have no constitutional right to a jury trial. After both sides submit evidence, the judge makes a decision on whether the charges have been proved. If the state fails under the proper standard of proof, the minor is discharged. If the allegations are proved beyond a reasonable doubt, the minor is declared a ward of the court and a disposition hearing is set, which is similar to a sentencing hearing in adult criminal courts.

Most urban juvenile courts have bifurcated adjudicational and dispositional hearings, which enables the probation department to prepare a background history of the minor that the court uses in deciding final dispositioning. The purpose of the social background investigation is twofold: 1) to assist the probation department in developing a treatment plan for the minor; 2) to help the judge decide a sentence that will promote the best interests of the child, while simultaneously ensuring the safety of the community. The information gathered during the social history investigation is forwarded to the judge in a pre-sentencing report. The report contains information about the incident under review, family background, the minor's behavior at home and in school, and any record of previous contacts with the juvenile court. A bifurcatèd hearing has the advantage of giving the probation department, the minor's attorney and the presiding judge a chance to explore alternative options in arriving at an appropriate sentence for the minor.

In rural juvenile courts, adjudicational and dispositional hearings occur together. Limited information on which the court can draw, results from: lack of available staff to bifurate these hearings and develop a social history; and restricted access to psychologists, family therapists and child care experts to whom most urban courts are privy. Rural probation officers, therefore, must rely on their intuition or "gut feelings" in developing treatment plans for juveniles and making recommendations to the court for dispositioning.

Sentencing in rural juvenile courts is weighed in favor of allowing youths to remain in the community with their families. A first-time offender normally receives a suspended sentence and may be ordered to pay restitution or perform community service work. If problems persist, the minor is placed on probation, which is the most commonly used disposition in juvenile courts (Streib 1978). In the rural juvenile justice system, the sentence of probation, however, is not much different from informal supervision due to limited resources and the lack of full-time probation officers.

The caseloads of rural probation officers include both adults and juveniles scattered over several counties. If a youth fails to keep probation appointments or refuses to participate in court-ordered programs, the probation officer (P.O.) has limited remedial options. The P.O. can revoke the minor's probation and recommend placement outside the community or can wait until the minor is 17 and then terminate the court's jurisdiction. Compared to the urban juvenile justice system, rural juvenile courts have fewer sentencing alternatives, and they function without many private sector programs and resources. Early Offender Programs and Intensive Probation Supervision Programs are lacking, along with affordable private sector services. Because income levels generally are lower in rural areas, often youths are not covered by insurance, and when their parents cannot afford private therapeutic care, their children may be sent to a state facility for psychological assessment and screening. Although they have fewer sentencing options, rural judges have learned to take advantage of local helping networks and resources.

A recent study examined the role orientations of Nebraska juvenile court judges and found that rural judges embraced a more "activist" mode of judicial functioning compared to the traditional role of "impartial decision-maker" preferred by urban judges (Provorse and Sarata 1989). Mobilizing innovative treatment plans and "pressuring" youths and their families to take advantage of these, albeit limited, resources reflect an "activist" judicial role orientation. Due to limited fiscal resources and youth services available in rural areas, "judges *must* adopt a more active stance to fund or create solutions which serve the needs of the community and protect the interests of the child" (Provorse and Sarata 1989: 11).

SUMMARY

Although the statutory language contained in most states' juvenile court acts is very similar, the application is different between urban and rural juvenile courts. Urban juvenile courts throughout the United States process thousands of cases annually and are equipped to handle a heavy volume of referrals. In urban court settings, a full-time professional staff performs specialized functions, such as: legal screening, intake adjustment interviewing, and psychological testing and evaluation. Judges in urban juvenile courts hear juvenile cases exclusively, and they are supported by a staff of professionals who are involved actively in the dispositional process of each case. Procedural safeguards prescribed in the 1974 and the amended 1980 Juvenile Justice and Delinquency Prevention Act (JJDP) are followed carefully in order to use court time efficiently, and to avoid legal procedural errors that could result in costly appeals. The result is a system of justice that is highly efficient, is predictable in the application of decision-making criteria, and is legalistic in orientation.

Rural juvenile courts operate more like the traditional *parens patriae* court. Greater responsibility is placed on the judge to uphold the rights of juveniles, and to determine what is in their best interest. Full-time attorneys are not present to protect a minor's legal rights, and rural parents rarely have the income to hire an attorney. Rural juvenile courts do not have the staff and resources to undertake a rigorous social history investigation of youths or their families. Practically speaking, this means that decision making at the dispositional stage is largely based on the experience and "wisdom" of the juvenile court judge. The lack of resources and limited range of sentencing alternatives forces the rural judge to be creative, and some have learned to use the services of local organizations, volunteer groups and informal helping networks. Although fewer pre-court diversion programs are available, not so many youths enter the rural juvenile justice system as they do in urban contexts because of "net-widening." This phenomenon of the urban system refers to the process whereby juveniles, ordinarily who would avoid court contact entirely, are brought into the juvenile justice "net" because pre-court diversion programs exist. An inherent strength of the rural juvenile justice system is a preference for solving youth problems in ways that minimize net-widening.

In 1999, the juvenile court will be 100 years old. As experts re-assess the court's basic philosophy and re-examine its operations, the most important challenge confronting rural juvenile courts is developing and maintaining resources and services to assist youths and their families. Whether they like it or not, rural justice officials must adapt to shrinking state and local funds for court programs and services. Better coordination with agencies outside the rural juvenile justice system is essential. The logistical problems of providing multiple services to rural families partially can be overcome through stronger inter-agency cooperation and planning, and more creative use of regional care sites. In the rural juvenile justice system, the recruitment and training of volunteers and para-professionals to serve as lay counselors and crisis intervention workers, can alleviate some service deficiencies. Rural court officials also must be more active in educating the local community about what the juvenile court can do to help youths and their families stay together, and why it is important to invest resources on behalf of children in ways that will improve their lives.

REFERENCES

Brakel, S. J., and G. R. South. "Diversion from the Criminal Process in the Rural Community," *American Criminal Law Quarterly*, 17, 1969: 122-173.

Cannon, B. C., and K. Kolson. "Rural Compliance with Gault: A Case Study," *Journal of Family Law*, 10, 1971: 300-326.

Chesney-Lind, M. "Girls in Jail," *Crime and Delinquency*, 34, 1988: 150-168.

Children's Defense Fund. *Children in Adult Jails*. Washington, DC: Children's Defense Fund, 1976.

Coates, R. B. "The Future of Corrections in Juvenile Justice," in A. R. Roberts, ed., *Juvenile Justice: Policies, Programs, and Services*. Chicago: The Dorsey Press, 1989: 281-297.

Community Research Associates. *Removing Children from Adult Jails: A Guide to Action*. Champaign, IL, 1980.

_____. *The Michigan Holdover Network: Short-Term Supervision Strategies for Rural Counties*. Champaign, IL, 1987.

Cottle, T. J. *Children in Jail: Seven Lessons in American Justice*. Boston: Beacon Press, 1977.

DeJames, J. "Issues in Rural Juvenile Justice," in J. Jankovic, R. K. Green, and S. D. Cronk, eds., *Juvenile Justice in Rural America*. Office of Juvenile Justice and Delinquency Prevention, Washington, DC: United States Government Printing Office, 1980.

Elliot, D. S., D. Huizinga, and S. S. Ageton. *Explaining Delinquency and Drug Use*. Beverly Hills, CA: Sage Publications, 1985.

Farley, O. W., K. A. Griffiths, R. A. Skidmore, and M. G. Thackery. *Rural Social Work Practice*. New York: Free Press, 1982.

Feld, B. C. "The Right to Counsel in Juvenile Court: An Empirical Study of When Lawyers Appear and the Difference They Make," *The Journal of Criminal Law and Criminology*, 79, 1989: 1185-1346.

_____. "Justice by Geography: Urban, Suburban, and Rural Variations in Juvenile Justice Administration," *The Journal of Criminal Law and Criminology*, 82, 1991: 156-210.

_____. *Justice for Children: The Right to Counsel in Juvenile Courts.* Boston: Northeastern University Press, 1993.

Gibbons, D. C., and A. Jolin. "Rural Delinquency Literature: What's There?," Paper presented at The American Society of Criminology. Toronto, Canada, 1982.

Hagen, B. H. "Rural Adolescents and Mental Health: Growing Up in the Rural Community," *Human Services in the Rural Environment*, 11, 1987: 23-27.

Heyman, S. R. "Capitalizing on Unique Assets of Rural Areas for Community Interventions," *Journal of Rural Community Psychology*, 3, 1982: 35-48.

Kempf, K. L., S. C. Decker, and R. L. Bing. *An Analysis of Apparent Disparities in the Handling of Black Youth Within Missouri's Juvenile Justice System* (Executive Summary). Department of Administration of Justice Center for Metropolitan Studies. St. Louis, MO: University of Missouri-St. Louis Press, 1990.

Keve, P. W. *The Consequences of Prohibiting the Jailing of Juveniles.* Unpublished report. Virginia Commonwealth University, Richmond, VA, 1984.

Klein, M. A. "Deinstitutionalization and Diversion of Juvenile Offenders: A Litany of Impediments," in N. Morris and M. Tonry, eds., *Crime and Justice: An Annual Review of Research.* Chicago: University of Chicago Press, 1979: 145-201.

Krisberg, B., P. Litsky, and I. Schwartz. "Youth in Confinement: Justice by Geography," *Journal of Research in Crime and Delinquency*, 21, 1984: 153-181.

Kurtz, P. D., and E. W. Lindsey. "A Locality Development Approach to Delinquency Prevention in Rural Areas," *Human Services in the Rural Environment*, 11, 1987: 9-15.

Libertoff, K. "The Runaway Youth Issue: Implications for Rural Communities," in J. Jankovic, R. K. Green, and S. D. Cronk, eds., *Juvenile Justice in Rural America*. Office of Juvenile Justice and Delinquency Prevention, Washington, DC: United States Government Printing Office, 1980.

Melton, G. B. "Community Psychology and Rural Legal Systems," in A. W. Childs and G. B. Melton, eds., *Rural Psychology*. New York: Plenum Press, 1983.

National Coalition of State Juvenile Justice Advisory Group. *First Report to the President, the Congress and the Administrator of the Office of Juvenile Justice and Delinquency Prevention*, 1986.

National Council on Crime and Delinquency. *Standards and Guides for the Detention of Children and Youth*, 2d ed. Washington, DC: United States Government Printing Office, 1961.

North Dakota Division of Juvenile Services. *The North Dakota Experience: Transition to Compliance*. Bismark, ND, 1991.

Office for Substance Abuse Prevention. *Prevention Resource Guide: Rural Communities*. National Clearinghouse for Alcohol and Drug Information: Rockville, MD, 1991.

Pawlek, E. J. "Juvenile Justice: A Rural-Urban Comparison," in J. Jankovic, R. K. Green, and S. D. Cronk, eds., *Juvenile Justice in America*. Office of Juvenile Justice and Delinquency Prevention, Washington, DC: United States Government Printing Office, 1980.

Polk, K. *An Exploration of Rural Juvenile Delinquency*. Lane County Youth Study Project: Eugene, OR, 1963.

Provorse, D., and B. Sarata. "The Social Psychology of Juvenile Court Judges in Rural Communities," *Journal of Rural Community Psychology*, 10, 1989: 3-15.

Roberts, A. R., ed. *Juvenile Justice: Policies, Programs, and Services*. Chicago: The Dorsey Press, 1989.

Roche, M. P. *Rural Police and Rural Youth*. Charlottesville, VA: The University Press of Virginia, 1985.

Rubin, J. T. "The Emerging Prosecutor Dominance of the Juvenile Court Intake Process," *Crime and Delinquency*, 26, 1980: 299-318.

_____. "The Juvenile Court Landscape," in A. R. Roberts, ed., *Juvenile Justice: Policies, Programs, and Services*. Chicago: The Dorsey Press, 1989: 110-141.

Sarri, R., and Y. Hasenfeld. "Brought to Justice? Juveniles, the Courts, and the Law," in R. Sarri and Y. Hasenfeld, eds., *National Assessment of Juvenile Corrections*. Ann Arbor, MI: University of Michigan Press, 1976.

Schwartz, I. M., L. Harris, and L. Levi. "The Jailing of Juveniles in Minnesota," *Crime and Delinquency*, 34, 1988: 133-149.

Streib, V. M. *Juvenile Justice in America*. Port Washington, NJ: Kennikat Press, 1978.

Waltman, G. H. "Main Street Revisited: Social Work Practice in Rural Areas," *Social Casework*, 67, 1986: 466-474.

Weber, G. K. "Preparing Social Workers for Practice in Rural Social Systems," in H. W. Johnson, ed., *Rural Human Services: A Book of Readings*. Itasca, IL: F. E. Peacock Publishers, 1980.

CHAPTER 11

American Indian Justice Systems and Tribal Courts in Rural "Indian Country"

by *Melissa A. Pflüg*

INTRODUCTION

This chapter addresses three issues: 1) United States federal Indian policy and statutes that establish, condition and constrain court and justice systems among rural Indian communities; 2) the structure, characteristics and concerns of tribal courts; 3) future challenges facing tribal justice systems. At the outset it is important to realize several factors about Indian justice systems and tribal courts. First, reservations are distinct communities established by the federal government within a broader contiguous geographic area that the government defines as "Indian Country." Unlike most reservations themselves, Indian Country includes both Indian and non-Indian inhabitants. Second, tribal courts function as one juridical institution within the reservation community. Third, the structure and function of tribal courts are conditioned and constrained largely by federal law. Fourth, because of the unique setting of both the rural tribal court within the reservation and the broader justice system as applied within Indian Country, jurisdictional "clashes" exist between the federal, state and tribal courts.

Today, there are approximately 150 Indian tribal justice systems operating in Indian Country and/or Indian reservations throughout the United States. These systems display distinct features from those of the wider American criminal justice system. Because of the nineteenth century federal Indian policy of reservationism, many Indian peoples were consolidated in bounded geographic areas. Tribal communities were created by the federal government within what it defines geographically as Indian Country. Contemporary Indian systems of justice, including the tribal court system, are conditioned and constrained both by shifting United States federal Indian policy regarding Indian "sovereignty" and a history of federal statutes. Tribal justice systems must address issues related to the general poverty, isolation, substance abuse and crime rates

191

found on reservations, and the sometimes hostile interactions between Indians and non-Indians that characterize many reservations and communities in Indian Country.

In addition to the above broad social issues that the tribal justice system must address, tribal courts encounter more specific difficulties. For example, most tribal court judges are not full-time court officials and these court systems do not include a probation staff. Counseling services, child care specialists and other professional resources usually are not available to the tribal court. Judges face problems of skepticism and fear by tribal members of bringing in non-Indian professionals who they consider "outsiders." Additionally, tribal court judges face the larger challenge of upholding traditional community values concerning justice within a context of non-Indian constitutional and international law, especially because of the unique circumstances of Indian Country.

Indian reservations are land properties held in trust by the federal government, today involving more than 50 million acres in the United States. Indian Country, however, has a wider application and includes counties containing reservations because, frequently, tribal members live in towns and lands outside the boundaries of the reservation itself. This surrounding area generally includes non-Indian residents. So, there are two jurisdictional issues implicit to the concept of Indian Country: 1) the political boundary of the tribal entity that is the reservation itself; 2) the boundaries of civil governments of the adjacent towns and counties (Sutton 1991: 7). Jim Bransky, an attorney with Michigan Indian Legal Services, suggests that the federal government's formal definition of Indian Country was intended to identify federal criminal jurisdiction over Indians under the Major Crimes Act (MCA) of 1885 (1988: 372). Subsequent to a 1948 amendment to the MCA, the Supreme Court has held that both civil and criminal jurisdiction applies to the definition of Indian Country (*Decoteau* v. *District County Court*, 1975 and *Moe* v. *Confederated Salish and Kootenai Tribes*, 1976). The concept of Indian Country, and federal criminal and civil jurisdiction over its boundaries, is rooted in the MCA, resulting in fundamental changes in traditional Indian systems of justice.

While the traditional Indian method of handling offenses was a matter of restitution based on council consensus, Congress, by passing the MCA, made clear its policy of the superiority of United States law over Indian systems of justice and granted jurisdiction to the federal courts over certain crimes committed by Indians within Indian Country. Today, after several amendments, the "major crimes" committed by Indians in Indian Country that fall under the exclusive jurisdiction of federal courts include: murder, manslaughter, kidnapping, rape, statutory rape, involuntary sodomy, assault with intent to commit rape, incest, assault with intent to commit murder, assault with a deadly weapon, assault resulting in serious bodily injury, arson, burglary, and robbery (18 U.S.C., 1153, 3242). The authority behind the MCA stems from the guardian-ward relationship between federal and Indian governments established by the United States Supreme Court.

Traditionally, tribal councils of elders presided over the "legislative," "executive" and "judicial" aspects of tribal governments, so tribal systems of justice were community forums. The tribe, therefore, had complete civil and criminal jurisdiction over its members and those in its territory. Generally, offenses were viewed more as ethical transgressions of "relationship" than as a matter of infringing on the man-made legal rights of others. Solutions were mediated by a council of elders instead of going through the non-Indian process of adversarial litigation (Peak 1989: 392; Pommersheim 1992: 438). Restitution for unethical actions focused on healing the relationship between the parties, which was regarded as being essential to maintaining the well-being of the entire community. Before the establishment of United States government Indian policy, an Indian people's authority over their lands and those found within it stemmed from their existence as a sovereign nation. However, traditional patterns of tribal sovereignty now have been limited by the United States government. United States federal Indian policy has changed traditional Indian governing structures, especially by insisting that the Bureau of Indian Affairs (BIA) act as arbitrating agency between the federal government and the separate tribes it recognizes as legitimate political entities. Within these recognized groups, most centralized on rural reservations, tribal courts and tribal boards of directors often have replaced traditional councils. Additionally, the nature of the court processes has changed dramatically, both in the aims and goals of adjudication and the structure of the courts.

United States federal legislation and court decisions have established reservationed communities of Indians, and have determined tribal court jurisdiction and the function of tribal courts. Before allowing separate reservation communities to establish independent tribal courts, Courts of Indian Offenses (CIOs) and Indian police forces were organized and supervised by the BIA. The CIOs and police forces, both differing in most respects from those located within traditional cultural patterns, were newly formed institutions serving as the criminal justice system in Indian Country. The reservation itself, Indian police, the tribal court system and the new structures of government by tribal boards of directors, are institutions *forced* on tribes and communities. Even the "tribes" themselves no longer are traditional but are new centralized political bodies resulting from federal reservation policies of the nineteenth century and the United States government's claims for continuing trust responsibilities over Indian reservation lands. The existence of centralized tribal governments, patterned on the model of the wider United States system, makes reservations juridical places distinct from the "places of relationships" that formerly maintained justice through traditional methods.

The situation has become particularly complex, especially in rural settings where reservations are small. Many tribal members live away from the reservation, and many non-Indians go to reservations for activities such as gambling and buying arts and crafts. The mixing of Indians and non-Indians on reservations means "crimes" no longer can be dealt with solely by a traditional Indian council, even though the Indians may claim sovereignty. Although the focus of these modern systems of Indian justice still is on maintaining harmonious relationships, in making decisions Indian court officials must account for their separation of power from federal and state systems, and they have to decide whether court powers are separate from the tribal board of directors. In tribal justice systems, procedures for handling particular types of cases tend to be based more on traditional community values than on the authority of man-made laws, and they tend to respond to community instead of simply individual needs and concerns. The general approach preferred by Indian justice systems is to appeal to community negotiation and such traditional forums as elders gatherings instead of court actions. So, the broad concept structuring Indian justice systems is prevention over intervention.

A fundamental concern of Indian justice systems today derives from legal questions about the nature of tribal authority, and definitions of self-government and sovereignty. The federal policy regarding tribal sovereignty was shaped to a large extent by the United States Supreme Court under Chief Justice John Marshall in *Cherokee Nation* v. *State of Georgia* (1831) and *Worcester* v. *Georgia* (1832). The first Cherokee case resulted in Indian tribes being defined as "domestic dependents" of the United States government, therefore, limiting tribal ability to appeal to international law, while in the second case, the Cherokee lost their jurisdictional authority to the state. The Burger Supreme Court, however, reinterpreted this latter decision and emphasized that in certain criminal cases, the tribe has the right to act as an independent sovereign instead of an arm of the federal government. The current Rehnquist Supreme Court, in an attempt to overrule tribal sovereignty entirely, holds tribes to be under the dominion of the federal protectorate. Shifting federal Indian policy, especially concerning tribal sovereignty, has had a great impact on tribally-run justice systems; for example, by fundamentally changing their structure and diminishing their authority.

FEDERAL STATUTES AND COURT JURISDICTION: CONDITIONS AND CONSTRAINTS

The issues of the definition of "sovereignty" and the status of reservation tribal groups relative to the interests of the United States are the basis for federal statutes that ultimately condition and constrain the jurisdiction of tribal courts. During their relationships with the French and British in the seventeenth and eighteenth centuries, Indian nations were sovereign entities that operated outside the legal domain of the European colonists. With the establishment of the United States as a sovereign nation, Indian nations increasingly were absorbed into the American system, and the issue of tribal sovereignty became of great concern to the federal government. As developed in United States law,

> The concept of sovereignty consists of two main components: the recognition of a government's proper zones of authority free from intrusion by other sovereigns within the society, and the understanding that within these zones the sovereign may enact substantive rules that are potentially divergent or "different" from that of other—even dominant—sovereigns within the system.
>
> —Pommersheim 1992: 421

Despite its definition, the United States did not consider that sovereignty applied to Indian nations and, consequently, federal Indian policy was never framed by this legal concept.

By the late eighteenth century, the federal government adopted a policy of forcibly removing Indian nations to reservations that it established, and it began engaging heavily in treaty-making in order to assert its legal jurisdiction over these newly established communities. To constrain Indian power, the federal government "gave" to Indian nations the status of being "internal sovereigns of a *limited kind*" (Pommersheim 1992: 417), which was translated as "domestic dependents." This definitional aspect of Indian status was the focus of two precedent-setting cases: *Cherokee Nation* v. *State of Georgia* and *Worcester* v. *Georgia*.

In the case of *Cherokee Nation* v. *State of Georgia* (1831), the Cherokee argued that they were a sovereign foreign nation and as such were entitled to sue a state under Article 3 of the United States Constitution. Chief Justice John Marshall upheld their argument provisionally. Instead of a foreign nation, which would fall under international law, Justice Marshall defined the Cherokee as a "domestic dependent nation." A policy of guardian/ward relationship emerged because the Supreme Court did not clearly differentiate between or define "foreign" versus "sovereign" nation. Michael Petoskey (personal communication), a tribal court attorney for the Grand Traverse Band of Chippewa and Ottawa in Michigan, identifies the result of this decision as establishing a law of covenant: a non-negotiated contract was created between the trustor (the Euro-American doctrine of discovery-conquest-ownership) and the land trustee (the U.S.), and between the land trustee and the beneficiary (the tribe). The contractual relationship was intended to define federal jurisdiction.

In *Worcester* v. *Georgia* (1832), Chief Justice Marshall decided that the state had exclusive jurisdictional power instead of jurisdictional powers existing concurrently. The decision in this case is significant, as it signaled a shift in federal Indian policy. The right of sovereignty and self-government of the reservation as separate from the state but not the federal government, shifted to a policy of state law having jurisdiction over the tribe.

Following the decisions in the Cherokee cases, subsequent legislation and court decisions in the 1880s constructed criminal justice systems on reservations and eroded tribal self-governance (Peak 1989: 398). Also, stemming from the Supreme Court's decision in *Ex Parte Crow Dog* (1883), a murder case involving two tribal members of the Rose Bud Sioux Reservation in South Dakota, the federal government began a process of establishing a federally-run Indian court system, the Courts of Indian Offenses (CIOs), under the authority of the Bureau of Indian Affairs (BIA). To further assert its authority over Indian affairs,

Congress passed the Major Crimes Act (MCA) in 1885, defining specific criminal cases to be adjudicated by the federal courts and bringing "federal law enforcement officers onto the reservation...and [*forbidding*] *tribal governments from using traditional punishments for criminal acts* [emphasis mine]" (Peak 1989: 399). These legislative acts and court decisions propelled the sequential erosion of tribal sovereignty and autonomy.

Soon after the MCA was passed, two cases again addressed the issue of the "limited" degree of tribal sovereignty. *Kagama* v. *United States* (1886) and *Lone Wolf* v. *Hitchcock* (1903) put tribes under the authority of the federal system by making them subject to the absolute or plenary power of Congress, so proclaiming ultimate jurisdiction over tribes (Pommersheim 1992: 418-19). This meant further erosion of tribal power and authority.

Shifting from a policy of Indian reservationism to one of cultural assimilation and tribal termination, Congress passed Public Law-280 (1954), granting six states concurrent criminal and civil jurisdiction over Indian reservations within those states' boundaries. Many tribal leaders objected to PL-280 because they viewed it as reflecting the federal policy of the termination of tribal units. Limiting exclusive tribal jurisdiction, PL-280 created the possibility of cases falling within all three jurisdictions concurrently. This is illustrated by the following example given by John Petoskey, a tribal court attorney for the Grand Traverse Band of Chippewa and Ottawa, Michigan (personal communication). If an Indian lived on a reservation, put a down payment on a truck owned by a non-Indian, brought it back to the reservation and then did not pay the balance owed, the non-Indian seller of the truck could go to the state court and sue the Indian for breach of contract. But, the Indian could counter-sue, arguing the financing instrument violated the Truth In Lending Act (a federal statute), so the case would move from the state to the federal court. If the case occurred in a non- PL-280 state, the initial contract was made within Indian Country and, therefore, tribal jurisdiction, and a subsequent case would be held in tribal court. Actually, this case would involve concurrent state and tribal jurisdiction, as the Indian takes the truck off the reservation and uses state roads, and the like, so the state does have an interest. One can see the existing confusion likely to lead to injustices for one, or all, parties.

With the disbanding of the termination policy, and as a product of Lyndon Johnson's emerging policy of self-determination for Indians,

Congress passed the Indian Civil Rights Act (82 Stat. 73, Title II—Rights of Indians; Civil Rights Act, PL-90-284; 1968), making *some* of the Bill of Rights for all Americans applicable to Indian tribes. The ICRA states:

No Indian tribe exercising powers of self-government shall—

(1)   make or enforce any law prohibiting the free exercise of religion, or abridging the freedom of speech, or of the press, or the right of the people peaceably to assemble and to petition for a redress of grievances;

(2)   violate the right of the people to be secure in their persons, houses, papers, and effects against unreasonable search and seizures, nor issue warrants, but upon probable cause, supported by oath or affirmation, and particularly describing the place to be searched and person or thing to be seized;

(3)   subject any person for the same offense to be twice put in jeopardy;

(4)   compel any person in any criminal case to be a witness against himself;

(5)   take any private property for public use without just compensation;

(6)   deny to any person in a criminal proceeding the right to a speedy and public trial, to be informed of the nature and cause of the accusation, to be confronted with the witnesses against him, to have compulsory process for obtaining witnesses in his favor, and at his own expense to have the assistance of counsel for his defence;

(7)   require excessive bail, impose excessive fines, inflict cruel and unusual punishments, and in no event impose for conviction of any one offense any penalty or punishment greater than imprisonment for a term of one year and a fine of $5,000, or both;

(8)   deny to any person within its jurisdiction the equal protection of its laws or deprive any person of liberty or property without due process of law;

(9)   pass any bill of attainder or ex post facto law; or

(10)   deny any person accused of an offense punishable by imprisonment the right, upon request, to a trial by jury of not less than six persons.

—25 U.S.C. 461

Many tribal leaders object to the ICRA. Vine Deloria, Jr., for example, argues: "With the passage of the 1968 Civil Rights Act, Indian tribes fell victim to the Bill of Rights," setting the stage "for total erosion of tribal customs" (1988: 238). Some tribes, the Pueblo in particular, are "fighting to get the law amended because the law allows reliance on traditional solutions only to the extent that they do not conflict with state and federal laws" (Deloria, Jr. 1988: 238). Nevertheless, the ICRA stipulates that tribal courts can determine land disposition. Tribal courts have jurisdiction over land disposition primarily because of Indian concerns over property distribution in cases of inter-ethnic marriages. For example, tribal communities face such questions as what and how property distributions should be made in cases of an Indian male from Onendaga society, which traces descent through the female line, marrying and then divorcing a non-Indian female, versus an Indian female from Ojibwa society, which traces descent through the male line, marrying and then divorcing a non-Indian male. Ultimately, the issue that such cases as these raise extends beyond land disposition to include child custody and, therefore, resulted in passage of the Indian Child Welfare Act.

The Indian Child Welfare Act (U.S. Code, Title 25: Indians. PL-90-608 2[4], 92 Stat. 3069; 1978) combined case law to determine jurisdiction over children who are members of a federally recognized tribal group. The Act reads that each tribe has exclusive jurisdiction over the welfare and adoption of its member children (except in the 6 PL-280 states), and has the responsibility to maintain a guardian-ward relationship over children who are tribal members. The Act was intended to protect against child abduction by the state welfare system. From 1915 until the passage of the Child Welfare Act, the placement status of an adoptee, even if adopted by Indians, was determined by the state's assessing the "best interest of the child;" that is, adjudicating whether the adoptee had to remain a resident or could leave the reservation after adoption. This Act put the matter of the welfare of Indian children under the authority of the tribal court.

The current jurisdiction of tribal courts stems from the implementation of tribal constitutions modelled after that of the United States. The tribal court system has several jurisdictional aspects: the tribal conservation court is one jurisdiction, as are civil and limited criminal jurisdictions. The criminal jurisdiction of the court has a territorial component; it applies to offenses not listed in the MCA committed by Indians on Indian lands, such as the reservation or other lands held in trust by the federal government for the tribe. As a result of the Supreme Court's decision in the *Oliphant* case (*Oliphant* v. *Suquamish Tribe*, 1978), currently tribal courts do not have criminal jurisdiction over non-Indians who commit offenses in Indian Country but only have civil jurisdiction. Additionally, the case raises a question of tribal court jurisdiction over Indians.

> In March 1977 the U.S. Supreme Court decided *Oliphant* v. *Suquamish*, another major decision affecting Indian criminal justice and, from the Indian practitioner's standpoint, bringing more problems to reservation justice and adding to role conflict. Succinctly, *Oliphant* established that tribal courts lacked *inherent* jurisdiction to try and punish Indian criminal offenders [emphasis mine].
>
> —Peak 1989: 404

This decision was an attempt by the Supreme Court to limit tribal power. Tribal attorney Jim Bransky identifies that:

> If a crime occurs outside Indian Country then the tribe does not have jurisdiction over the matter, even if the accused is a tribal member. An exception to this rule is tribal jurisdiction over a member's exercise of treaty off-reservation hunting and fishing rights. If a crime occurs in Indian Country, is not one of the "major crimes," and both the accused and victim are Indian, then the tribe has exclusive jurisdiction over the case. In prosecuting the case, the tribe must comply with the ICRA [Indian Civil Rights Act], which limits the punishment to one year in jail or $5,000, or both. If a non-Indian commits a crime against an Indian in Indian Country, then the federal government has exclusive jurisdiction under the General Crimes Act [1817] (18 U.S.C. 1152).
>
> —1988: 373-74

Because of the decision in the *Oliphant* case, determining whether the tribal court has criminal jurisdiction requires asking and answering three questions: 1) did the crime take place in Indian Country? 2) are the accused and the victim Indian or non-Indian? 3) is the crime one that is addressed in the MCA?

Unlike the criminal arena, the federal government has made little effort to restrict tribal civil jurisdiction, especially in the area of domestic matters, including marriages and divorces and child custody. In addition to having sole authority to adjudicate civil disputes of tribal members, civil authority covers the activities of non-Indians within Indian Country. Tribal courts have the authority to adjudicate such civil infractions by non-Indians as taxation, business licensing, hunting and fishing plus zoning violations (Bransky 1988: 375).

STRUCTURE, CHARACTERISTICS AND CONCERNS OF TRIBAL JUSTICE SYSTEMS

The structure, characteristics and concerns of contemporary tribal justice systems largely are due to federal legislation, the process of establishing reservations, shifting definitions of tribal political and legal status, and the fact that tribal courts are emerging cultural institutions. The structure of contemporary courts was established after the 1930s, when tribal organizations adopted written constitutions based on authorization by the BIA. Tribal court systems can be structured in one of two ways: 1) on the BIA sanctioned *U.S. Code of Federal Regulations*; 2) by independent tribal constitutions allowing the court to function more closely following tribal tradition and community values. Two examples of court systems structured by tribal constitutions are the Grand Traverse Band of Chippewa and Ottawa in Michigan, and the Lac du Flambeau Chippewa in Wisconsin.

Article V of the Grand Traverse Band's Constitution stipulates the structure and characteristics of their tribal court:

Section 1. Judicial Power Vested. The judicial power of the Grand Traverse Band shall be vested in a tribal court system. The tribal court system shall be composed of a court of general jurisdiction (hereinafter referred to as the "Tribal Court"), an appellate court (hereinafter referred to as the "Tribal Appellate Court"), and such lower courts as the Tribal Appellate Court may establish.

Section 2. Jurisdiction. The judicial power shall extend to all cases arising under this Constitution, ordinances, regulations, and/or judicial decisions of the Grand Traverse Band and shall be exercised to the fullest extent consistent with self-determination and the sovereign powers of the Tribe.

Section 3. Composition of the Tribal Court System.
(a) Tribal Court. The Tribal Court shall be a court of general jurisdiction and shall consist of one (1) judge and one (1) associate judge who shall meet as often as circumstances require.
(b) Tribal Appellate Court. The Tribal Appellate Court shall consist of three (3) judges. At least one (1) of the three (3) judges shall be an attorney licensed to practice before the courts of a state in the United States.
Section 4. Appointments and Compensation.
(a) Appointment to the Court of General Jurisdiction. The judges of the Tribal Court and such lower courts as the Tribal Appellate Court may establish shall be appointed by an affirmative vote of five (5) of the seven (7) members of the Tribal Council for a term of four (4) years.
(b) Appointment to the Appellate Court. Each judge of the Tribal Appellate Court shall be appointed by an affirmative vote of five (5) of the seven (7) members of the Tribal Council for a term of six (6) years.
(c) Compensation. The Tribal Council shall have the power to establish the level of compensation for each judge; provided that the compensation due to each individual judge shall not be diminished during his/her appointment.
Section 5. Eligibility for Appointment and Service. Any person shall be eligible to serve as a tribal court judge only if he/she:
(a) Is a member of the Grand Traverse Band who has attained the age of eighteen (18) and/or is an attorney licensed to practice before the courts of a state in the United States;
(b) Is not presently a Tribal Council member or running to become a Tribal Council member; and
(c) Has not been convicted, within ten (10) years of such appointment, of any felony by a court of competent jurisdiction.
Section 6. Judicial Independence. The Tribal Judiciary shall be independent from the legislative and executive functions of the tribal government and no person exercising powers of the legislative or executive functions of government shall exercise powers properly belonging to the the judicial branch of government; provided that the Tribal Council shall be empowered to function as the Judiciary of the Grand Traverse Band until the judges prescribed by this Article have been appointed; provided further that the first Tribal Council elected

under this Constitution shall make appointments to its courts within ninety (90) days after its members are elected.

Section 7. Practice and Procedure. The Tribal Judiciary shall by general rules establish, modify, amend, or simplify the practice and procedure in all courts of the Grand Traverse Band.

Section 8. Removal of a Tribal Judge. The Tribal Judiciary may remove any judge by an affirmative vote of a majority of all other members of the Judiciary for:

(a) Unethical conduct, as defined by the American Bar Association Code of Judicial Conduct;

(b) Physical or mental disability which prevent the performance of judicial duties;

(c) Persistent failure to perform duties;

(d) Gross misconduct that is clearly prejudicial to the administration of justice; or

(e) Ineligibility, under Section 5 of this Article, to serve as a member of the Tribal Judiciary.

Section 9. Vacancies in the Tribal Judiciary. Any vacancy in the Tribal Judiciary shall be filled by the Tribal Council in the same manner as the original appointment for the balance of the unexpired term.

—Petoskey 1988: 368

What is noteworthy about the structure of the Grand Traverse Band's court system is that the judiciary is independent from the tribal governing board. Other systems provide for concurrent exercise of executive, legislative and judicial functions by the tribal governing board and the court.

The structure of the justice system among the Lac du Flambeau Chippewa tribe in Wisconsin is such that the Tribal Council has ultimate authority over all tribal members but has no jurisdiction over non-Indians. It is, however, a check on the tribal court. The Tribal Council is made up of members of the tribal governing board and community members who oversee the tribal court. The court system is comprised of one Chief Judge, two associate judges, a magistrate, a clerk of courts and a prosecutor. A person may appeal a ruling to the associate judges and a third judge from another reservation's tribal court who is chosen by the Chief Judge. Tribal members must go through the appeals process; they cannot directly go to the tribal governing board for reprieve from a ruling by the Chief Judge. Also included in the justice system is an Indian Child Welfare Office and a tribal police force. The tribal police force was deputized by the Vilas County, Wisconsin, Sheriff's Department in January 1993 and, therefore, has increased authority over non-Indian violators on the reservation. For example, before the tribal police force was deputized, jurisdictional authority was limited, as illustrated by the following hypothetical case. If a non-Indian exceeded the speed limit in a school zone on the reservation and was stopped by a tribal police officer, the officer could ask for the driver's operating license and inquire whether or not the driver was a tribal member. However, if the driver was not a tribal member, no citations could be issued. If a non-Indian exceeded the speed limit through the same school zone on the reservation and was stopped by a state policeman or a county deputy, the driver could be issued a citation. These anomalies indicate the limited power of tribal authorities over non-Indian offenders, even on the reservation, without deputization of the tribal police force.

Now, non-Indians routinely appear in tribal court. For example, Sp. Hon. Ernest St. Germaine, Chief Judge, Lac du Flambeau Tribal Court, relates (personal communication):

> I recently had a non-Indian appear in my court with a traffic citation. After questioning him and discovering that he was not a tribal member, I gave him the option to have me dismiss it but turn it over to the District Attorney for disposition or for us to proceed in our court. He opted to proceed in our court, which we did. Now, non-tribal members have that option.

In addition to having a unique structure, tribal courts are characterized by the types of offenses they can, and do, adjudicate. Besides traffic violations, some of the types of civil offenses adjudicated in tribal courts include: treaty violations, especially those related to hunting and fishing on reservation lands; domestic violence; littering and destruction of property; drunkenness and disorderliness; truancy and juvenile delinquency; and child abuse and neglect.

Sentences for civil and non-MCA criminal infractions include fines but because of poverty rates, many people cannot pay. Therefore, greater emphasis is placed on community service to uphold the tradition of justice being a matter of mediating ethical transgressions of "relationship." Many tribal judges see their role primarily as being educational and secondarily punitive. Jail terms are issued infrequently. Reluctance to issue jail terms results from a number of factors. Generally, it is a financial burden for the tribe, as it must pay the county for use of its jail. A more significant reason for the low incidence of jail terms is that:

> One of the chief customs in Indian life is the idea of compensation instead of retribution in criminal law. Arbitrary punishment, no matter how apparently suitable to the crime, has had little place in Indian society. These customs have by and large endured and many tribes still feel that if the culprit makes a suitable restitution to his victim no further punishment need be meted out by the tribe.
>
> —Deloria, Jr. 1988: 237-38

The special structure and characteristics of tribal courts produce a number of concerns for Indian judicial authorities. One concern is the problem of possible inconsistencies in decisions of cases where there is cross-jurisdiction. Two of the main concerns of tribal courts today are hunting and fishing violations, which often put tribal members in conflict with Department of Natural Resources (DNR) authorities, and gambling casinos. For example, among the Lac du Flambeau Chippewa, fishing rights are enforced by the tribal court. Tribal Chief Judge, Sp. Hon. Ernest St. Germaine, relates one case appearing before his court (personal communication):

> Three tribal members were out spearing during the off-reservation treaty spearing season. GLIFWC Agents are positioned at the boat landings to count and measure fish when spearers are done. Often, State DNR Wardens will observe this process. The State Warden apparently hid in the bushes farther down the shoreline to observe the spearers from that vantage point. According to his testimony, he observed the spearers from a distance of "oh, 300 yards, or so" across the water with binoculars. He observed them "spear a fish, take it in the boat, take it off the spear, measure it, see that it was too big, then place it in the water over the side of the boat." He marked his place on shore and with landmarks, determined where the fish was floating, then went to get another warden with a boat to make the arrest. This was about an hour after

dark. He then returned an hour later with another warden and a boat, and made the arrest.

[There are] Several things to consider in this case. First, the State Warden is obviously knowledgeable about the process of spearing a fish. He knows the procedure. You bring it in the boat, knock it off the spear, allow it to stop flopping, then, using a specially made board, measure the fish. Spearers are allowed only a certain number of walleye for each permit. They are allowed four fish over that size. The question is, did the warden testify about what he actually saw, or what he thought he saw based on his knowledge of that process? Did he actually see this happen from that distance an hour after dark, even with binoculars? Could he really see them measuring it? Did they dump the fish over the side, or were they washing the board off in the water, which they commonly do after measuring because the fish slime would obscure the markings on the board if they didn't? Next, would they have left the fish floating, or would any sane spearer stab the walleye's air bladder first, to make it sink? Why, then, didn't they do this to the one over-sized walleye that they had in their possession, and to which they admitted they speared, and for which they accepted the citation? They had been cited for waste of natural resources for the several fish which were found floating on the lake. Those I dismissed because there was no direct evidence to link the spearers with those fish, other than speculative testimony of a warden who believed he saw them spear one fish and dump it. My case in point is that...If [you] were standing in the bushes an hour after dark with binoculars watching the spearers, what might [you] have imagined [you were] seeing those spearers do? Would [your] testimony be enough to find them guilty? If you were standing three football fields away from Hardees and a man walked out the door, does he have a burger and fries, or is he carrying a baby pamper for his child? Obviously a burger and fries, because after all, he was in Hardees, right?

After finding them not guilty of wasting natural resources, I also addressed them at length about a traditional cultural meeting about the Circle of Life. In the end, we may or may not know their guilt or innocence, but the Creator knows. If indeed they have violated one of the Creator's laws, then the victims will be our children, and our children's children. One day, the walleye will go away if this is what is happening to them. Our children may hear accounts of walleye spearing, and our children's children may ask, "What is a walleye?" Cultural teachings are the foundation of my court.

In addition to hunting and fishing violations, many court officials have concerns stemming from the existence of gambling casinos on reservations. Some view gambling operations as tearing apart the threads of traditional society. Another example that Chief Judge St. Germaine relates is a case concerning activities associated with gambling (personal communication):

A woman who was a tribal member and an employee of the casino, who had small children at home, was accused of neglecting her children because she was spending all of her time at the casino, not only working, but gambling and drinking. She was brought into my court, and I imposed conditions which she was required to meet, including alcohol and drug assessments, follow-through with any recommendations including treatment, refrain from using alcohol, provide an alcohol-free environment for her children, seek personal counseling, and attend parenting classes. When she didn't follow any of these, which were part of a court order, I found her in contempt and imposed a fine. When she didn't pay, I placed her under house arrest because at the time, our tribal court had no funds by which we could place her in the county jail. (This has changed, as the Tribal Council recently passed a resolution authorizing the use of tribal funds for jail terms. My how things are changing in our court now that this news has gotten around the "res.")

Many adults spend a great deal of their time at the casino, instead of "at home being parents to their children." I'm advocating that no one be hired at the casino who doesn't have a high school degree or a GED. Yet, at the same time, I had a father in court last week, in his 30s, six children, who has his first job...at the casino. He was neatly dressed, clean, sober, and proud of his new job. He has no education. But, his wife ran off with his first-ever paycheck, and locked the three youngest children in the bedroom while he was at work. I am reconsidering my position.

Another concern facing Indian justice systems is that new tribal governing boards, established to comply with BIA criteria for recognition, change traditional systems of justice in significant ways. Justice systems are not always made up of tribal elders but are composed of members who are elected from different bands and factions of reservations. While elders and traditional leaders may run for an office on the governing board, the new system allows younger people, and people with special interests, to rise to positions of power. There has been a shift in leadership away from decentralized councils of band leaders governing by consensus, to a centralized governing body of individuals elected to represent constituents in a unified tribal government. The effect of this has been an erosion of traditional ways.

FUTURE CHALLENGES FACING TRIBAL JUSTICE SYSTEMS

Tribal courts and Indian justice systems face a number of challenges in the future. A primary concern of tribal courts and Indian justice systems is how to amend the intrusive role of the United States government, the BIA and state governments in drafting and preparing original tribal constitutions, and in amending those already in existence. This is particularly critical with regards to the provision to establish and limit tribal court jurisdiction over cases involving Indians and non-Indians. In planning and implementing effective justice programs, many public and tribal officials, judges and attorneys are still asking "Who has jurisdiction—the tribe, the federal government or the state?" Boundaries of authority have not been clearly established.

Because the tribal court system is not a traditional Indian method of dispute resolution, both court officials and the institution of the court must gain credibility within and without Indian Country. Like all court systems, especially those in rural settings, tribal courts must work to maintain distance from the political concerns of the governing board. Justice systems using the governing board for appeal face a critical challenge of being apolitical. Acquiring a competent judicial staff and network of professional resources is another challenge. Many potential judges aspire to train at such institutions as the National Indian Justice Center and the Judicial College at Reno, Nevada but this goal is hindered by lack of financial ability. Additionally, there are the challenges of maintaining a staff once it is trained, and of acquiring adequate funding to attract workers in the first place. Also, there are the broad challenges of planning criminal justice systems and implementing revised programs.

A major challenge to tribal courts is the conflict between Indians and the BIA over planning appropriate criminal justice strategies. Through its Division of Law Enforcement Services (DLES), the BIA introduced its Reservation Law Enforcement Plan in 1977 as a source for identifying law enforcement problems and needs under the supervision of the BIA. DLES proposed a two-step program: 1) compiling and reporting information for the past five years and anticipating future trends; 2) proposing solutions within a five-year window of the future.

Nelson and Sheley identify a number of problems in the DLES plan common to many other criminal justice system plans, especially those targeted for rural settings (1985: 184). The tribe is restricted in defining its own problems. Crimes to be addressed are pre-defined and prioritized based on the FBI Index Offenses: homicide, rape, robbery, aggravated assault, burglary, larceny, and motor vehicle theft. Indians may perceive the seriousness and nature of "crimes" in different terms. Under the DLES plan, the assessment of crime relies on official enforcement statistics, raising two inherent problems in this context: their reliability and their validity are questionable both in the rural non-reservation and reservation settings. Indian criminal justice practice and records-keeping have been marginally accurate at best and, traditionally, Indian peoples are reluctant to report victimizations to outside law enforcement officials. Consequently, there is a critical need for accurate crime data reflecting individual tribal and reservation circumstances. Under the DLES plan, tribes would be subject to criminal justice plans based on BIA generated data, and the resulting policies would, therefore, threaten to reflect bureaucratic requirements more than community needs.

The DLES plan is a prime example of the fact that criminal justice policies applied to Indians, as articulated by the federal government and implemented by the BIA, are founded on the wrong premise. They account for neither the Indian view of justice as a matter of prevention—rooted in a philosophy of establishing, maintaining and expanding social relationships through proper ethical behavior—nor for deviance, traditionally, being dealt with primarily by council consensus. "Many national leaders have encouraged Indian judges to write lengthy opinions on their cases incorporating tribal customs and beliefs with state and federal codes and thus redirecting tribal ordinances toward a new goal of combining punishment, rehabilitation and compensatory solutions" (Deloria, Jr. 1988: 238-39). Actually, this proposal by national leaders may be more reflective of a bureaucratic intent to have tribal judges and their courts get lost "in the system" than a statement acknowledging the inherent value of traditional Indian systems of justice. After all, tribal court judges still ask "Who will pay attention, and who will do anything?"

Looking at the history of BIA administration of crime control programs, Nelson and Sheley offer a general approach to criminal justice planning on reservations, taking into consideration both the tribal goal of self-determination and BIA influence.

> The basic goal of a criminal justice program for a reservation must be involvement of the tribe both in the definition of the crime problem and in the implementation of the plan. Beyond this, the criminal justice plan must recognize both formal and informal deterrents to crime. That is, the traditional formal social control response to crime, i.e., law enforcement, must be complemented by programs designed to take advantage of informal forms of social control already extant within the tribes. Precisely which types of informal social control will by emphasized depend upon tribal culture, definition of the crime problem, and the degree to which tribes wish to involve themselves in crime prevention.
> —Nelson and Sheley 1985: 189

Crime deterrence through informal social control is the traditional method: breach of conduct is constrained coercively by attachments to, and respect for, elders who uphold the validity of traditional cultural norms, and individual commitment to traditional goals and activities.

At base, direct tribal involvement is crucial to both the reservation criminal justice planning process and ultimate success of the program. Tribal courts must remain faithful to traditional meanings and definitions of "justice" (Pflüg 1992a, 1992b, 1995). Many Indian peoples see a fundamental difference between "Equal Justice *Under* the Law," which is the basis of American constitutional jurisprudence, and their traditional view that justice cannot be subsumed under man-made laws (Pflüg, forthcoming). "The twenty-one instructions that guide our life keep us in harmony. They are not laws. They weren't created by people. They were a gift from the Great Spirit which brings us together," said one elder. They interpret justice not as supporting laws but rather the opposite: man-made laws should be simply tools to use when necessary to uphold justice. Justice is interpreted by Indians as reinforcing and reflecting traditional, culturally prescribed, patterns of ethical behavior.

Perhaps the best articulation of many Indian peoples' view of U.S. law is in terms of "fences," "bulwark" and "ownership." An elder said, "The U.S. uses laws to try to protect itself, and to control others. And we all know that what it controls, it thinks it owns—right down to our ancestors." Another elder said, "The American legal system is a lot of absolute rules and regulations made up by lawyers which they use to control others." A third elder said, "They've taken our lands, and they've even tried to take our culture. And, what have we ever been given in return? Lines and boundaries and reservations." These elders' comments say everything about the fact that many Indian people see non-Indian law in terms of defensive imagery equally powerful to fencing property, to creating territorial or state or national boundaries, and to establishing rules to separate human beings from each other. The social world for many Indian peoples, however, derives from fusion, not fission. They see U.S. law as totally different from their model for establishing and maintaining proper interpersonal relationships. The traditional way to order and guide relationships is through gift exchange, understood as a continuum of sharing and reciprocity, not by man-made laws and threats and punishments (Pflüg 1995). However, they see the United States government as having reciprocated very little. Consequently, Indians interpret relations with the United States as being completely asymmetrical, and United States law as operating with a total lack of exchange. To them, the law withholds and it owns—which for Indian peoples is the worst kind of ethical behavior.

Mediation of relationships, whether harmonious or conflicting, through gift exchange expresses that ethical acts of responsibility ultimately bond people together in dynamic relationships. With an ethos and worldview structured by the characteristics of a gift economy, Indian peoples view acts that mediate between disagreeing people not as being part-and-parcel a matter of arbitration or adversarial litigation but as just and ethical negotiation. They interpret the United States legal system as having a fundamentally opposite perspective to their own deriving from principles associated with market exchange. As they understand this system, "arbitration" is the key concept. An elder noted, "I don't think the United States legal system asks people what their needs are. The law just decides for us what programs are going to be started in our own backyards." Not being framed within a system of gift-giving, many

Indians view United States law as legitimizing the continuing attempts by American policy makers to suppress their sovereignty efforts. They view federal policy skeptically as a medium for validating social relations, therefore, taking the frame of reference way beyond the legal/justice system itself.

A traditional view of the superiority of justice over law is echoed by the Lakota who end all prayers and public addresses with an appeal to "all my relatives," which reinforces the theme that the goal of personal life is to uphold interpersonal relations through proper ethical behavior. This suggests that tribal courts and Indian justice systems face the challenge of determining how behavioral/ethical transgressions against "kin" should be treated, whether the parties in a case are actual family members or the relationships are extended out to include the community and even the total Indian and non-Indian cultures. The focus must remain on traditional patterns of relationships and not on rights per se.

Many Indian peoples believe that the outside world has closed the door on them, prejudice against them may never be overcome, and federal and state policy is structured deliberately to set them up for defeat. This is obvious to them when the BIA is not responding to critical social concerns such as high crime rates and rampant alcoholism and diabetes, which they equate with non-Indian ways of life. As one elder put it, "Not only is the government trying to overtly destroy us by keeping us fragmented, it's sitting back and letting us—maybe hoping that we will—self-destruct by adopting non-Indian ways. It's up to us to get back on the Red Road." This could not say more about the fact that Indian peoples recognize their survival depends on their own initiative.

Since justice constitutes a world of meaning and action, so must the implementation and execution of this newly imposed legal system. Today, tribal courts are charged with upholding both justice and laws. "In a developing tribal court jurisprudence, attention to such issues is especially critical, lest tribal courts inadvertently reproduce the distortions that permeate majoritarian courts and their jurisprudence" (Pommersheim 1992: 436). It may be too much to ask them to do this, in the light of the fundamental differences existing between the two "laws."

Officials in tribal justice systems must account for a unique history and culture, as well as the needs of individual clients. Success of Indian-conceived justice systems in Indian Country requires that a unique "jurisprudence of place" be combined within the context of constitutional and international law. This need stems from the context of Indian Country and the status of sovereignty.

SUMMARY

Tribal court jurisprudence today is going through a process of significant change. In an attempt to reflect and uphold indigenous tribal integrity, court officials and justice system planners are faced with blending innovative concepts of justice with constitutional and international law. The enduring challenge for tribal courts is their role in helping to define and establish a permanent tribal sovereignty against the backdrop of a non-sympathetic and ignorant non-Indian justice system. They quickly are becoming significant tribal institutions and as such they must work to realize the goal of sovereignty and, therefore, the achievement of justice within the broad realm of Indian-U.S. relations. The need is to develop a true tribal jurisprudence of "place" committed to upholding traditional concepts of justice.

Despite enormous obstacles of rural isolation, poverty, elevated crime rates, and conflicting definitions of sovereignty and court jurisdiction, Indian justice systems continue to reflect the fact that Indian peoples have not been passive victims—history has not just happened *to* them. Instead, Indian peoples have continued to act with constructive intentionality. In this, tribal courts play a key role in maintaining tribal identities and resisting the ongoing forces of assimilation. However, to achieve a satisfactory blend of both judicial systems, there is a need for Indians and non-Indians alike to be aware of the real issues—the conflicting aims of the two systems, and the differing structures and dynamic characteristics of each.

REFERENCES

Bransky, J. J. "Tribal Court Jurisdiction," *Michigan Bar Journal*, May 1988: 370-376.

Deloria, V., Jr. *Custer Died for Your Sins*. Norman, OK: University of Oklahoma Press, 1988.

Indian Child Welfare Act. U.S. Code, Title 25, 92 Stat. 3069, PL-90-608 2[4]; 1978.

Indian Civil Rights Act. 25 U.S.C. 461, 82 Stat. 73, Title II—Rights of Indians; Civil Rights Act, PL-90-284; 1968.

Major Crimes Act. 18 U.S.C. 1151, 1153, 3242.

Nelson, R. A., and J. F. Sheley. "Bureau of Indian Affairs Influence on Indian Self-Determination," in V. Deloria, Jr., ed., *American Indian Policy in the Twentieth Century.* Norman, OK: University of Oklahoma Press, 1985: 177-196.

Peak, K. "Criminal Justice, Law, and Policy in Indian Country: A Historical Perspective," *Journal of Criminal Justice*, 17, 1989: 393-407.

Petoskey, M. "Tribal Courts," *Michigan Bar Journal*, May 1988: 366-369.

Pflüg, M. A. "'Breaking Bread': Metaphor and Ritual in Odawa Religious Practice," *Religion,* 22, 1992(a): 247-258.

_____. "Politics of Great Lakes Indian Religion," *Michigan Historical Review*, December 1992(b): 15-32.

_____. "'The Last Stand?': Odawa Revitalizationists v. U.S. Law," in D. Westerlund, ed., *Questioning the Secular State.* London: Charles Hurst, Publishers, Ltd. and New York: St. Martin's Press, 1995.

_____. *Reclaiming a Sovereign Place: Myth and Ritual in Odawa Revitalization.* In progress.

Pommersheim, F. "Liberation, Dreams, and Hard Work: An Essay on Tribal Court Jurisprudence," *Wisconsin Law Review,* 1992: 411-457.

Sutton, I. "Preface to Indian Country: Geography and Law," *American Indian Culture and Research Journal*, 15, No. 2, 1991: 3-35.

CASES CITED

Cherokee Nation v. *State of Georgia*, 30 U.S. (5 Pet.) 1 (1831).

Decoteau v. *District County Court*, 420 U.S. 425, 427 n.2 (1975).

Ex Parte Crow Dog, 109 U.S. 556 (1883).

Kagama v. *United States*, 118 U.S. 375 (1886).

Lone Wolf v. *Hitchcock*, 187 U.S. 553, 565 (1903).

Moe v. *Confederated Salish and Kootenai Tribes*, 425 U.S. 463, 478-79 (1976).

Oliphant v. *Suquamish Tribe*, 435 U.S. 191 (1978).

Worcester v. *Georgia*, 31 U.S. (6 Pet.) 515, 556 (1832).

CHAPTER 12

Right-Wing Extremism and
the Problem of Rural Unrest

by *Robert A. Wood*

INTRODUCTION

The purpose of this chapter is to describe the activities of right-wing extremists and their role in the unrest that characterizes much of rural America today. In addition to providing an account of the conditions that exist, this work also seeks to detail the constraints and challenges that the activities of these groups present to law enforcement and to others.

There are many different forms of extreme right-wing organizations in the United States today, and categorizations or typologies vary to a great degree (see White 1991). A further complication is that each group has its own particular agenda and motivations. Despite their many differences, there are some ideological themes that are shared (Gurr 1988). Politically, there are a wide range of notions common to the extreme Right, among them embracing white supremacist and Neo-Nazi ideals cloaked in the jargon of patriotism and religion. Loosely knit, with neither a national organization nor single leader, many are paramilitary survivalists who argue that the federal reserve system and income tax are unlawful, that state and federal officials exceed their authority, and that only the county level of government may rightfully pass and enforce laws. Most view themselves as defenders against a conspiracy by Jews, minorities, lawyers and governmental officials—especially federal judges and the IRS—to destroy the Constitution, the United States and Christianity.

CHRISTIAN IDENTITY

The other major area that provides a common dimension among many of these groups is religious fundamentalism under the auspices of the Christian Identity Movement. As in their approach to politics, the extreme Right neither embraces a unified body of religious theory nor is there total agreement among all Identity adherents. Although, inherently, its doctrine is racist and anti-Semitic, not all believers in Identity are connected to the violent activities of the far Right. However, for years, many in the Identity Movement have had ties to extremist elements. Consequently, there are several basic themes and assumptions that commonly are found in the writings and other pronouncements of Identity theology and right-wing organizations:

1) Anglo-Saxons are the true descendants of the Israelites of the Old Testament with whom God made his covenant, and they are His chosen people (most Christian theologians believe the descendants of the Israelites are Jews). They are the last true defenders of the faith and the United States is the true State of Israel, the last bastion against evil.

2) God's laws are absolute and the only ones that people are obligated to follow. Because His laws have been disregarded, the United States is on the brink of disaster and Armageddon is imminent. Loyalty is not owed to institutions that are corrupt and have lost favor with God. Man's laws especially are invalid because the United States government is controlled by Jews, a "Zionist Occupational Government" (ZOG). The news media and economic institutions also are directed by Jews.

3) Three types of people exist. Whites (God's chosen) are of a higher order than either Jews (the "Seed of Satan") or blacks. Since members of the last group have no souls, they are sub-human and represent "false starts" before God perfected whites. They also are manipulated by Jews against the Aryans.

4) Because Jews are the children of the devil, they are responsible for all of the evil that has occurred throughout history and are the spiritual and moral enemies of white Christians. Armageddon is viewed as a military confrontation between God's chosen (the Aryan race) and the forces of Satan (Jews, blacks and other minority groups).

5) For white Christians, there are no practical distinctions among race, religion and nationality (Finch 1983; Barker 1986; Zeskind 1986a).

The most extreme version of Identity advocates that Jews should be exterminated to end the conflict with whites.

Although most Identity ministers refer to this proposal with slightly veiled references, one member of a group called The Order made plain at his trial in 1985 that he was taught Jews "...were the progeny of the devil and it was the responsibility of the white race to destroy the Jew" (King September 1985: 7). While it has been estimated that less than 50% of those linked to Identity support the sometimes overt rhetoric of white supremacy about racism and violence, it permeates the basic teachings of the movement.

The beliefs of Identity are of great importance in understanding the actions of the far Right. It has been argued that the framework of extremist organizations usually are identified with one or more of the following: Christian conservatism, racial purity, or political conservatism. Many of the assertions made by the latter two areas are directly related to the theoretical justifications provided by Christian conservatism as detailed by Identity churches. Although all groups of the extreme Right do not adhere to Identity's biblical teachings, groups who support views of radical or political extremism share similarities with the positions advocated by many Identity ministries (Barker 1986).

As a result an important philosophical rationale for the social, economic and political theories of the Right is provided, whether one is advocating a race war that would "deliver our people from the Jews and achieve total victory for the Aryan race" or objecting to the exercise of any governmental influence and power in general. One student of the far Right has stated that:

> Identity's implications are broad. It provides answers to political, moral, military and racial issues. It careens from religion to politics to cosmology, teaching virtually every subject of interest to the radical Right as it goes...[providing] an explanation and a villain for virtually every social ill.
> —Finch 1983: 75

One of the most important considerations is Identity's potential as a unifying force. By sharing the common bond of religion, groups of the Right that are not galvanized in terms of their political positions are presented with a cohesive racial, religious and national identification. Put another way, Identity merges two factions of the far Right that, traditionally, have been at odds with each other; those who stress race, and those who emphasize religious bigotry (Weinberg 1987). Various independent factions of the Ku Klux Klan are provided with a common purpose, and groups associated with the Posse Comitatus, which has no national leader or organization, have the opportunity to forge meaningful ties. James Coates has discussed the fact that before the adoption of Identity by the extreme Right, many observers noted a "circular firing squad" mentality whenever like-minded groups attempted to unify. Each faction was so preoccupied with its own agenda that it was unwilling to cooperate with others (1987).

To a real degree, then, the Identity Movement has provided a foundation for a loose alliance among different organizations throughout rural America. A good example of this trend is the efforts of the Aryan Nations, a Neo-Nazi group that has been described as an "umbrella" organization affiliated with, and supporting the activities and goals of, a number of diverse groups. Interrelationships among various organizations of the Right have included cross-memberships, joint paramilitary exercises, a sharing of arms and money acquired through illegal activities, and information disseminated through a computer network and various publications (Barker 1986). These linkages have grown to such an extent that in spring 1988, 14 leaders and members of various factions were tried by the federal government for seditious conspiracy, albeit unsuccessfully. Investigators have discovered, however, that "the tie that binds" these extremists is not so much organizational in nature as religious, based on the Christian Identity Movement.

This is not meant to imply that total agreement and harmony presently exists among these groups, or that it is likely to be achieved at any time soon, largely because of their opposition to any governmental authority beyond the county level. While this is an important impediment to establishing formal unification, an Idaho law enforcement officer who monitors the activities of the far Right has stated that:

> The Aryan Nations, as well as other right-wing groups have learned lessons from the radical Left's efforts in collaboration. Establishing effective, efficient, and ongoing linkages with other organizations is almost as productive in achieving goals as successfully forming a single, unified, organizational structure. The capacity to be able to draw upon manpower and physical resources from a broad based coalition to a directed purpose is in itself, a significant power position.
> —Barker 1986: 16-17

SOCIO-ECONOMIC CHARACTERISTICS

Drawing on data from a number of sources, Leonard Weinberg has emphasized the rural background of many of those who are associated with extremist hate groups (1987). The movement during the 1940s largely was an urban one with most organizations having their headquarters in the large cities of the midwest and northeast. By contrast, during the 1980s it was found that the leaders of the far Right had a distinctive rural or small-town southern origin. Among them were a surprisingly high proportion of small businessmen, lawyers, teachers and journalists. One of the most notorious and violent factions, The Order, was found to be mostly middle-aged, white protestant, blue-collar workers who were brought up in small towns or medium-size cities in the west.

In addition to the above, it is interesting to note the characteristics of the members of one of the biggest and enduring factions of the extreme Right, the Posse Comitatus. A "typical" member has been described as a white, gun-owning male who grew up in a rural area, still resides there, and who has had confrontations with authorities, possibly including charges for income tax evasion. Although likely a "minister" in a church to avoid paying taxes, usually he is a "deep and bedrock" fundamentalist Christian who rationalizes his actions as "following the Law of God." While having only a limited education, he might be well-read, especially in common law and U.S. history. The individual probably belongs to, or at least sympathizes with, other tax revolt or paramilitary organizations, and he tenaciously adheres to his beliefs regardless of the consequences. Last, he is likely to be a self-employed mechanic, farmer or repairman (Finch 1983; Yeager 1994). This is of special consequence because the Posse serves as a bellwether for gauging the popularity of the far Right for, unlike other Neo-Nazi organizations, its members are "...usually steady, hardworking, and a normal part of their communities. They have been usually radicalized by the deteriorating economic conditions in rural America" (Zeskind 1986b: 11).

Finally, research suggests that the rank-and-file membership of right-wing organizations and its leadership come from different socio-economic classes. While confirming the essence of the profile of the typical member described above, Jeffrey Handler concluded that leaders had higher incomes, white collar jobs and were better educated (1990).

MEMBERSHIP AND RECRUITMENT

Indications are that active membership in the more "traditional" sectors of the white supremacist movement have declined since the mid-1980s. In 1987, Suall estimated that 4,500 to 5,000 individuals belonged to the various factions of the Ku Klux Klan, a drop of 15% to 25% from 1983. Comparable decreases also were cited for other conventional Neo-Nazi organizations, attributable largely to in-fighting among the leadership and arrests that have been made by federal authorities. It also is important to note that as their numbers have decreased, these groups have become increasingly more violent in their activities (for example, see Yeager's 1994 discussion of the Posse Comitatus in this regard). Despite these trends, according to other sources, the number attracted to the extreme Right remained fairly constant during the 1980s at about 15,000 to 20,000 activists, plus some 150,000 sympathizers who attend rallies and meetings, and who buy literature or make financial contributions (Lutz and Zeskind 1987).

This apparent contradiction is explained by the fact that despite some setbacks of their own, the most successful segments of the white supremacist movement have been those associated with Identity theology that has been used as a method to enlist individuals into extremist groups. As the leader of the Aryan Nations, Richard Butler, has pointed out, "The Church is the outreach of faith. The Aryan Nations is the action arm" (King October 1985: 31). A private organization that studies the activities of right-wing groups has concluded that:

> Identity has also developed a series of distinct theological beliefs around areas of concern to large numbers of Christians. Organizers use these distinct beliefs as a recruiting tool among people whose initial interest in Identity is primarily religious. In this regard Identity is similar to other Bible-based religious cults. Identity plays a dual role—it provides religious unity for differing racist political groups and it brings religious people into contact with the racist movement.
>
> —Prairiefire, Inc. 1986: 63

Identity's "outreach of the faith" and propaganda associated with the far Right includes the dissemination of information to members and potential recruits through several sources. During the 1980s, a computer link, the "Aryan Liberty Net," included one file entitled "Know Your Enemy" and contained data on the Anti-Defamation League of the B'nai

B'rith, United States Communist Party and "race traitors and informers." Today internet news groups are regularly used by a number of factions to disseminate information. Sermons and teachings are broadcast over radio; for example, through the late Sheldon Emry's *America's Promise Radio Network* that claims a nationwide listening audience. Newsletters, booklets, pamphlets, newspapers and cassette tapes are distributed through the mail, as well as by other methods. A collector of right-wing literature who lives in the upper midwest found materials from the Aryan Nations and the "Crusade for Christ and Country" at truck stops in the south and northwest. Pieces authored by members of the Posse Comitatus were found on automobiles at shopping centers in North Dakota, and were being wholesaled out of a car at one Minnesota VFW. It also was discovered that some groups' publications share the same authors. *Behind Communism*, a booklet "documenting the Jewish origin and control of communism" was offered for sale from an America's Promise literature list based in Phoenix, Arizona and was available at a Posse Comitatus meeting in Fargo, North Dakota. A Christian Committee in Ohio offered some of the same materials found in the Posse Comitatus' *U.S. Citizen's Handbook for Justice*, although no mention was made of that organization.

Despite various estimates, the exact strength of the far Right is unknown because of its clandestine nature. At least part of this is attributable to the relative seclusion of rural areas. The Posse Comitatus has long been considered to be the largest single component of the far Right by those who monitor the activities of radical groups. In the Great Plains and midwest alone, estimates a decade ago placed the number of "hard core" extremists at 2,000 to 5,000 with approximately 7 to 10 times as many sympathizers (Levitas and Zeskind 1986). Part of the difficulty of arriving at credible estimates is that many who resist governmental authority deny any connection with radical groups in an attempt to avoid the scrutiny of law enforcement. As others also have noted (for example, see Zeskind 1986b), in many cases organizations function under cover names such as the "Educated Citizens of Iowa," "America First" (Wichita, Kansas), the "Patriots," or "Constitutionalists." More recently, it has been estimated that "patriot" and militia groups may number as many as 100,000 (Morganthau 1995).

TACTICS

Ted Gurr observes that while we are able to accurately provide a social-economic profile of right-wing extremists and the common themes associated with their political and religious beliefs, the actual behavior of individuals and groups differ dramatically (1988). He has provided a useful framework for analysis by identifying four distinct types of activities that characterize the far Right: those which are 1) legal; 2) of borderline legality; 3) non-violent but illegal practices; 4) violent.

Legal Activities

During the 1980s the serious decline of the economic and social base in rural areas, especially in those locales tied extensively to farming, produced widespread unrest and protest. Disruption of public hearings, farm foreclosures and court procedures have become commonplace since the middle of the decade. While such social awareness groups as Prairiefire, Inc., and the Center for Democratic Renewal have explained that the most visible and active organizations in rural America are affiliated with democratic and progressive ideals, they also have expressed serious concern over the propaganda efforts and political opportunism of the far Right. These activities are hardly novel:

> Throughout American history anti-Semitism and white supremacy have taken root in rural areas, where some populist politicians blamed farmers' problems on mythical Jewish bankers who were supposedly manipulating the economy to evil ends.
>
> —Bishop 1988: E5

One portion of this legacy has been the emergence of the so-called "Soft Posse" groups that frequently label themselves as "Christian Patriots" or "Constitutionalists."

Zeskind has described the movement as a "semi-anarchic collection of groups dedicated to a peculiar interpretation of the U.S. Constitution" (1987: 16). Although expressing a fundamental belief in "Christian" law and economics based on their own reading of the Bible, and subscribing to covert racism and anti-Semitism, most do not join the Ku Klux Klan, Aryan Nations and other Neo-Nazi groups in calling for violence against the federal government and minorities. Instead, many perceive them-selves as being legal experts and harass officials through the use of "paper bullets" in the form of quasi-legal strategies such as the filing of frivolous lawsuits against judges, IRS agents and other public figures. One example is a 50-page packet entitled "Republic Redress v. Democracy," which comes complete with sample legal documents for those wishing to encumber the legal system (Coates 1987). Unfortunately, those with extreme financial difficulties, especially farmers, have been most frequently solicited by groups that energetically marketed their products through the mail, newsletters and seminars.

Borderline Activities

Many white supremacists have expressed the belief that they are at war with the "Zionist" federal government. While "hate groups" like the Ku Klux Klan obviously have been a factor in American politics for decades, the advent of organizations acquainted with techniques associated with survivalism and guerilla warfare have been a relatively new area of concern for those in law enforcement. The result has been extensive paramilitary training that consists of comprehensive schooling in weapons and military tactics, as well as the stockpiling of weapons and ammunition. Many believers participate in these actions based on the premise that the total moral, economic and military collapse of the United States is near, and that preparation is needed for the second coming of Christ. These beliefs originate from a combination of the propensity for violence among those on the extreme Right, the teachings of Identity and the popularity of survivalism among many in rural America (Zeskind 1986a; Coates 1987).

Many paramilitary activities have taken, and continue to take, place in permanent compounds located in isolated rural areas. Hoffman has observed that the degree of the threat posed by right-wing extremist groups is documented by the far reaching geographical extent of their activities, the varied causes that they espouse and the similarities of the agendas that they promote (1989). For many years, the Covenant, Sword of the Arm of the Lord (C.S.A.) instructed many members of the far Right in survival training and other skills at its encampment on the Missouri-Arkansas border. In the mid-1980s, authorities raided the complex and arrested four members of The Order and C.S.A. leader James Ellison, who subsequently was convicted of racketeering charges and sentenced to 20 years in prison. Regular gatherings and other activities also have taken place at the Aryan Nations compound near Hayden Lake, Idaho. Other locations for paramilitary education during the decade of the 1980s were known to exist in West Virginia and

Oklahoma, and although they did not possess a permanent site, the now defunct White Patriot Party in North Carolina engaged in regular weapons training. Finally, the Christian Patriots Defense League (CPDL) included advice on weapons and tactics for years as part of their "Freedom Festivals" in rural Missouri and southern Illinois until anti-paramilitary legislation in Missouri outlawed the activities in 1985.

Today, paramilitary activities have become even more overt in many areas of the country. Although they are most visible in Michigan and Montana, it has been estimated that hundreds of citizen militias have formed in anywhere from 24 to 36 states for the purposes of practicing techniques associated with assault maneuvers, reconnaissance, ambushes and self-defense. The avowed purposes of these groups include general opposition to gun control, assisting law enforcement with civil emergencies and opposition to what is viewed as an abuse of power by the federal government. Two incidents, in particular, are cited by the militias as examples of where citizens need to be prepared to defend themselves: the 1992 siege and gun battle between federal authorities and Randy Weaver, a white separatist wanted on gun charges in Idaho, and the 1993 raid of David Koresh's Branch Davidian compound by Alcohol, Tobacco and Firearm agents at Waco, Texas.

An overall assessment of the activities of these groups is still in the formative stage. Most authorities believe that while these militias are not as dangerous as the ones formed by the Aryan Nations, Posse Comitatus and others in the 1980s, membership in the current militias is more widespread. Concerns that white supremacists are very active among the groups is also growing; for example, connections between a Montana militia and the Aryan Nations have been uncovered (McHugh 1994; New York Times Wire Story 1994; Schneider 1994; Fargo Forum 1995; USA Today 1995). At the time this chapter was finalized, it was not clear if those accused of the bombing of the Oklahoma City, Oklahoma federal building were connected to a militia. Whether or not such links are discovered, it is likely that law enforcement will more closely scrutinize these groups in the future.

Illegal, but Non-Violent Activities
Some of the more typical ploys used by this segment of the far Right involve endeavors to place common law liens against the property of government officials. The attempted use of common law eviction notices also are not unusual when property has been foreclosed. These tactics

have not been successful in terms of achieving substantive legal results but in many instances have proven to be a burden on those who must process them through the judicial system.

Two other examples illustrate the type of "Soft Posse" self-help tactics with which law enforcement officials have had to contend. First, in 1987, a Kansas activist was arrested in connection with a complicated loan scheme whereby "sight drafts," worthless vouchers made to look like bank drafts, were used to pay debts. Based on a non-existent entity called "Common Title Bond and Trust Company," it was thought that at the end of 1987 that over $300 million in worthless sight drafts were circulating in Canada, the Dakotas, Iowa, Kansas, Minnesota and Nebraska. In a second scheme, six tax protestors from Minnesota, South Dakota and Colorado were convicted for establishing "warehouse banks" to conceal the income of its members. It was estimated that the National Commodities and Barter Association exchanged up to $500,000 each day for its 20,000 participants to help them avoid taxes.

Violence

Several instances illustrate the activities of the extreme Right that have taken the form of violence. On February 13, 1983, for the first time in North Dakota's history, and for the first time nationwide since 1972, members of the United States Marshal's Service were killed in the line of duty. In retrospect, the shootings by Gordon Kahl and others at Medina, North Dakota are important because they signaled the rise of Right-Wing terrorism in the United States during the 1980s. As a result of the incident, the Posse Comitatus and other radical groups became the focus of national attention among both the law enforcement community and the public at large.

The search for Kahl, a survivalist and long-time resident of the region, illustrates the problem of tracking and apprehending a suspect in a sparsely populated countryside. As one of the marshals in charge of the investigation stated, "A person could traverse the whole state without ever driving on a blacktop, especially if he knew his way around" ("Officials" 1983: A12). For the federal agents and North Dakota's small force of officers covering the state, this required the implementation of tactics not typically employed by experts in conventional fugitive investigations. These included exhausting grid-type searches, the deployment of convoys over long distances and the cordoning off of small towns while they were searched. A toll-free number and the largest reward ever offered by the United States Marshal's Service also were established.

One official attributed a lack of substantive leads to a fear of reprisals but he was probably closer to the truth when he recognized the empathy that many residents had for Kahl. Some individuals did not agree with his actions but they shared his suspicion of the federal government and disdain for the income tax, while still others were more explicit in their support and believed that the killings were necessary. Even before his death in June 1983, in another shootout in Arkansas, Kahl's supporters sought to make him a martyr and folk hero with at least two ballads being written to sing his praises and rationalize his actions.

The events associated with Gordon Kahl have had important repercussions for extremists and law enforcement agencies alike. As a result of the widespread manhunt, the Justice Department began to detect links among organizations of the radical Right. Kahl had attended Aryan Nations functions, and it is clear that his activities were a precursor to the violence of the far Right that has become common in recent years. It should come as no surprise that Kahl often has been cited as a hero and martyr by extremists nationwide.

The reaction of law enforcement agencies throughout the United States to the shootings was swift. Within days, the Nebraska Highway Patrol stepped up its intelligence gathering activities of suspected Posse members, officials in Kansas recommended the purchase of semi-automatic weapons to meet a perceived threat, and Missouri legislators called for quick passage of a law designed to control paramilitary activities. The FBI and Bureau of Alcohol, Tobacco and Firearms began investigations in 26 states, one of which led to the conviction of a group in northwestern Minnesota in March 1983 for conspiring to commit at least four "kidnapping-hostage style" bank robberies. Information gained from their arrests directly led to an April 1985 raid of the National Commodity and Barter Association that operated a tax evasion/money laundering scheme in seven cities and five states, and was linked to the Posse Comitatus.

One of the most violent groups among the far Right has been The Order (also known as the *Bruderschweigen* [Silent Brotherhood] or White American Bastion), an offshoot of the Aryan Nations. On April 12, 1985, 23 members of the group were indicted for a series of spectacular crimes, most of which were committed in 1984: murder, attempted murder, armed robberies of banks and armored cars netting about $4 million (most of which has never been recovered), conspiracy, arson, counterfeiting, and bombings.

Not all members of The Order were believers in Identity theology but the activities and goals of the group were compatible with the beliefs of some who adhere to the religion. The Order's primary objectives were the financing of activities that would lead to the overthrow of the "Zionist Occupational Government" (United States government), and the prompting of an apocalyptic race war. At least in part, these activities were inspired by *The Turner Diaries*, a fantasy about a fascist revolution during the 1990s. In this instance, the teachings of Identity not only became a rationalization for a system of beliefs but also a call to action. By the middle of 1986, all members of The Order were believed to be either killed or imprisoned.

Violent acts among the far Right have continued since the demise of The Order, but are in a state of flux. Typically, "...periodic outbursts of concentrated violence are frequently followed by a dramatic decline in terrorist operations.... Thus there appears to be a cyclical pattern to terrorism in the United States" (Hoffman 1989: 5). This is due in large part to a vigorous, and for the most part successful, campaign by the federal government to imprison the members and leaders of the various Neo-Nazi groups. During the 1980s, over 150 white supremacists were prosecuted and more than 50 were incarcerated, including 38 members of The Order (Salholz and Miller 1988).

The most notable failure to obtain convictions occurred in February 1988 when 14 individuals linked to the far Right, including many of the most prominent advocates of violence, were found innocent of a number of charges after a seven-week trial in Fort Smith, Arkansas. The most serious allegations involved plotting the overthrow of the federal government, the establishment of a "Whites Only" homeland in the Pacific northwest, the attempted murder of federal officials, and the interstate transportation of stolen money. Among the defendants were members of the Aryan Nations, The Order, Ku Klux Klan, Posse Comitatus and C.S.A., many of whom already were serving time for previous crimes. Most of the accused also were adherents of Identity and included such leaders as Richard Butler, Robert Miles and Louis Beam. Indications are that members of the jury did not believe the government's chief witness, former C.S.A. leader James Ellison and accepted defense attorney contentions that he had made up the conspiracy charges in order to receive a reduction in the 20-year sentence he was serving for racketeering.

SUMMARY, FUTURE TRENDS AND PROSPECTS

While this failure represents a significant setback, there is no doubt that in the long run, the federal government's efforts have resulted in a weakening of the far Right's influence. However, these efforts have been far from conclusive and extremists are likely to remain a viable force in rural America for four major reasons. First, there is general agreement among those who monitor extremist groups that as they become more desperate they will also become increasingly militant. Hoffman has speculated that increased government prosecutions may actually lead to increased violence in retaliation (1989). During the year between the indictment and trial of the white supremacists, membership drives and organizational activities openly continued. Additionally, although attempts at broad-based recruitment have failed to this point, they also may experience a resurgence with changing circumstances, for example, a decline in the economy.

Second, in the past the extreme Right has demonstrated a capacity to adapt their tactics to ensure their survival. There are indications that this is taking place once more with many groups replacing overt violence with more elaborate propaganda campaigns and political organizing. This new approach is illustrated by Tom Metzger who became the focus of much of the white supremacist movement in the late 1980s, partially due to the legal difficulties of many of the far Right's other leaders. Head of the California-based White Aryan Resistance, Metzger has emphasized the use of technology and has produced 45 one-half hour programs entitled "Race and Reason" that have been broadcast over public access stations in 10 states (Center for Democratic Renewal January 1988).

Many different violent "Skinhead" factions also have emerged among working class, inner-city youth. Described as "militantly patriotic, xenophobic and racist," they have their origin in Great Britain where they were linked to Neo-Nazi groups (Hoffman 1989: 10). From 1985, they grew from an estimated 1,500 members in 12 states to approximately 3,500 in 40 states in the early 1990s (Connely and Freed 1994). Members have been arrested in a number of locales for assaults against minorities and for arson, robbery and narcotics charges. To many observers, the Skinheads represent a serious long-term threat because of their potential as a recruitment base for extremists, a need that has not been met in the past. Other factions of the Ku Klux Klan also have been increasingly active in their search for new members during the late 1980s with marches in Georgia, North Carolina, Maine and Ohio, reportedly meeting with substantial success.

Third, the radical Right remains a possible threat because of the very nature of the movement itself. Although many of the more violent segments of the Right have at least temporarily reduced their activities as a result of pressure from law enforcement, it is important to keep in mind an assessment made by the FBI concerning domestic terrorism in the 1980s:

> Terrorism is cyclic in nature. Activities occur because of certain issues; when the issues fade or the terrorists are arrested, the activities will generally subside. But different issues will arise and different terrorists will come forth to commit new acts. And so the cycle continues.
>
> —Harris 1987: 13

Last, based on an assessment of present economic indicators (see Chapter 13), the potential for future violence and continued unrest in rural America is great. The role of deteriorating economic conditions and the concomitant increase in extremist recruiting efforts among rural Americans has been well documented (Audsley 1985; Melnichak 1985; Levitas and Zeskind 1986; White 1991). This is an important consideration because, as previously mentioned, members enlisted into white supremacist groups are often normal, hardworking members of rural communities who have become radicalized by degenerating economic conditions. Events of the last decade have provided supporting evidence for Joseph Melnichak's proposition that "police units in America's 'heartland' are no longer immune to domestic terrorism," and have demonstrated that those in rural law enforcement must be as vigilant as their urban counterparts (1985: 17).

REFERENCES

Audsley, D. "Posse Comitatus: An Extremist Tax Protest Group," *TVI Journal*, 6, No. 1, 1985: 13-16.

Barker, W. E. "The Aryan Nations: A Linkage Profile." Unpublished manuscript, Kootenai County Idaho Sheriffs Office, 1986.

Bishop, K. "Fourteen on Trial: Judging the Danger on the Right Fringe," *The New York Times*, March 6, 1988: E5.

Center for Democratic Renewal. "Metzger Begins Move to the Top," *The Monitor*, 10, 1988: 5.

Coates, J. *Armed and Dangerous: The Rise of the Survivalist Right.* New York: Hill and Wang, 1987.

Connely, M., and H. Freed. "Breeding Hate," *Annual Editions, Criminal Justice 94/95*, 1994: 17-18.

Finch, P. *God, Guts, and Guns.* New York: Seaview/Putnam, 1983.

Gurr, T. "Political Terrorism in the United States: Historical Antecedents and Contemporary Trends," in M. Stohl, ed., *The Politics of Terrorism.* New York: Marcel Dekker, 1988.

Handler, J. "Socioeconomic Profile of an American Terrorist," *Terrorism*, 13, 1990: 195-213.

Harris, J. W., Jr. "Domestic Terrorism in the 1980s," *FBI Law Enforcement Bulletin*, 56, 1987: 5-13.

Hoffman, B. "Terrorism in the United States, Recent Trends and Future Prospects," *TVI Report*, 8, No. 3, 1989: 4-11.

"Hundreds of Militias in USA," *USA Today*, April 24, 1995: A4.

King, W. "Neo-Nazi Describes Assassination Plans," *The New York Times*, September 14, 1985: 7.

_____. "Racist Aryan Nations Groups Indicts New Disciples," *The New York Times*, October 20, 1985: 37.

Levitas D., and L. Zeskind. "Background Report: Racist and Anti-Semitic Organizational Intervention in the Farm Protest Movement," in *Rural Leadership Training Manual: Building Constructive Responses to the Radical Right*. Des Moines, IA: Prairiefire, Inc., and Atlanta: Center for Democratic Renewal, 1986: 15-36.

Lutz, C., and L. Zeskind. *They Don't All Wear Sheets: A Chronology of Racist and Far Right Violence: 1980-1986*. Atlanta: Center for Democratic Renewal, 1987.

McHugh, D. "They Cite Their Disgust with Government," *The Detroit Free Press*, October 13, 1994: 1A, 12A.

Melnichak, J. M. "Domestic Terrorism in America," *TVI Journal*, 6, No. 1, 1985: 17-19.

Morganthau, T. "The View from the Far Right," *Newsweek*, May 1, 1995: 36-39.

New York Times Wire Story. "Militias Stand Against Gun Control," *The Fargo Forum*, November 14, 1994: B7.

"Officials Believe Kahl Used Rural Harvey Hiding Place," *The Fargo Forum*, April 19, 1983: A12.

"Once in Shadows, Militias Now Armed and Furious," *The Fargo Forum*, April 24, 1995: A5.

Prairiefire, Inc., "Identity Christianity," in *Rural Leadership Training Manual: Building Constructive Responses to the Radical Right*. Des Moines, IA: Prairiefire, Inc., and Atlanta: Center for Democratic Renewal, 1986: 63-70.

Salholz, E., and M. Miller. "Curbing the Hatemongers," *Newsweek*, September 19, 1988: 29.

Schneider, K. "Apocalypse When?.... Fearing a Conspiracy, Some Heed a Call to Arms," *The Harbor Light Community Newsweekly*, November 30-December 6, 1994: 1, 3.

Suall, I. *The Hate Movement Today: A Chronicle of Violence and Disarray*. New York: Anti-Defamation League of B'nai B'rith Civil Rights Division, 1987.

Weinberg, L. "The Radical Right and Varieties of Right-Wing Politics in the United States." Unpublished manuscript, 1987.

White, J. *Terrorism: An Introduction*. Pacific Grove, CA: Brooks/Cole, 1991.

Yaeger, C. H. "Armageddon Tomorrow! The Posse Comitatus Prepares for the Future," *TVI Report*, 11, No. 2, 1994: 16-20.

Zeskind, L. *The "Christian Identity" Movement: A Theoretical Justification for Racist and Anti-Semitic Violence*. Atlanta: National Council of the Churches of Christ in the U.S.A., 1986a.

_____. "The Far Right," in *Rural Leadership Training Manual: Building Constructive Responses to the Radical Right*. Atlanta: Center for Democratic Renewal, 1986b: 7-14.

_____. "Back to Barbarism: Hate Group Activity," *Engage/Social Action*, 15, No. 6, 1987: 10-19.

PART VI

THE FUTURE OF RURAL CRIMINAL JUSTICE

This section contains one chapter, "Rural Criminal Justice: Current Themes and Future Directions," which is co-authored by the editors of this volume. First, we summarize the "Conditions, Constraints and Challenges" from the previous 12 chapters and highlight the perspectives of the contributors to the text. Six major themes are identified and discussed.

Second, a brief profile of socio-economic conditions in rural America is presented. The impact of the farm crisis of the 1980s and trends in the early part of the current decade are explored. This overview and other data provide an important context for the final portion of the chapter where predictions are made for the future of both crime and criminal justice agencies in rural areas. We suggest that some existing patterns are likely to continue, while others may change.

CHAPTER 13

Rural Criminal Justice:
Current Themes and Future Directions

by *Robert A. Wood, Thomas D. McDonald,* and *Melissa A. Pflüg*

INTRODUCTION

This chapter has three major purposes. First, we provide a summary of the "Conditions, Constraints and Challenges" that have been the focus of the previous selections in this text. One major theme is that the economic, social and political settings of rural America shape the conditions that produce constraints and challenges for the criminal justice system. We begin with a review of the state of crime in the rural setting, then move to a discussion of the factors that impact criminal justice agencies in the rural context.

Second, we present a brief socio-economic portrait of rural America. This is necessary to place our observations about what might happen in years to come into proper perspective. The major idea that emerges in this section is that the term "rural" is both complex and diverse.

Third, based on the selections in this volume and on the research of others, we offer our views of the direction that rural crime and criminal justice may follow in the future. A central contention of this section is that those environmental conditions that currently have a negative impact seem likely to intensify.

CONDITIONS, CONSTRAINTS AND CHALLENGES

Crime and Violence

Although the major emphasis of the contributions found throughout this work was on criminal justice agencies and related phenomena, three authors focused on the nature of crime in rural locales. Kevin M. Thompson (Chapter 1) and Nanci Koser Wilson (Chapter 9) provided an overview of current conditions by reviewing available data concerning types of offenses and frequency of crime. Robert A. Wood (Chapter 12) discussed crime, violence and other activities of extremist groups in rural America.

Thompson's analysis in "The Nature and Scope of Rural Crime" found that over time, urban arrest rates were approximately three times greater than those in rural locales. The gap between the two settings widens somewhat when the focus is on violent crime, while burglary rates account for a greater proportion of all crime in rural areas as compared to the total volume of offenses in urban centers. Differences in the ratio of arrest rates for violations of public order, such as curfew offenses and prostitution, are fairly large (with a greater frequency in urban settings), while the distance narrows when one considers data for more serious crimes such as homicide and rape. Last, juveniles were found to be proportionally under-represented in rural statistics.

In Wilson's piece, "The Industrialization of Wilderness: Women, Crime and Rurality," the author specifically explored data relating to gender as well as making rural-urban comparisons. She concluded that rural crime rates generally are lower than in urban locales, women commit fewer crimes than men and women who reside in rural areas have lower rates when compared to anyone else. Women tend to be arrested for income-producing crimes, their victims are more frequently men and they are less likely to be violent.

While not utilizing a specific crime data base, "Right-Wing Extremism and the Problem of Rural Unrest" by Wood provided an overview of the operations of radical organizations in rural areas. Although individuals in these groups share a common core of beliefs, and we can profile their socio-economic characteristics, they engage in a wide range of behaviors. These activities as a whole present important challenges to rural and small-town law enforcement.

The Criminal Justice System

The remaining nine pieces in the text reviewed the administration of justice within the framework of the rural setting. Chapter 2, "Some Economic Realities of Rural Criminal Justice," by Thomas D. McDonald, presented a general discussion of economic conditions, constraints and challenges. Other selections focused on an analysis of the operation of law enforcement (Chapters 3 and 4); rural courts, including juvenile and Indian justice systems (Chapters 5, 6, 10 and 11); and corrections (Chapters 7 and 8). The purpose here is to discuss the ideas that were common to many of these works. Although these topics are treated separately, the elements discussed are interrelated and as a result influence one another. Also, each of these factors has important consequences for the administration of justice. The following six themes are discussed:

1) descriptions and definitions of rurality vary;
2) comparisons of rural and urban criminal justice agencies reveal both similarities and differences;
3) agencies are part of the community in which they operate and are influenced by their environment;
4) rural criminal justice is less bureaucratic and formal than its urban counterpart;
5) most actors in rural agencies perform multiple roles;
6) many rural areas lack adequate resources, which directly affects personnel, services and facilities.

A striking aspect of the literature on rural criminal justice is that there is a great deal of diversity concerning the meaning of what is "rural." As noted in our introduction to this text and elsewhere in the reader, the idea of rurality does not imply homogeneity any more than in the case of urban centers. Consequently, our contributors viewed and defined the notion in many different ways.

Both Victor H. Sims in "The Structural Components of Rural Law Enforcement: Roles and Organizations," and Herman Wood and Sanford Schwartz in "Structure of Rural Corrections" suggested that concepts of "rural" and "urban" are not always dichotomous but are more appropriately viewed as a continuum; in some areas the distinctions become blurred. For instance, rural enclaves may be surrounded by urban settings, while in other situations there is a convergence or overlapping of the two areas as large cities expand. As a result, mutual interdependence takes place and the character of relevant institutions in both may be affected.

In other cases, rural settings are characterized by geographical isolation. Law enforcement may find that some areas are hard to patrol because of great distances, courts may have a difficult time functioning as planned and the processes associated with corrections may be made more difficult. Additionally, those who engage in illegal activities, such as extremist groups, may be afforded more secrecy.

At times even our contributors who wrote on the same general topic did not agree on what exactly constituted "rurality." For example, in "Structures and Roles of Rural Courts," Anne M. Bartol utilized a definition from the literature that characterized rural courts as having fewer than *two* full-time general jurisdiction judges, and as being most commonly located in counties with populations below 60,000. Carroll Edmondson, on the other hand, in "Rural Courts, the Rural Community and the Challenge of Change," viewed rural courts as any limited or general jurisdiction trial court with no more than *three* full-time judges in locales of less than 60,000.

On another dimension, virtually every work in this volume contained relative comparisons between rural and urban data and/or procedures. A common theme to these selections was that the rural setting possessed some commonalities with the urban environment, yet the former had characteristics that make it unique. For example, in "Stress in Small-Town and Rural Law Enforcement," Curt R. Bartol contended that while police in both types of environments experience stress related to the performance of their duties, much of the existing literature makes the mistake of assuming that the same factors for each context are relevant.

Other conditions that exist also have important consequences for the administration of justice in rural agencies. McDonald (Chapter 2) emphasized that the setting within which law enforcement and courts operate has major impacts. A central theme of Edmondson's piece (Chapter 6) was how rural society has molded conditions that directly shape constraints and challenges for rural courts. Other works in this book echoed these sentiments in their own particular areas of concern and have noted different influences of the larger environment. For instance, Melissa A. Pflüg detailed how "American Indian Justice Systems and Tribal Courts in Rural 'Indian Country'" have been shaped and constrained by federal legislation. The result has been the development of a unique structure and jurisdiction.

Another major theme that appeared in a number of pieces emphasized that when compared to urban centers, rural criminal justice agencies are less bureaucratic and deal with cases on a more informal basis. The idea of operating on the basis of "comity," a sense of accommodation, politeness and courtesy, as opposed to adversariness, was analyzed in many of the selections. This process has important consequences for how defendants are treated. For example, Randall R. Beger in "Rural Juvenile Courts: A Structural Assessment" described the processing of cases on the basis of close personal relationships and verbal agreements, as opposed to strict adherence to written rules. Among other factors, he discussed the difficulty that arises when evaluating some programs associated with juvenile justice, such as the benefits of diversion programs for youth (if they exist).

Two other illustrations of the real life impact of the informality that pervades rural criminal justice agencies also are instructive. Edmondson (Chapter 6) described how comity may weaken constitutional due process protections, encourage delay in the disposition of cases and treat strangers to the community unfairly. He noted that this expectation of accommodation also operates in urban courts but the underlying forces fundamentally are different. This reinforces a point made earlier in this section; rural and urban agencies may appear to operate in a similar fashion but the particular factors that drive these procedures may not be the same. Wood and Schwartz (Chapter 8) also explained how this more personal style of decision-making can impact such decisions as pre-trial release and sentencing. In some cases, key decision-makers have personal connections not only with the accused but also their families.

The notion that actors within the system in rural areas frequently are generalists who must play multiple roles was also a very common topic. This is true of police in the small-town setting who must wear many different "hats," including that of a social worker (Sims, Chapter 3), and of the country sheriff who functions in the capacity of a law enforcer, jail supervisor, politician and administrator (McDonald, Chapter 2). Further, judges routinely may perform duties associated with adjudicators, counselors and probation officers. In small jails, one employee may be responsible for cleaning up, dispatching, providing transportation for offenders and booking suspects. When speaking of these duties of the "corrections generalist," Wood and Schwartz (Chapter 8) use the phrase "jack-of-all-trades;" this concept applies equally to many others in the system.

Last, the theme of a lack of resources was pervasive in our contributors' selections. This condition, in particular, presents many challenges. All stages of the system (law enforcement, courts and corrections) are constrained when they attempt to hire, educate and retain qualified personnel. In relation to small-town and rural police, low salaries lead to problems in developing and fostering leadership skills (Sims, Chapter 3). Our four pieces that included information on rural courts (A. Bartol, Chapter 5; Edmondson, Chapter 6; Beger, Chapter 10;

Pflüg, Chapter 11) all have noted that a lack of adequate finances may lead to the hiring of lay (non-lawyer) and/or part-time judges who in many cases pursue other outside interests or careers that may have priority. Prosecuting attorneys also are often part-time employees. Funding frequently does not sufficiently exist to staff municipal and county jails. Several selections also have discussed how budgetary conditions limit the pool of qualified candidates from whom agencies can choose.

Budgetary considerations have other important consequences; auxiliary or peripheral services also suffer and typically were characterized as inadequate. For instance, small-town police departments lack the necessary means to hire full-time psychologists to counsel officers on stress (C. Bartol, Chapter 4). All six contributors who authored selections on rural courts and corrections highlighted a lack of diversion, counseling, rehabilitation, child care and other support programs for offenders and their families.

Another problem stemming from the lack of available funds that was identified is the existence of substandard physical facilities. This has not been so much of a concern for most rural and small-town law enforcement agencies as it has been for some rural courts; the problem is most acute for rural correctional facilities. In her piece on "County and Municipal Jails," Lois A. Guyon described life and conditions in these facilities from both a historical and modern perspective. One of her key arguments was that over time there has been relatively little change. Wood and Schwartz (Chapter 8) also discussed the physical plants of these organizations.

RURAL AMERICA: A SOCIO-ECONOMIC PROFILE

One of the key themes noted throughout much of this volume has been that like all organizations, those agencies related to criminal justice are part of the general communities in which they operate and are shaped to a degree by external forces. These influences themselves are complex and intertwined. It is our belief that one of the most important features that will impact the future of rural criminal justice will be the status of rural economic conditions. These, of course, are related to social and political considerations. To understand fully the basis on which we explore future possibilities, it is necessary to briefly review historical and current circumstances concerning the vitality of rural America.

During the 1970s, many rural areas were prosperous and had a high rate of economic growth. This was in sharp contrast to the next decade, when many regions outside metropolitan locations experienced an economic crisis unequaled since the great economic depression of the 1930s, prompted in large part by problems related to agriculture. The statistics and trends associated with the farm crisis make for melancholy reading at best. Land values, export markets and overall demand for agricultural goods declined during the 1980s, while debt climbed dramatically. Records for farm foreclosures that have stood for 50 years were broken, and while 21% of the nation's farmers were classified as suffering from "severe financial stress" the figure climbed to one-third in the midwest and Great Plains (Murdock and Leistritz 1988). Between 1980 and 1988, the government estimated that 274,000 farms went out of business and the number of individuals engaged in agriculture declined by one-sixth during that period (Cohen 1988). Equally important was the impact that these trends have had on other segments of rural America. Failing businesses led to declining employment, tax revenue and capital for investment. These factors contributed to a reduced population in many rural areas, a phenomenon that had many important consequences. Among these were the exodus of many well-educated and civic-minded citizens, which in turn hindered the development of innovative solutions to economic dilemmas (Murdock and Leistritz 1988). Rural constituencies also lost political influence after the 1990 census when congressional and legislative redistricting occurred. The resulting impact not only was a loss of members in the House of Representatives on the national level but also fewer rural representatives in states like North Dakota, which for the first time became dominated by urban sites as defined by the Census Bureau.

Related social problems also were extensive. Problems such as stress, suicide, depression, substance abuse, domestic strife and violent crimes all rose dramatically in rural areas. Rural poverty increased by one-third between 1978 and 1986, and in the late 1980s it was estimated that 10% to 20% of America's homeless were in rural locales (Cohen 1988). A reduction in the ability of government and social service agencies to deal adequately with these problems left a relatively large number of individuals with permanent social and psychological difficulties (Murdock and Leistritz 1988).

The United States Department of Agriculture has provided us with a longitudinal, and somewhat more optimistic, profile of conditions in rural

America (USDA 1995). Compared to relative historical trends, there have been many changes that have had a beneficial impact. For example, improvements have taken place in electrical, telephone and highway systems. Home ownership has increased, as has the quality of those dwellings. High school graduation rates also now approximate those in urban centers.

As of 1992, only 7.2% of those employed in rural locales were engaged in farming compared with 14.4% in 1969. Today, two-thirds of rural workers are in the service industry (recreation, resorts, finances, real estate, etc.) and manufacturing. As a whole, the 1980s have been followed by a slow, although uneven, economic recovery.

The USDA also has noted that underlying these generalities are a great deal of diversity, with rural life varying greatly from one region to the next. They concluded that:

> Some rural areas simply have not enjoyed many of the benefits of progress over the last 50 years. They have largely been left behind, still struggling with poverty, unemployment, inadequate infrastructure, and a lack of viable opportunities. Others, that have seen improvements, lack the resources and skills necessary to compete in the future economic environment. These, if they remain unprepared, will be left behind.
>
> —1995: 9

Leistritz and Hamm have provided an overview of the economic difficulties found in portions of rural America (1994). While noting that the last decade has been one of economic restructuring for the United States, generally, conditions in non-urban areas have been especially difficult. A major reason has been that although we can emphasize the diversity that is present among rural regions, each area tends to rely on only one or a few basic industries. Change in just one of these key sectors leads to the possibility of vulnerability. As a whole, the general pattern is one of disadvantage when compared to urban areas (USDA 1995).

These conditions have had several major consequences for many rural locations. Among these is an increasing gap for key indicators concerning income compared to urban centers. In a comparison of metropolitan and non-metropolitan statistics, the USDA highlighted persistent and widening discrepancies between per capita earnings (1995).

Leistritz and Hamm also emphasized this point when they observed that since the end of the 1970s, per capita income in rural counties declined relative to urban sites and by the early 1990s was only about 75% of their counterparts (1994). It is important to understand that this overall pattern of urban advantage exists despite the predominant type of economic activity found in rural counties, although areas mainly dependent on tourists and retirees have suffered smaller losses.

Another aspect of these declining economic conditions is the existence of persistent rural poverty. From 1970 to 1990, rural poverty rates actually declined in non-metropolitan areas overall, and also in relative terms when compared to urban areas. In 1970, the ratios were 1.37 to 1 of rural to urban poor respectively; 1.09 to 1 in 1980; and virtually 1 to 1 in 1990 (personal communication, North Dakota Census Data Center). For a number of rural counties, however, poverty continues to be a chronic problem.

As with poverty, descriptions associated with rural population trends are mixed. The 1970s saw a period of economic growth that was greater than for both suburban and urban locations. This halted years of outward migration but this success abruptly ended with the farm crisis and recessions of the 1980s. By the close of the decade, rural areas saw a net loss of a half-million people each year. The period from 1990 to the present has been more varied. Some areas that serve as "retirement destinations" and recreation areas have grown in population, while farming counties continue to decline, although at a slower rate than in the past (Leistritz and Hamm 1994; USDA 1995).

We have presented a socio-economic portrait that has emphasized change, variability and complexity (USDA 1995). A wide range of conditions exists, and each locale may face a unique set of constraints and challenges. Overall, much of rural America is facing difficulties that are related to community decline precipitated by economic difficulties (Leistritz and Hamm 1994), and in some instances extreme poverty. The themes and overview presented above become important ingredients in our predictions for the future directions of both crime and the criminal justice system.

FUTURE TRENDS AND PROSPECTS

A central theme of Bennett's book on the future of crime in America was that the social conditions that then existed were not static but would be subject to the forces of change (1987). She coined the term "crimewarps" to describe a complex set of elements that would lead to the alteration or displacement of existing patterns. Here we will describe what we perceive to be potential directions for both rural crime and criminal justice.

At the outset, we must emphasize that our conclusions are suggestive, and as such, cannot be viewed as inevitable forecasts. Wardlaw has made the point that "futurology" is an uncertain and hazardous business, and he noted that a variety of authors have warned that detailed speculation almost never is accurate (1989). Further, he noted that there is the potential that when security personnel make predictions, there is the risk that they will make mistakes in one of two basic directions. First, individuals may fail to identify changes in existing conditions that ultimately occur; second, and more likely, there may be too much pessimism about the future. He also wrote that those who consider violence, in particular, may give less weight to data that point to a more positive outcome because they are less intriguing. Although we are not security personnel, we recognize the importance of Wardlaw's observations.

The last qualification is that no one set of predictions may apply equally to all rural settings. As discussed in the previous sections of this chapter, a great deal of diversity exists concerning socio-economic conditions and opportunities in "rural" America, and there is even substantial disagreement over what exactly constitutes "rurality."

To explain possibilities for the future we will return to some of the major themes that we described earlier as "Conditions, Constraints and Challenges." At points, we rely on predictions made by our contributors, and at times we incorporate information from other sources. As in the first section of this chapter, we begin with an overview of various aspects of crime and then move to a discussion of rural criminal justice agencies.

Crime and Violence

As measured by arrest rates, it is clear that rural crime has not steadily increased over the past two decades. During this time period, rural crime actually peaked in 1980, reached an almost 10-year-low in 1984, and then began to increase once more, although by no means in a straight, upward trajectory (see Figure 1, Thompson, Chapter 1). We have reason to believe that this general erratic pattern will continue. A related issue is whether rural-urban rates are drawing closer together. This does not seem to be the case, with most studies concluding that the relative differences between the two have remained fairly constant over time (see, for example, Thompson, Chapter 1; Weisheit et al. 1994).

We must note, however, that the relationship between rural and urban rates undoubtedly will continue to vary based on the actual type of crime involved. For example, violent crime may continue to be disproportionately overrepresented in urban centers and crimes against property proportionately higher in rural locales.

Further, it has long been recognized that economic considerations are crucial variables in predicting increased rates of crime (see Bennett 1987; Weisheit et al. 1994), especially those related to theft and violence. For example, low incomes, unemployment and poverty with their related difficulties are key variables. In those rural communities where these conditions persist, for example in the south and elsewhere, we can reasonably speculate that rates of crime may remain the same, or even intensify, if conditions do not improve.

The work of Nanci Koser Wilson (Chapter 9) indicated that another specific category in which crime is likely to increase is among women. Except for sexually related crime (such as prostitution), recent trends suggest that overall arrest rates for rural women are increasing and are beginning to converge with those of women in urban America. At the same time, the types of offenses for which rural women are arrested do not appear to be changing. Wilson predicted that sexual crimes by women are not likely to increase but to the extent that women become impoverished and head households, they are likely to commit income-producing crimes, such as theft. She also made this observation for urban women.

An additional perspective that exists is that a comparison between rural and urban crime rates is not so meaningful as changes in longitudinal patterns. It has been suggested by Fischer that a "spillover" effect takes place and urban rates (either up or down) and forms of urban crime set the tone for rural areas (1980). Bennett has labelled this geographical movement as the "march" or urbanization of rural crime (1987). This is one possible explanation as to why the gap between urban and rural rates (as reported by the FBI's Uniform Crime Index) has remained fairly constant over time. Additional support for this thesis is found in the recent spread of urban gangs and drugs to less populated areas. It is logical that crime could disperse more easily to rural settings in those locations where the two areas are merging with one another as a result of urban growth (Thompson, Chapter 1). To the degree that these patterns continue to exist, we may predict with confidence that major cities will act as an "early warning system" for rural crime.

As noted in the introduction to Part V of this text, there are several issues that Weisheit et al. identify as special or emerging concerns that may be of developing importance to rural law enforcement (1994). These are: gangs, substance abuse, vice and organized crime, violence, hate crimes, arson, and activities involving agriculture and wildlife. While these authors urged that their findings in this area be interpreted with care because much information came from the popular press (sometimes based on anecdotal evidence), they also expressed the belief that these areas deserve further attention by researchers.

Finally, we believe that the behaviors associated with right-wing extremists (some participating in hate crimes) will continue to persist. Based on the past, it is more likely than not that their activities will be cyclical (ebb and flow), and that they will continue to provide challenges to law enforcement because they have proved their capacity to adopt tactics to changing conditions. They previously have established themselves and recruited new members where economic conditions have been poor, such as in the south and midwest during the 1980s. As discussed in this chapter, it is quite possible that poverty will persist in some rural locations. We would expect these areas to remain fertile focal points for the efforts of these groups.

The Criminal Justice System

In the first major section of this chapter, we reviewed a number of themes related to the "Conditions, Constraints and Challenges" for criminal justice agencies. Two major points that were made need to be re-emphasized. First, several of these factors are interrelated and have an impact on one another. Second, individually and as a group, these considerations have important consequences for how defendants are apprehended and processed by the system. As they relate to our current overview of possible trends and prospects, the interplay between these observations will become even more evident.

At this point, we return to a central theme: criminal justice agencies are affected not only by internal procedures but also by the environment in which they operate. Based on this premise, we can reach several conclusions and make general predictions for both continuity and change.

Previously, we noted that one contention by many of our contributors was that rural criminal justice is less bureaucratic and formal than its urban counterpart. In part, this is a reflection of the informality that characterizes much of rural life. An aspect of this general approach has been described as "comity," or a method of accommodation among various actors in the system instead of adversariness (see A. Bartol, Chapter 5 and Edmondson, Chapter 6). Because of its close tie to rural culture, comity is likely to remain unaltered and continue to have a major impact on the way defendants are treated by the system. Edmondson (Chapter 6) concluded that a restructuring of rural courts in some areas under a unified court model largely left this process unaffected, despite formal organizational change.

In our previous sections, we also discussed how many practitioners in rural agencies are expected to play multiple roles, and how much of the system lacks adequate resources that directly affect personnel, facilities and peripheral services. There are several indicators that suggest the likelihood that in the long term these trends will continue and even possibly intensify.

We already have suggested that where economic conditions such as poverty are present, there is a chance that crime will increase, including a rise in offenses against property and persons. Economic difficulties in a community also can logically be expected to have an impact on the resources that are made available to rural criminal justice agencies. Others, such as Weisheit et al., have made similar observations (1994). Assuming that there will be more demand in the event crime increases, there also might be fewer resources with which to respond. As a whole, we believe that criminal justice agencies will be called on to perform at the same level, or higher, with less assets in the future. This conclusion largely is based on our review of socio-economic factors previously discussed in this chapter, and on what we believe is a likely scenario for the near term.

The current political climate points to an era of declining federal assistance to both rural and urban communities as efforts focus on cutting federal spending to reduce the deficit or decrease taxes. If this occurs, local and state governments will be expected to share more of the burden for programs related to criminal justice. Either they may choose to raise taxes to replace a loss of federal revenue or cut existing budgets. While some may opt for the former, others undoubtedly will follow the last course of action, especially to the degree that the pressure for "less government" affects politicians and government at those levels. Decreasing populations and the resulting decline in an adequate tax base in many communities already have complicated the problem of adequately funding many rural criminal justice agencies and related social services. In still other cases, governmental officials and/or politicians have given priority to other needs outside of the criminal justice system.

Presently, the focus of public attention has been on the apprehension of offenders by the police, followed by the sentencing decisions of the courts and finally the processes associated with corrections. If these trends continue, as we assume they will, the facilities and needs of law enforcement will continue to be the best funded of the rural agencies and corrections the least.

In this environment of reduced resources, rural America will continue to compete with urban centers. To the extent that the past is an accurate predictor of the future, the outcome will not be extremely positive in this regard, and the more highly populated urban areas will continue to receive priority. In sum, challenges and constraints shaped by external conditions are not likely to improve dramatically in most areas but will, quite possibly, be exacerbated. A brief return to an exploration of current socio-economic conditions puts the consequences of the possible script described above in its proper perspective.

Cook and Mizer have presented a typology that underscores the differences and complexities that exist concerning economic and social conditions in the rural United States (1994). First, they classified 2,259 of 2,276 "non-metro" counties into one of six categories based on type of economic dependency: farming (556), manufacturing (506), non-specialized (484), services (323), government (244), and mining (146). Obviously, no one industry dominates all aspects of the rural economy.

Further, the authors grouped 1,197 of these counties into one or more of five policy types that dominate a locale: persistent poverty (535), commuting communities (381), transfers-dependent (381), federal lands (270), and retirement destinations (190). Trends that exist in both sets frequently are regional, with rural areas in one part of the nation being similar to those in the same general locale but different from those in another. Clearly, it is inappropriate to speak of a single set of rural opportunities or problems.

A more detailed review of four of these 11 categories, government- and farming-dependent counties from the economic types, and persistent poverty and transfers-dependent counties related to the policy categories, becomes important for our purposes. While a distrust of government frequently has been cited as a characteristic of rural areas (for example, in explaining the success of some right-wing extremists), ironically, there co-exists another dimension, that of economic reliance.

Government-dependent counties (9.8% of rural entities) are the location for a high level of federal, state and local activities such as higher education, health care, penal institutions, military bases and headquarters for park services. Earnings from these activities range from 25% to 77% of all revenues, and they average 38%. A mean of 75% of these monies comes from local and state governments, and 25% are from the federal government. These areas tend to be adjacent to urban centers, and they experienced population and earnings growth instead of decline in the 1980s. Regardless, of all economic dependency categories (as opposed to policy types), this cluster experienced the highest average rate of poverty, due partly to large numbers of military personnel and low-income college students. If federal cutbacks materialize, and include further closing of military installations and decreases in financial aid to students, reasonably we could expect these conditions to intensify.

There also has been much speculation that federal cuts will impact farm programs as part of efforts to reduce the size of the federal government and budget. Farming-dependent counties are the most numerous of the economic dependent units (24%) but they contain only 9% of the rural population. These areas are located predominantly in the midwest from North Dakota to Texas (over 50%), with most of the remainder in the south (30%) and west (17%). These locales especially were hard hit by the out-migration of population (-11%) during the 1980s. In 1990, over two-thirds of these counties had no towns larger than 2,500 and populations averaging only 38% that of all rural areas. These counties also have large percentages of people who are potentially dependent on government aid. For every 100 adults of working age, 87 individuals were either 17 and younger, or 65 and over, giving these areas the highest ratio of any economic or policy type in Cook and Mizer's scheme (1994). When combined with the government-dependent counties described earlier (which had the highest average rates of poverty among the economic types) these entities account for over one-third of all rural counties and 22% of the non-urban population.

Finally, two policy types, persistent poverty and transfers-dependent counties, become extremely important for our purposes. The former represents 24% of all non-metro counties, 19% of the rural population and 32% of all rural poor. They are predominantly concentrated in the south (83%) and on Indian reservations in the north and west.

Transfers-dependent counties (17%) have economies that are based on federal, state and local government payments, such as unemployment, social security, pensions and welfare. Expenditures from these and other programs range from 25% to 45% of total income, and counties are regionally concentrated in the south (64%), midwest (26%) and west (10%). They tend to be the less populous rural counties and many are totally rural in character.

Because both persistent poverty and transfers-dependent counties heavily overlap (233 counties fall into both categories), they exhibit some of the same socio-economic traits. Typically, both areas have disproportionate numbers of minorities, female headed households, the undereducated, and those with physical or mental disabilities. The transfers-dependent areas also contain a larger share of the elderly (including the retired), in addition to those populations that are characteristic of poverty. Overall, persistent poverty and transfers-dependent entities account for 30% of all rural counties.

It is important to note that there is an important overlap between the economic dependent and policy types. For example, government-dependent counties included 84 persistent poverty areas and 89 transfers-dependent counties. The numbers for farming-dependent entities were 135 and 63 respectively.

SUMMARY

It is against this rather somber portrait that we generally predict that if federal and other budgetary reductions materialize, those factors that tend to have a negative impact on criminal justice agencies will intensify in many rural locations. While it is hard to forecast exactly what the future holds, it seems certain that immediate resolution of many of the difficulties described above is not realistic.

At the same time, nothing is inevitable concerning the predictions that we have made. Several factors also may alter future directions. First, new developments in technology and security procedures associated with the detection of crime may have a positive impact. Second, many rural areas in the 1970s witnessed relatively high rates of growth and economic prosperity. Leistritz and Hamm have suggested that recently there has been renewed interest in rural economic development (1994).

They noted increased activism by state and local government, a new emphasis on entrepreneurship, expansion of some existing businesses and the development of innovative economic strategies to spur development.

Although we have emphasized the problems of many rural areas, some counties are prospering by emphasizing service industries, retirement amenities and recreational facilities. Ironically, even prosperity may not be the total answer for all difficulties. For instance, Weisheit et al. have noted that each set of economic conditions, even growth, may present new opportunities for criminal activity and unique challenges to law enforcement (1994).

Innovative policy makers have the ability to assess their individual situations and respond to change by implementing programs that reflect their expertise and imaginative management techniques. Several of our contributors have highlighted such ingenuity among rural criminal justice practitioners, and we have reason to believe that this will continue to be the case.

Whatever the course of the future, the vitality of the nation rests in part on a healthy rural environment (USDA 1995) and its criminal justice agencies. Transforming this recognition into rational policies may not be an easy charge, even under the best of circumstances. Regardless, it is obvious that change will continue and there will be new conditions, constraints and challenges. We are just as confident that new responses and solutions will emerge. Also, it is clear that because of the variation and complexity that exist, these answers must be tailored to fit each local community's needs and expectations.

REFERENCES

Bennett, G. *Crimewarps: The Future of Crime in America.* New York: Anchor Books, 1987.

Cohen, S. "Rural Homeless: A Growing Problem Across the Nation," *The Fargo Forum,* December 18, 1988: A17, A24.

Cook, P., and K. L. Mizer. *The Revised ERS County Typology: An Overview.* Washington, DC: United States Department of Agriculture, Economic Research Service, 1994.

Fischer, C. S. "The Spread of Violent Crime from City to Countryside, 1955 to 1975," *Rural Sociology,* 45, No. 3, 1980: 416-434.

Leistritz, F. L., and R. Hamm. *Rural Economic Development 1975-1993.* Westport, CT: Greenwood Press, 1994.

Murdock, S. H., and F. L. Leistritz. *The Farm Financial Crisis: Socioeconomic Dimensions and Implications for Producers and Rural Areas.* Boulder, CO: Westview Press, 1988.

United States Department of Agriculture, Economic Research Service, *Understanding Rural America.* Agriculture Information Bulletin No. 710. Washington, DC: United States Department of Agriculture, 1995.

Wardlaw, G. *Political Terrorism: Theory, Tactics and Countermeasures.* New York: Cambridge University Press, 1989.

Weisheit, R., D. Falcone, and L. Wells. "Rural Crime and Rural Policing," in *National Institute of Justice: Research in Action.* Washington, DC: United States Department of Justice, 1994.